THE WRATH OF THE LAMB

THE WRATH OF THE LAMB

BY

ANTHONY TYRRELL HANSON
United Theological College, Bangalore

WIPF & STOCK · Eugene, Oregon

Wipf and Stock Publishers
199 W 8th Ave, Suite 3
Eugene, OR 97401

The Wrath of the Lamb
By Hanson, Anthony Tyrrell
Copyright©1957 SPCK
ISBN 13: 978-1-60899-724-4
Publication date 6/8/2010
Previously published by SPCK, 1957

This Edition reprinted by Wipf and Stock Publishers
by arrangement with SPCK, London.

CONIUGI DILECTISSIMAE
HUIUS LABORIS OMNIS
PARTICIPI

ACKNOWLEDGEMENTS

I DESIRE first to acknowledge the untiring help I have received from my wife in typing out several drafts of this work under by no means ideal conditions of climate and in the midst of many other labours. I also wish to record my appreciation of the encouragement and help given me by the late Canon J. E. L. Oulton, D.D., sometime Regius Professor of Divinity in the University of Dublin. I am grateful to the Reverend T. P. Dunning, C.M., and his colleagues at All Hallows College, Dublin, for kind assistance in procuring a book for me which was not to be found in any of the great libraries of Britain, and to the Librarian of the United Theological College, Bangalore, and the Reverend Marcus Ward, D.D., for the willing way in which they sent me books from their admirable theological library at a time when I was in a remote part of Hyderabad. I wish to thank Professor S. H. Hooke, D.D., for answering several enquiries on various points, and Professor H. H. Rowley, D.D., for a searching criticism of the first draft of this work. I am indebted to Professor D. Nineham for his kindness in verifying a number of references for me; and finally I would record my thanks to the director of the S.P.C.K. and to the staff for the efficient way in which they have enabled me to do my own proof reading at a distance of six thousand miles.

CONTENTS

ACKNOWLEDGEMENTS	*page* vi
FOREWORD	ix
1. THE WRATH IN THE PRE-EXILIC PERIOD	1
2. POST-EXILIC DEVELOPMENTS	
The Problem of the Wrath and the Mercy of God	13
The Impersonal Wrath	21
Apocalyptic Wrath	26
The Cup of Wrath	27
A Summary of the Conception of the Wrath of God in the Old Testament	36
3. THE WRATH IN THE INTER-TESTAMENTAL PERIOD	
The Apocrypha	41
Jewish Apocalyptic Literature	47
The Rabbis	54
The Hellenizers	55
4. THE WRATH IN PAUL'S WRITINGS	68
5. JUDGEMENT IN THE SYNOPTIC GOSPELS AND ACTS	112
6. JUDGEMENT IN HEBREWS, THE JOHANNINE WRITINGS, THE PASTORAL AND CATHOLIC EPISTLES	
The Epistle to the Hebrews	132
The Fourth Gospel and Johannine Epistles	141
The Pastoral and Catholic Epistles	151
7. THE WRATH IN THE APOCALYPSE	159
A Summary of the New Testament Evidence concerning the Wrath of God	178
8. THE WRATH OF THE LAMB AS AN ELEMENT IN CHRISTIAN DOCTRINE	181
APPENDIXES:	
1. The Correct Rendering of Habakkuk 2.15,16	202

CONTENTS

2. The Date of Jeremiah 25.15–31 and 51.1–58 — 204
3. The Translation in the Septuagint of Words for the Divine Wrath — 206
4. W. D. Davies' Suggestion that Paul thought of Christ as the New Torah — 210
5. The Meaning of πυρὸς ζῆλος in Hebrews 10.27 — 213
6. The Wrath of God and Faith in Christian Thought compared with the Concepts of *Karma* and *Bhakti* in Hindu Thought — 215

BIBLIOGRAPHY — 224

INDEXES
1. References and Citations — 235
2. General Index — 246

FOREWORD

THERE are some themes which can be traced through the whole Bible. They first appear in the Old Testament; then, modified and developed, they reappear in the New Testament and help to express the significance of Jesus the Messiah. Such for example is the idea of sacrifice: in a book such as Hicks' *The Fulness of Sacrifice* we can see this theme followed out from the earliest parts of the Old Testament right up to its highest and profoundest expression in the Epistle to the Hebrews or the Gospel of St John. This present book deals with a conception which certainly is found in both Old and New Testaments, the conception of the wrath of God. But it seems at first sight difficult to believe that the wrath of God is really on a par with a great central theme like that of sacrifice: the wrath of God, it may be felt, is appropriate enough in the Old Testament, where men's minds were not yet ready to receive the full revelation of the love of God; but surely the wrath of God cannot be considered as an essential part of New Testament thought. Must it not be put in the same category as St Paul's views on women covering their heads in church—an idea which may have had its relevance in the times of the writers of the New Testament, but cannot be considered as essential for Christians in all ages to accept?

That there is some justification for this view cannot be denied; too often Christian thinkers have interpreted the phrase "the wrath of God" in the New Testament as if it had exactly the meaning which it has in many parts of the Old Testament, and then made it play an important part in their doctrine of the atonement. The consequence has been that with the rise of biblical criticism in the first half of the last century, many theologians have either repudiated the notion of the wrath of God altogether as unworthy of God's character revealed in Christ, or else tried to explain it away. Perhaps the first to do this was A. Ritschl, a German theologian who rejected the concept of the wrath of God as unworthy of inclusion in a scheme of Christian theology.[1]

---

[1] A. Ritschl, *The Christian Doctrine of Justification and Reconciliation*, Vol. III, p. 323 (E.T., Edinburgh 1900).

FOREWORD

To-day, with the return to a more biblical theology and the great emphasis on orthodox tradition, the tendency has been, in as far as the wrath of God has received any notice, to reinstate a somewhat Old Testament interpretation of God's wrath in Christian doctrine: e.g. R. V. G. Tasker's *The Biblical Doctrine of the Wrath of God* (London 1951) and A. B. Macaulay's *The Death of Jesus* (London 1938). But this is hardly satisfactory either: the life, death, and resurrection of Jesus Christ must make some difference to what we believe about the wrath of God. Is there perhaps a Christian doctrine of the wrath of God?

The main contention of this book is that there is: this book is named "The Wrath of the Lamb" not just because this is a striking title, but because there is to be found in the New Testament a doctrine of the wrath of God which is profoundly modified by the revelation of the love of God in Jesus Christ, and is at certain points essentially related to the Cross of Christ. The phrase "the wrath of the Lamb" comes from the Book of Revelation, and it was a study of Revelation that suggested the idea of tracing the conception of the wrath of God through the Bible. As a result of that investigation I am convinced that there is a definitely New Testament doctrine of the wrath and that this doctrine finds its climax and deepest expression in the Book of Revelation. There is something paradoxical indeed in the very thought of the wrath of God occurring in a religion that is based on a belief in the love of God, and it is even more paradoxical that the most Christian expression of that thought should be found in the Book of Revelation, which seems at first sight to be in some respects the least Christian and most Jewish book in the New Testament. But a religion which believes in the true incarnation of God in human nature must be full of paradoxes anyway; and if this book succeeds in showing that the writers of the New Testament in their treatment of the wrath of God are more Christian than many Christian theologians who have written since their day, it will not have failed in its purpose.

1

THE WRATH IN THE PRE-EXILIC PERIOD

PROBABLY the oldest part of the Bible in which we meet with the wrath of God is the older narrative contained in 1 and 2 Samuel. Scholars agree that this was written by someone who had first-hand knowledge of the court of Solomon, and perhaps even of David also. It has been suggested that the author of this narrative might have been Abiathar, the priest at David's court. There are two passages in this narrative where the wrath of God is specially prominent: 2 Sam. 6.7, 8 and 24.1. The first of these runs as follows:

> And the anger of the Lord was kindled against Uzzah; and God smote him there for his error; and there he died by the ark of God. And David was displeased, because the Lord had broken forth upon Uzzah.

The divine wrath here seems to have little to do with either justice or morality. The phrase translated "for his error" is not very clear in the Hebrew, but it does not represent one of the words normally used to describe a deliberate sin.[1] Moreover, the pious king David is obviously annoyed because he thinks that Uzzah was unjustly or unnecessarily killed. We also see here that the divine wrath takes the form of a direct visitation: Uzzah was not thought of as having died of a disease.

There is another passage connected with this, though wrath is not specifically mentioned in it, 1 Sam. 6.19. This passage does not seem to belong to the same ancient narrative as 2 Sam. 6.7, 8, but it is no doubt earlier than the Deuteronomic school which originated in the seventh century B.C.[2] In this passage we read how God "smote the men of

---

[1] The word in the M.T. is עַל־הַשַּׁל, which is meaningless. LXX offers ἐπὶ τῇ προπετείᾳ and the Vulgate "*super temeritate*". Some suggest the words in the M.T. are the remains of the words found in the parallel place in 1 Chron. 13.10: "because he put forth his hand to the ark". Smith (I.C.C., Edinburgh 1899, in loc.) suggests that the M.T. conceals words which originally described the exact location of the event.

[2] Smith (op. cit., Introd., p. xix) suggests that 1 Sam. 6 was originally a separate document, and was later incorporated in the later historical narrative by the author of that narrative.

Bethshemesh, because they had looked into the ark of the Lord". The actual figures of men slain given in the R.V., though they faithfully reproduce the Hebrew, are very probably not the original figures written by the author of this passage. The Septuagint suggests that the original number was only seventy. But in any case we have here a similar event to that described in 2 Sam. 6.7, 8: sudden death is ascribed to God's hand, and we may reasonably guess that this event too was ascribed to the wrath of God. Here too the action of the wrath seems to be direct (the fact that these seventy deaths were perhaps due to bubonic plague does not alter this), and the wrath is not really moralized. The "error" of the men of Bethshemesh seems no more a real sin than was that of Uzzah.

The second passage in the ancient narrative where wrath appears prominently is 2 Sam. 24.1 [1]:

> And again the anger of the Lord was kindled against Israel, and he moved David against them, saying, Go, number Israel and Judah.

Subsequently we read how, in punishment for the sin of numbering the people, David is offered three alternatives, famine, defeat in war, or pestilence. Finally, when David has chosen pestilence, the Lord relents, and verse 25 runs:

> So the Lord was intreated for the land, and the plague was stayed from Israel.

Here there is no clue as to why God was angry: though the R.V. translates "again the anger of the Lord was kindled", the Hebrew does not imply that the anger was caused by some previous sin, such as David's adultery with Bathsheba. The author of the passage apparently sees no necessity of inquiring why God should be angry. The wrath here is not quite as direct as it is in the deaths of Uzzah and of the men of Bethshemesh; we learn that it may be inflicted through the agency of famine, or war. But it is still manifested in an unusual occurrence, pestilence. With this passage we may compare 1 Sam. 26.19, also from the ancient narrative. David is protesting his innocence to Saul, and he courteously suggests that Saul in persecuting him may have

---

[1] Smith thinks that this chapter belongs to the ancient narrative in 1 and 2 Samuel (op. cit., Introd., p. xxvii). In any case there can be little doubt about its early date.

been instigated by God.[1] If so, this is a sign of God's wrath, because in David's opinion Saul's persecuting him was a sin. His words are:

> If it be the Lord that hath stirred thee up against me, let him accept an offering.

If David's supposition is correct, the Lord must be appeased by an offering, a sign that his anger has been aroused. So here also we have wrath with no apparent moral content; at least David sees no reason to inquire why God should have been angry with Saul. We cannot tell how the wrath was conceived as expressing itself here, since presumably Saul had not yet been punished for his sin of persecuting David. David suggests that he may avoid punishment by making an offering. It is interesting that both here and in 2 Sam. 24.25 God's wrath can be appeased by an offering.

So in the earliest part of the Old Testament, where the divine wrath is met with, it is thought of as not necessarily accountable or rational, or morally motivated. It expresses itself in unusual occurrences, especially in sudden death, and it may be appeased by an appropriate offering.

In the older parts of the Pentateuch (the parts called J and E by nineteenth-century scholars) much the same conception of the divine wrath meets us, though there is more emphasis on the moral motive lying behind God's wrath. All the same, there are several passages where the wrath seems to have no moral motive, or an inadequate one: in Ex. 19.22,24, the priests and people are warned not to approach the mountain of Sinai too close, "lest the Lord break forth upon them". The Hebrew word used is the same as that used in 2 Sam. 6.8; the wrath here seems to be something uncontrollable and not altogether accountable. In Num. 11.10, Moses is described as being displeased because the Lord was angry with the people, just as David is displeased in 2 Sam. 6.8. The wrath here is not unmotivated; it was caused by the people's weeping. But it seems to a pious man like Moses to be unreasonable. Another instance of unaccountable wrath occurs in Num. 22. 22: "And God's anger was kindled because [Balaam] went." In verse 20 God has

---

[1] The word for "stirred up" here is the same as that translated "moved" in 2 Sam. 24.1, סוּת.

commanded Balaam to go, so it seems unreasonable that he should be angry because Balaam went. Even modern commentators, who are not concerned to put a respectable construction on the oldest parts of the Old Testament, try to find reasons for this anger.[1] But it seems more natural to understand that God is represented as being angry with Balaam for his own inscrutable reasons—a state of affairs which it does not occur to the writer of the story to question.

In Num. 16.31–5 Dathan and Abiram are swallowed up by the earth and destroyed by fire (there seem to be two narratives here). Here wrath, specifically mentioned, is direct and manifested in an unusual occurrence. In other places it is inflicted by less direct means, e.g. Num. 21.6, where God is angry with the people and sends fiery serpents[2]; in Num. 12.10 Miriam provokes the divine wrath and is punished by leprosy. In Num. 25.11 Phinehas is described as appeasing the divine wrath by slaying two persons who had offended God. In all these four instances an attempt has been made to account for the occurrence of the wrath. In fact the oldest parts of the Pentateuch may be said to show the same conception of the divine wrath as we find in the earliest historical narrative, but to modify it in the direction of moralizing it and also of ascribing secondary causes, such as disease, to the wrath. But we are still far from the conception of the divine wrath as automatically provoked by sin, or as traceable in all adversity. In this respect the conception of the wrath which we have so far met forms a marked exception to the generalization which many scholars have made about divine wrath in the Old Testament. For example, Sanday and Headlam in their commentary on Rom. 1.18[3] say that the wrath of God in the Old Testament is specially connected with the Covenant, being inflicted on Jews for breaking the Covenant and on Gentiles for oppressing the Covenant people. This, though true of later parts of the Old Testament writings, cannot be said to apply to the parts we have considered so far. In Num. 11.1, for example, God is angry with the people for wanting to go back to Egypt; in Num. 12.9 he is angry with Miriam for disputing Moses' authority, and in Num. 32.10 he is angry

---

[1] E.g. Gray, I.C.C. in Exodus (Edinburgh 1903), in loc.
[2] Elliott-Binns (West. Comm., London 1927, in loc.) thinks that this passage is the work of a redactor.
[3] I.C.C. (Edinburgh 1907).

with the report of the spies. In none of these instances could it be said that the divine anger is caused by a transgression of the covenant. Wheeler Robinson in *Record and Revelation*[1] writes: "Adversity is always felt as God's wrath." This can hardly apply to the oldest parts of the Old Testament: for example, there is no suggestion that the defeats at Shiloh or Gilboa were instances of God's wrath. In them the wrath is normally seen in some striking or unusual occurrence, not in every kind of adversity.

In 2 Kings 3.27 occurs something which is unique in the Bible, the wrath of an alien God. Israel is besieging the king of Moab in one of his cities; in his extremity the king sacrifices his eldest son on the city wall. The historian comments: "And there was great wrath against Israel." Most modern commentators[2] agree that this must refer to the wrath of Chemosh, national deity of Moab. More conservative editors jib at this conclusion; for example, Barnes[3] attributes the wrath to Jahweh, but this only gives another example of irrational wrath. Slotke,[4] a modern Jewish editor, shows great ingenuity in avoiding the attribution of the wrath to Chemosh, suggesting Jahveh, the king of Edom, and even the army of Judah as possible alternatives! But there can be little doubt that the author of this passage believed in the reality of Chemosh's wrath, for he makes it a reason for Israel's subsequent retreat. It is interesting to note that we have another source of information about Chemosh's wrath, the Moabite Stone. Omri's oppression of Moab is attributed to the wrath of Chemosh: "For Chemosh was wroth with his land."[5] We should notice that Chemosh's wrath in 2 Kings 3.27 is not exactly irrational, but it does not seem to have any moral content, being caused simply by the powerful sacrifice of the king of Moab.

Wheeler Robinson's statement that "adversity is always felt as God's wrath" is eminently true of the Book of Deuteronomy and of those parts of the Old Testament influenced by the Deuteronomic

---

[1] P. 342 (Oxford 1938).
[2] E.g. Skinner (Century Bible, in loc.), and Albright (*Archaeology and the Religion of Israel*, Baltimore 1942, p. 162).
[3] Cambridge Bible (1908), in loc.
[4] Soncino Comms. (London 1950), in loc.
[5] See G. A. Cooke *A Text Book of North Semitic Inscriptions* (Oxford 1903).

school. This means in effect that in the Book of Deuteronomy the wrath is fully moralized. It is also normally inflicted by indirect means, e.g. defeat in war. There are a number of instances of direct wrath, but these are traditional incidents already described as direct in earlier narratives. But even in Deuteronomy the divine wrath is not necessarily connected with transgressions of the covenant; for example, in Deut. 1.34 God is angry with the people for complaining, and in 3.26 he is angry with Moses "for the people's sake".

The first of the written prophets, Amos, makes no specific reference to the divine wrath, but in his immediate successor, Hosea, the wrath is quite prominent.[1] For example, Hos. 5.10 runs: "I will pour out my wrath upon them like water." In 8.5 God says: "Mine anger is kindled against them [Israel]." In 13.11 God is condemning the rapid changes of kings which took place after the death of Jeroboam II in 743 B.C. He says: "I have given thee a king in mine anger, and have taken him away in my wrath." The sense is that the appointment of Jeroboam I at the time of the disruption of Solomon's kingdom was a sign of God's wrath in the same way that the decay of the kingship in Hosea's day was a sign of God's wrath. In these passages the divine wrath seems to have a strong emotional content.[2] The wrath is manifested by indirect means in the processes of history, but it is the very personal wrath of Jahweh. This is supremely manifested in Hos. 11.8,9:

> Mine heart is turned within me,
> My compassions are kindled together.
> I will not execute the fierceness of mine anger,
> I will not return to destroy Ephraim:
> For I am God, and not man.

The point of saying, "I am God and not man", is that, unlike unstable humans, God will not let a passing emotion such as anger divert him from his eternal purposes of love. It is only in moments of great

---

[1] It is no accident that Amos does not at all refer to God's wrath. He emphasizes the justice of God where Hosea speaks of his love. As justice is more impersonal than love, so the conception of the divine wrath, which at that time was thought of in very personal terms, is more congenial to Hosea.

[2] Notice especially the use of the strong word עֶבְרָה in 5.10; apparently it does not come from √עבר, though Hosea may have believed that it did. See art. ὀργή in *Th.W.z.N.T.*

emotion that Hosea refers to the divine wrath: wrath is in fact Jahweh's strong personal reaction to Israel's sin. The direct, sometimes irrational, wrath of the earliest historical narratives and the earliest parts of the Pentateuch was not sufficiently moral for the eighth-century prophets. Nor had the thought of the wrath as a principle operating in history occurred to them, so it remains as a more or less passing emotion (for they were not afraid of anthropomorphism). It is this personal note in Hosea that brings him so close to the New Testament conception of God's love. The reason why the New Testament writers do not follow his conception of the divine wrath is partly that the Cross gave them a new insight into the nature of the wrath, and partly that they were in their day the heirs of a later doctrine of the impersonal wrath, which represented in its way a deeper understanding of God's ways with men. Hosea sees the conjunction of wrath and love in the divine nature as something of a contradiction: one conflicts with the other. The New Testament writers for the most part knew, or dimly apprehended, that conflict resolved. But at least Hosea does see the problem; there are only two other passages in the Old Testament of which this can be said.[1]

There are not very many references to God's wrath in the undisputed writings of Isaiah the son of Amoz, and five of them consist of the repetition of a refrain:

> For all this his anger is not turned away,
> But his hand is stretched out still.

(See Isa. 5.25; 9.12,17,21; 10.4.) In 9.8—10.4 various kinds of disasters are attributed to Jahweh's wrath: foreign invasion, death in war, drought, famine, civil war. We are nearer the post-exilic conception of all adversity as a manifestation of the divine wrath; but it is still very much the personal act of Jahveh, and there is nothing automatic about it. The wrath is always mediated by the operation of history or nature. This is very clearly expressed in 10.5:

> Ho Assyrian, the rod of mine anger, the staff in whose hand is mine indignation!

Most scholars agree that the phrase "in whose hand" was not in the

---

[1] Psalm 85 and Isa. 63.7—64.12.

original[1]; so Isaiah does not express the unprecedented thought of a Gentile nation being given God's wrath as its weapon. But Isaiah does claim that what to an outsider would seem a fairly common event in history, the conquest of a small nation by a large one, is really the working out of the wrath of God.

When the parts of the Book of Jeremiah that are probably not from his pen have been separated, there emerges a very sensitive, and indeed thoughtful, conception of the wrath of God, given the period in which he lived. Jeremiah often refers to the divine wrath, and he often uses the metaphor of "pouring out". He also compares the wrath to fire. Cf. 44.6:

> Wherefore my fury and mine anger was poured forth, and was kindled in the cities of Judah and in the streets of Jerusalem; and they are wasted and desolate, as at this day.[2]

The nearest modern equivalent to this figure is an incendiary bomb! The wrath was for Jeremiah very closely associated with the effects of the wrath, just as the word of the Lord is not to be separated from the effects of that word. The word also is compared to fire. Cf. 23.29:

> Is not my word like fire, saith the Lord;
> And like a hammer that breaketh the rock in pieces?

We think also of Jahveh's word described as "a burning fire shut up in my bones", in 20.9. The word burns to be proclaimed, and when it is proclaimed it is followed by its fulfilment, so much so that it can be identified with its fulfilment, as in 23.29. Similarly the wrath of God is primarily the effects of sin. It is not so much an affection of God as an effect of God's nature manifest in history; cf. 4.4; 6.11. In this last the fury of the Lord is actually "poured forth upon the children in the street". In this respect Jeremiah's conception of the divine wrath is nearer that of the New Testament than that of any of his predecessors. On the other hand, the New Testament conception of the wrath as a spiritual state and also as an impersonal process is never suggested in Jeremiah. For him Jahveh was a personal God, and therefore his wrath

---

[1] E.g. Skinner (Camb. Bible, 1900), Wade (West. Comm., London 1911), Gray (I.C.C., Edinburgh 1912).

[2] Some scholars would attribute this passage to Baruch rather than directly to Jeremiah, but we may believe that the metaphor came from the prophet himself.

was personal. In this he is a true successor of Hosea. Thus in its development in the Scriptures the idea of the divine wrath undergoes an almost complete transformation: it began as something like a capricious emotion. The prophets and law writers moralized it, but retained the emotional element. In the New Testament the emotion disappears and the wrath is nothing else than the effects of breaking the laws of God's moral universe.

We can however trace in Jeremiah a certain sensitiveness in his treatment of the wrath of God. He does not use the phrase "to provoke the wrath of Jahveh" without misgivings. This is a phrase which is specially prominent in the Deuteronomic writings and so would naturally be in use in Jeremiah's day. But in each of the two places where he uses it we can detect signs of hesitation or regret. The first is 7.18,19:

> ... that they may provoke me to anger. Do they provoke me to anger? saith the Lord; do they not provoke themselves, to the confusion of their own faces?

Duhm[1] translates "provoke me to anger" as "cause me grief". It is a protest against the notion that Jahveh can really be annoyed by their deliberate sin: "How childish to think that they can spite Jahveh by such conduct!" (Peake).[2] The other reference is 8.19:

> Why have they provoked me to anger with their graven images?

This exclamation comes in a context of terrible grief at the wilfulness of the people of God. The previous verse runs:

> Oh that I could comfort myself against sorrow!
> My heart is faint within me.

The whole passage down to the end of the chapter is one of agonizing regret. It is the thought that his people could grieve Jahveh in this way that causes Jeremiah not anger but sorrow.

In two places Jeremiah describes himself as in some sense "full" of God's anger. The first is 6.11:

> I am full of the fury of the Lord. I am weary of holding it in. Pour it out upon the children in the street.

---

[1] Ed. Jeremiah (Tübingen-Leipzig 1910–11), in loc.
[2] Ed. Jeremiah and Lamentations (Century Bible, Edinburgh 1910), in loc.

Compare this with 20.9, where the same language is used of the word of God. The word is the wrath, which is the effect of the wrath, and it must be fulfilled because it is Jahveh's word. The contrast with Deutero-Isaiah is interesting; there (e.g. Isa. 51.20) those who are "full of the wrath of the Lord" are those who are suffering from its effects. Here the prophet is described as "full of the fury" because he is full of the message proclaiming the effects of the fury. Compare also 23.9:

> I am like a drunken man, and one whom wine hath overcome, because of the Lord, and because of his holy words.

In each of these cases Jeremiah is "a vessel of wrath" in an active not a passive sense. This has some significance for the interpretation of Rom. 9.22.

Ezekiel is in many ways the true successor to Jeremiah in his treatment of the divine wrath. He refers frequently to God's anger, almost always in order to describe the contemporary disasters of his people. Also, like Jeremiah, he sees the wrath as very much associated with its effects. Like Jeremiah, he uses the figure of fire very frequently, and also the metaphor of "pouring out". A good example of the identification of the wrath with its effects is Ezek. 16.38:

> I will bring upon thee the blood of fury and jealousy.

Similarly in 16.42 he says:

> My jealousy shall depart from thee,

meaning "the effects of my jealousy shall depart from thee". Compare also 23.25:

> And I will set my jealousy against thee, and they shall deal with thee in fury.

The first clause here represents the divine wrath as a hound tracking down its victim. In the second clause the Hebrew reads "thy fury". If this reading is right "thy fury" must mean "the fury thou (Oholibah = Jerusalem) hast caused in Jahveh". The fury is looked on as a sort of weapon which Jahveh gives to Judah's enemies to use. Cf. Isa. 10.5.

Though Ezekiel stands in Jeremiah's tradition, he shows himself less sensitive in his anthropomorphic language about the wrath.[1] The word meaning "to provoke to wrath" (*kṣh* and cognates) is used three times, and the word for jealousy (*kn'* and cognates) is a favourite one with Ezekiel. Another instance of his anthropomorphism is in his frequent use of the concept of "quieting" or "expending" the divine wrath. This gives a strongly emotional content to God's wrath; but it is important to notice that it is always Jahveh, not man, who satisfies his own wrath. It is only in much earlier times and also to some extent in later times, that the thought of man appeasing the wrath of God appears. On the whole Ezekiel thinks of the wrath as manifested more against Judah and Israel than against the Gentiles. But he does speak in several places of God being angry with Judah's oppressors, especially after the fall of Jerusalem.[2] This is significant, as we shall find that it is only after the fall of Jerusalem that God's wrath is much thought of as manifested against the Gentiles. In this respect Ezekiel marks a watershed: in him we see the wrath of God being turned from Israel to the Gentiles.

Before leaving the pre-exilic period we should perhaps ask the question: Why in this period is the divine wrath thought of so much as manifested against Israel and so little against the Gentiles? The only places in the Pentateuch where God is specifically described as angry with the Gentiles as such are Ex. 15.7 and Deut. 32.27,35. These both occur in the Songs, about whose dates there is considerable dispute.[3] Another example occurs in 1 Sam. 28.18, which probably does not belong to the earliest historical narrative. In Isa. 28.21 the prophet says:

> The Lord shall rise up as in Mount Perazim,
> He shall be wroth as in the valley of Gibeon.

It is not certain to what event Isaiah is referring, but in any case it seems to be to some signal victory over the Gentiles. We should note however that Isaiah only cites it in order to show that Jahveh was angry

---

[1] Cf. especially 38.18,19: "My fury shall come up into my nostrils." About the genuineness of this verse, *vide infra*.

[2] See 25.14,17; 30.15; 36.5,6; 38.18,19. This last is from the Gog passage. There seems to be a tendency to-day to accept this passage as from Ezekiel's pen. With Cooke (I.C.C., Edinburgh 1936, in loc.) compare Albright, *From Stone Age to Christianity* (Baltimore 1946), p. 249.

[3] There seems some reason to believe that they are later than the earliest parts of the Pentateuch but are pre-exilic.

with his own people in the prophet's day.[1] One other instance of divine wrath against the Gentiles occurs in Jer. 49.37. When we put these few instances against the many passages where God's wrath is declared against his own people, we cannot help questioning Wheeler Robinson's dictum in *Record and Revelation*, p. 342: "In spite of the prophets... the belief remained that wrath was specially directed against the enemies of Israel." The surprising thing is that up to the Exile the divine wrath is so rarely proclaimed against the Gentiles. For example, neither the destruction of Sodom and Gomorrah nor the overthrow of the Egyptians in the Red Sea is described as a manifestation of God's wrath. The reason may perhaps lie in another characteristic of the divine wrath which we have noted in this period, its personal nature. Jahveh was the personal God of Israel. He did not have personal dealings with the Gentiles to the same extent that he did with his own people. Wrath was thought of as a very personal thing, and perhaps it was half-consciously felt that the divine wrath was not an altogether appropriate thing to expect among those who were not thought of as God's people.

[1] Isa. 10.24–7; 30.27–33 are of doubtful authorship.

2

POST-EXILIC DEVELOPMENTS

THE PROBLEM OF THE WRATH AND THE MERCY OF GOD

IN Deutero-Isaiah, the prophet who arose while the Jews were in exile in Babylon and who exercised his ministry roughly between 549 and 537 B.C., there is one interesting passage where a sort of contrast appears between the wrath and the love of God. Isa. 48.9 runs:

> For my name's sake will I defer mine anger,
> And for my praise will I refrain for thee, that I cut thee not off.

The notion of Jahveh restraining his anger we have already met in Hosea. Here however the motive is a less profound one than the divine love which Hosea's insight enabled him to recognize. God restrains his anger "for his name's sake", which sounds more like pride than love. On the other hand "the name of Jahveh" has a very deep connotation; we might translate the phrase "because of my nature"—"His nature and his name is love."

In Isa. 42.25 we find an unusual thought, the suggestion that Israel actually failed to recognize God's wrath:

> Therefore he poured upon him (Israel) the fury of his anger . . . yet he knew not.

The word for "know" here is that used throughout the Old Testament for intimate knowledge, not just awareness (*yada'*). The parallel "laid to heart" shows that the meaning is not just that Israel was unaware of the divine displeasure, but that the nation was not able to see into the inner meaning of what it was suffering, i.e., that God's wrath was a punishment for their sins. This shows how completely by this time the wrath of God had been identified with its effects in history, and points forward to the New Testament conception whereby the wrath is something "revealed", i.e. it needs faith to apprehend it, just as it needs faith to recognize the love of God also. There is a hint of this in Jer. 23.20 as well. In the earliest times no one could possibly have failed to recognize the action of the wrath of God as they understood it.

Zechariah speaks in one passage of appeasing God's anger, Zech. 6.8:

> They have quieted my spirit in the north country.

The meaning is that Jahveh's wrath against the Gentiles is about to be appeased by a disaster in the Middle East. This is not an example of man deliberately appeasing the divine wrath; it is to be appeased by the process of human history. Zechariah uses for "appease" one of the words previously used by Ezekiel[1]; but whereas Ezekiel speaks of quieting God's wrath, Zechariah says "God's spirit". This may be a deliberate modification. In both Deutero-Isaiah and Zechariah the divine anger is directed primarily against the Gentiles, and from now on expressions of the divine wrath against the Gentiles become very frequent.

It is generally agreed that chapters 56–66 of the Book of Isaiah belong to the period after the Exile, though there is great uncertainty as to what particular time it is to which the various prophecies contained in this section belong. It is perhaps significant that there are several passages in this section which throw light on contemporary conceptions of the divine wrath. The exile instigated the deepest thinkers in Israel to meditate on the nature of sin, wrath, and grace. In Isa. 57.16, 17 and 60.10 wrath and mercy are juxtaposed:

> For I will not contend for ever,
> neither will I be always wroth;
> for the spirit should fail before me,
> and the souls which I have made.

Here mercy alternates with wrath. Similarly in the second passage we read:

> For in wrath I smote thee,
> but in favour have I had mercy on thee.

Mercy checks and limits justice as revealed in wrath. With one exception, this is as far as Old Testament writers advanced in their attempts

---

[1] נוּחַ; the other in Ezekieli s כָּלָה.

to reconcile the divine wrath with the divine love. They either said that wrath goes a certain way but is ultimately checked by mercy, or that God's love goes very far but that ultimately he has to give way to his wrath. Certain New Testament writers saw that the Cross offers a much deeper solution to the problem. But many Christian theologians advanced no farther towards a solution of the problem than did the Old Testament writers.[1]

There are two other passages where Jahveh's wrath is expressed in strong and vivid terms. In 59.17, 18 Jahveh in resentment against the enemies of Israel puts on

> garments of vengeance as a cloke. . . . According to their deeds, accordingly he will repay, fury to his adversaries, recompense to his enemies.

This is, as G. A. Smith insists,[2] a highly emotional passage; we are still at the original prophetic conception of wrath as a strong emotion in Jahveh, aroused by extraordinary sin. This passage affords an interesting comparison with the New Testament. It is quoted in Eph. 6.13–17, but the different context in which it is used shows the wide chasm that separates Old Testament from New Testament in this respect. The terms used in the Old Testament for the intervention of Jahveh on behalf of Israel are used in the New Testament to describe the weapons of the Christian in the battle of life. The Old Testament suggests the Incarnation in that it does describe an intervention of God in history, but here he intervenes by slaying his enemies, not dying for them. In the New Testament the intervention of God in history also manifests the wrath of God, but in a different, and far more profound way, as we shall see.

The second of these two "Trito-Isaiah" passages shows the characteristics of the first in an even more marked manner. In Isa. 63.1–6 we have a magnificent and appalling picture of Jahveh returning from the slaughter of his enemies, probably Edom.[3] His garments are still red with the blood of those whom he has slain. We notice in this that

---

[1] Oesterley and Robinson attribute both these passages to the Exile on the eve of the return (*A History of Israel*, Vol. II, Oxford 1932, in loc.).

[2] Ed. Isaiah, London 1927, in loc.

[3] Kissane (ed. Isaiah, Dublin 1943, in loc.) suggests that all reference to Edom may be obviated by translating "from Edom" as "red" and "from Bozrah" as "from the winefat".

pragmatic element in the divine wrath which is so prominent in Jeremiah and Ezekiel. In 63.5 the parallel to "Mine own arm brought salvation to me" is "My fury, it upheld me". Here is an outburst of the strong personal wrath of Jahveh. We may say in fact that in these two passages from "Trito-Isaiah" we have two great pictures of what the divine wrath looks like if you imagine a divine intervention in history without the Cross.[1]

There follows immediately a passage, Isa. 63.7—64.12, which seems to have no connection with the preceding one. It is by no means easy to fix its date; in view of 64.11, some date when the Temple was in ruins seems necessary. Yet it does not seem to belong to the period of the Exile. There is much to be said for the view that it may be a "Samaritan Lament", a pathetic cry from the Jews driven from the Temple by Ezra in 397, or their descendants. Some scholars suggest 350 B.C. as a likely date, when the Temple may have been damaged in the revolt against Artaxerxes Ochus.[2] The prophet here seems to suggest that the people are unable to help themselves. Jahveh's wrath is itself an obstacle to their reform. Thus 63.17 runs:

> Oh Lord, why dost thou make us err from thy ways,
> And hardenest our heart from thy fear?

And 64.6b—7a continues:

> And our iniquities, like the wind, take us away,
> For thou hast hid thy face from us,
> And consumed us by means of our iniquities.[3]

The passage ends (64.9):

> Be not wroth very sore, oh Lord,
> Neither remember iniquity for ever.

---

[1] In fact these two pictures are not unlike some of the adventures narrated of Krishna or Rama in Hindu mythology. These are both claimed as incarnations of Vishnu and might fairly be described as semi-divine interventions in history without the Cross.

[2] Cheyne (ed. Isaiah, London 1884, in loc.) suggested 350 B.C., followed by Box. Duhm favours 516–450 B.C. Kissane (op. cit., in loc.) suggests a late exilic date.

[3] The R.V. margin in translating "thou hast delivered us into the power of our iniquities" follows LXX and Syriac, which implies a reading וַתְּמַגְּעֵנוּ. The St Mark's Monastery text of Isaiah found in the Dead Sea Scrolls reads ותמגדנו, (see M. Burrows, *The Dead Sea Scrolls*, Vol. I, New Haven 1950, in loc.). This word is a *vox nihili*, but is nearer what the LXX implies. This variant reading strongly confirms the interpretation of the passage given here.

This passage is unique in the Old Testament, in that here only is it suggested that sin is the consequence of the divine wrath as well as being its cause. Bredenkampf[1] and Delitzsch[2] both quote here Luther's dictum *"peccatum est peccati poena"*, sin is the punishment of sin. This passage contains no commonplace complaint of Israel's excessive punishment. It shows in fact a profound insight into the nature of the divine wrath, an insight which we meet again only in the New Testament itself. The prophet's complaint is that the very process of the wrath itself involves his people in still further sin. They are in the power of their own sins, and are unable to extricate themselves by their own efforts. Here alone in the Old Testament the process "sin—wrath" is continued to read "sin—wrath—sin" *ad infinitum.* In this respect the prophet's conception of the divine wrath comes very near to that of the New Testament. Wrath brings about a condition of helpless sinfulness, says the prophet. Wrath is such a condition, says St Paul (see below, Chapter 4). But when we turn to the remedy which this anonymous prophet proposes, we realize that we are still in the Old Testament. He asks for an intervention of God, but this intervention is still thought of in terms of this world. The proposal comes in 64.1 following:

> Oh that thou wouldest rend the heavens,
> That thou wouldest come down,
> That the mountains might flow down at thy presence . . . etc.

The intervention is thought of in terms of Sinai rather than of Bethlehem or of Golgotha. Our author does not think of the divine wrath, however, in the later categories of the Old Testament,[3] which themselves have their place in New Testament thought, that is he does not think of the wrath as something automatic and impersonal. His solution to the predicament of his people, restricted though it is by the limits of Old Testament thought, reminds us a little of the free grace which we meet in the New Testament. It is to Hosea rather than the Chronicler that we must look for a parallel in the Old Testament. The very fact that his solution of the problem lies in a divine theophany shows that in his scheme of things salvation is by grace rather than by

---

[1] Ed. Isaiah (Erlangen 1887), in l oc.
[2] Ed. Isaiah (E.T., Edinburgh 1890), in loc.
[3] Or, if this passage is fourth-century, contemporary categories.

law. So in the fundamental conceptions of wrath and grace, inevitably so intimately linked, this prophet marks a watershed. He has realized that God's wrath cannot be simply regarded as God's punishment for sin and left at that. Wrath itself involves further sin, which itself brings down wrath, and so on. He sees that the only solution to this situation is a move, a decisive intervention, from God's side. What he did not see, what no one in the Old Testament saw (with the brilliant exception of the author of Isa. 52.13—53.12), was the way in which God was ultimately to intervene. If this is really a "Samaritan Lament", it is indeed a remarkable fact that one of the deepest insights about the divine wrath in the Old Testament should come from the outcast, not the orthodox.

The eighty-fifth psalm is also in its way an attempt at solving the same problem, though its solution may be less profound than that of the author of Isa. 63.7—64.12. The poet faces in a remarkable way the co-existence of wrath and mercy in Jahveh. The dating of the Psalms is usually extremely difficult, and this one is no exception. On the whole more scholars incline towards a date in the late Restoration period after Nehemiah.[1] This would make it a possible contemporary of the passage we have just been discussing. There can be little doubt that the poet is looking forward to the Messianic age: if any psalm is entitled to the epithet "messianic" surely this one is. It is important to realize, as Kirkpatrick observes,[2] that the virtues mentioned in the latter part of the psalm are divine attributes, not human qualities. The psalm falls into two parts; in the first, verses 1 to 7, the Psalmist is concerned with the present condition of Israel, and it is in this part that the explicit references to the divine wrath occur. In the second part, verses 8 to the end, he speaks of future reconciliation. The references to the divine wrath are as follows (verses 4–6):

> Thou hast turned away all thy wrath,
> Thou hast turned thyself from the fierceness of thine indignation.
> Turn us, O God of our salvation,
> And cause thine indignation to cease from us.
> Wilt thou be angry with us for ever?
> Wilt thou draw out thine anger to all generations?

---

[1] E.g. Briggs (ed. I.C.C., Edinburgh 1907); Oesterley (ed. London 1939).
[2] Ed. Psalms 42–89 (Cambridge 1914), in loc.

POST-EXILIC DEVELOPMENTS

The past anger probably refers to the Exile, the present anger to the hardships his people were suffering when the poet was writing. In the second half of the poem the Psalmist draws a picture of Jahveh's wrath and Jahveh's mercy reconciled. Cohen[1] comments: "The thought that peace, in the broader sense of wellbeing in addition to harmony, is the fruit of righteousness, is prominent in the Bible and Rabbinic literature." But this is to dull the edge of the argument: the poet gives us contrasted attributes of God and imagines them reconciled. His arrangement is "scissors formation", that is, he cites two contrasting attributes, A and B, in one line; then he cites a corresponding couple, in the order B and A, in the next line. Thus verses 10–11:

> Mercy and truth are met together;
> Righteousness and peace have kissed each other.
> Truth springeth out of the earth;
> And righteousness hath looked down from heaven.

"Mercy" (*chesed*) is Jahveh's loyal and steadfast love; it corresponds to "peace" (*shālōm*), which is Jahveh's blessing on reconciled Israel. "Truth" (*'emeth*) is the quality in Jahveh whereby he is true to himself, to his holiness, the quality whereby he cannot pass by sin. It corresponds to "righteousness" (*tsedeq*). These two words give us as it were God's norm whereby the crooked standards of the world are judged. Compare Ps. 111.7,8:

> The works of his hands are truth (*'emeth*) and judgement (*mishpat*);
> All his precepts are sure (*ne'emanim*).
> They are established for ever and ever,
> They are done in truth (*'emeth*) and uprightness (*yāshār*).

'emeth is here associated with judgement and uprightness. Similarly N. Snaith in *The Distinctive Ideas of the Old Testament* (London 1944) says of *tsedeq*: "*Tsedeq* certainly stands for the establishment of justice in the land. We would not detract to any degree from the importance of that, but, important as it is, it is but half of the truth. It is incidental that *tsedeq* stands for justice. It is incidental because *tsedeq* actually stands for the establishment of God's will" (page 69); and again on page 77: "*Tsedeq*, with its kindred words, signifies that standard

---

[1] Ed. Psalms (Soncino ed., London 1945) in loc.

which God maintains in the world. It is the norm by which all must be judged." In the Messianic Age, according to the author of Ps. 85, the establishment of God's will in the land will no longer be inconsistent with God's love and Israel's prosperity. We can therefore represent verse 10 thus:

The vertical lines show the contrasted attributes of Jahveh which are to be reconciled in the future. The horizontal lines link up the two aspects of each of these pairs of attributes. We might call the top line his love and the bottom line his judgement. Perhaps verse 11 shows how this reconciliation is to be effected. Righteousness looks down from heaven because truth springs out of the earth, and "truth" is here perhaps the faithfulness of the faithful remnant in the Messianic age. Our poet thus was fully aware of the problem set by the wrath and the mercy of God, and he looks for the solution only in the Messianic age. In this he was right, and that is why Ps. 85 is so appropriate for Christmas. What he could not foresee was the manner of their reconciliation in the Cross of the Messiah.

The Book of Job is most interesting for our purpose, because in it the author explicitly rejects the orthodox doctrine about God's anger, the belief that misfortune was necessarily a sign God's wrath. First Eliphaz, the leader of the orthodox friends, lets it be known that God's anger punishes the wicked (Job 4.9):

> By the breath of God they [the wicked] perish,
> And by the blast of his anger they are consumed.

Job himself apparently accepts this doctrine that misfortune is a sign of God's wrath, but the difference between himself and his friends is that he protests against God being angry with *him*. In 10.17 Job says:

> Thou renewest thy witnesses against me,
> And increasest thine indignation upon me.

And in 14.13 he actually asks to be protected by God from God's wrath:

POST-EXILIC DEVELOPMENTS

> That thou wouldest keep me secret, until thy wrath be past.

This is in line with the other passages in Job where Job appeals, so to speak, from God unrighteous to God righteous. Then there are several places where Job seems to be emphasizing the irrational violence of God's wrath. Cf. 9.5:

> [God] removeth the mountains, and they know it not,
> When he overthroweth them in his anger.

In 16.9 Job makes an even more startling accusation:

> He hath torn me in his wrath, and persecuted me;
> He hath gnashed upon me with his teeth.

There is no word in the Hebrew for "me" after "torn" and there is some reason for thinking that "persecuted me" may have originally been "and he attacks me".[1] Hence one scholar suggests that the right translation is: "His wrath hath rent him and he assaileth me." This would be a most daring statement: God cannot even control his own wrath! In any case the passage gives a very violent picture of God's anger. Compare also 19.11. All these passages have no doubt the same intention, to attack the orthodox doctrine of the divine wrath, to suggest that misfortune is not necessarily a sign of divine wrath, nor are violent convulsions of nature. This is supported by what God says when he appears to Job out of the whirlwind (40.11): "Scatter forth the inflictions of thy wrath." Job is in fact being told by God: "If you can govern better than I, pray assume my prerogatives. I have a deeper way of managing affairs."[2] The author of Job, profounder in his unorthodoxy than his contemporaries in their orthodoxy, saw that the doctrine of the divine wrath current in his day was inadequate. He does not offer a more adequate one himself.

THE IMPERSONAL WRATH

Some time after the Exile we find among a certain school of writers a marked tendency to speak of the divine wrath in a very impersonal manner. It first appears, though not prominently, in the latest part of

---

[1] This means reading וַיִּשְׂטְמֵנִי for וַיַּשְׂמְטֵנִי. Kissane (ed. Dublin 1939, in loc.) reads טָרַף for טָרַף אַפּוֹ.

[2] Compare Strahan (ed. Job, Edinburgh 1915), in loc.

the Pentateuch to be composed, often called the Priestly Document. The author of this part of the Pentateuch does not refer to the divine wrath very often, only five times in fact. Of these, two are expressed in strangely impersonal terms. In Num. 14.34 God says:

> Ye shall know my alienation.

The root meaning of this word (Hebrew $t^e n\bar{u}'\bar{a}h$) seems to be "aberration". The Septuagint translates it "my fierce wrath".[1] Even more impersonal is Num. 16.46:

> There is wrath gone out from the Lord.

There can be little doubt that this phrase is used in order to avoid attributing too personal a wrath to Jahveh.

When we reach the Chronicler (perhaps 350 to 250 B.C.) we find a writer who feels that to attribute wrath as a normal emotion to God is too anthropomorphic, and consequently his references to the divine wrath show a marked impersonalizing tendency. The Chronicler has no hestitation in speaking about God's wrath as an element in history, indeed he attributes every misfortune suffered by Judah, especially defeat in war, to the divine wrath. But that wrath is normally spoken of as a mysterious, impersonal force which arises like some natural phenomenon. It is usually provoked by idolatry. Except for incidents reproduced from Samuel and Kings, the wrath is never direct (even Uzziah's punishment in 2 Chron. 26.19 is a disease). The Chronicler almost always prefers to use an impersonal construction for the wrath of God, nor does he often describe Jahveh as sending the wrath. The wrath happens like an earthquake or a sunrise; cf. 2 Chron. 19.10:

> And so wrath came upon you;

also 1 Chron. 27.24:

> And there came wrath for this upon Israel.

See also 2 Chron. 32.25,26;[2] 2 Chron. 36.16,[3] In several places he leaves out a verb altogether; e.g. 2 Chron. 19.2:

> And for this thing is wrath upon thee from before the Lord.

---

[1] The Hebrew is תְּנוּאָה. The LXX is τὸν θυμὸν τῆς ὀργῆς μου.

[2] The Hebrew verb used here is בָּא.

[3] The verb used is עָלָה.

Compare also 2 Chron. 28.9,11,13. Equally significant is the fact that in many instances God's name is not attached to the wrath at all; it is simply called "wrath"; e.g. 1 Chron. 27.24; 2 Chron. 19.10; 24.18; 28.13; Ezra 7.23. Compare also Neh. 13.18:[1]

Yet ye bring more wrath upon Israel by profaning the sabbath.

There is in fact only one place in the Chronicler's history where God is described as being angry, as opposed to this mysterious and impersonal presentation of the divine wrath. This occurs in Ezra 9.14:

Wouldest thou not be angry with us till thou hadst consumed us?

This occurs in Ezra's prayer of penitence. It is a question how much of this prayer should be attributed to Ezra and how much to the Chronicler's editing. But in any case a phrase might be allowed in the intimacy of prayer which would be out of place in a more theological history.

The significance of this treatment of the divine wrath in the Chronicler's work must not be underrated. We need to look no further for the origin of Paul's doctrine of the wrath of God (see below, Chapter 4). In view of his conception of the wrath of God, it is only to be expected that the Chronicler should wish to modify some of the earlier material which he was handling. In two passages connected with the wrath we find him doing this. In 1 Chron. 15.13 the death of Uzzah is attributed to the fact that mere laymen, and not the Levites, bore the Ark (see our comment on 2 Samuel 6.7,8). The second passage is 1 Chron. 21.1, where it is not Jahveh but Satan who instigates David to number the people (see our comment on 2 Sam. 24.1). What the Chronicler objected to in these passages was not that Jahveh was described as acting directly and personally in anger, but the suggestion that Jahveh's wrath was amoral or irrational. Indeed it is the Chronicler's very systematization of the wrath that is his main contribution to the biblical conception of the wrath of God.

An interesting parallel to the Chronicler's treatment of the divine wrath is found in Ps. 78.21,31:

And anger also went up against Israel.

---

[1] This phrase seems to come from a passage which is Nehemiah's own composition, but Batten (ed. Ezra-Nehemiah, I.C.C., Edinburgh 1913, in loc.) considers that this actual phrase is inserted by the Chronicler.

The word for "went up" is *'ālāh*, as used in 2 Chron. 36.16.[1] This may be an indication of the psalm's date; several scholars place it in the late Persian period.[2] The Chronicler's conception of the wrath of God is also found in Proverbs and in Daniel. Cf. Prov. 11.4:

> Riches profit not in the day of wrath.

See also Prov. 11.23:

> The expectation of the wicked is wrath.

There can be little doubt that these passages refer to the divine wrath. The author (or authors) of Proverbs can use less impersonal language, e.g. 24.18:

> And he [God] turn away his wrath from him.

But the impersonal note is more marked.

In the Book of Daniel the divine wrath is portrayed in more impersonal, allusive, and majestic terms than in any other book of the Old Testament. This is partly no doubt because the author was writing a pamphlet for a resistance movement and dared not be too explicit in his references, but it is also because he is the heir of the Chronicler's tradition of impersonal wrath, and he conceived of this wrath as a mysterious and impersonal agency, not as the strong divine emotion of the prophets.[3] The first reference is Dan. 8.19:

> Behold, I will make thee know what shall be in the latter time of the indignation.

Here the wrath is primarily not God's emotion, but what is (from the point of view adopted by the author) destined to happen to Israel in the time of Antiochus Epiphanes. Driver interprets "the latter time of the indignation" as "the end of the coming persecution", no doubt rightly.[4] We find an even more impersonal and allusive reference in 9.27:

---

[1] But this psalmist does not object to saying that God was angry, as the beginning of verse 21 testifies.

[2] E.g. Briggs and Oesterley.

[3] H. H. Rowley in *The Servant of the Lord* (London 1952, pp. 237f.) argues strongly for the unity of authorship of the book.

[4] Ed. Daniel (Cambridge Bible, 1912), in loc.

And even unto the consummation, and that determined, shall wrath be poured out on the desolator.

There is no word in the Hebrew corresponding to "wrath"; we have a rare word (*nech^{e}rātsāh*) meaning "decision"; but this "decision" is poured out, and there can be no doubt that the R.V. is right in translating "wrath". In the previous verse (9.26) we may perhaps detect an even more hidden allusion to the wrath:

And his end shall be with a flood.

Charles refers this to the High Priest ("the Prince of the Covenant"). The phrase is applicable to the end of the ungodly rather than of the faithful,[1] but this is quite suitable for any of the collaborationist High Priests of the time of Epiphanes. In 11.22 the same word (*sheṭeph*) is used of the High Priest Onias III, and here Driver translates: "Swept away in the flood of divine judgement." So all these three passages may fairly be taken as extraordinarily impersonal and allusive references to the divine wrath. See also 11.36:

And he [Epiphanes] shall prosper till the indignation be accomplished.

Here the wrath is to be exercised on Israel and there is no suggestion that Epiphanes should incur it. It is very significant that perhaps the latest writer in the Old Testament should revert to the pre-exilic prophetic tradition in seeing the divine wrath as exercised primarily on Israel, and also that he should adhere so decidedly to the side of the Chronicler in his concept of the impersonal wrath. It is in a way a pointer to the New Testament, where both the impersonal wrath and the apocalyptic conception of the wrath as eschatological meet and are transformed.

There is one notable exception to the impersonal conception of the wrath in Daniel. It occurs in 9.16, where Daniel is making his prayer of penitence:

Let thy anger and thy fury... be turned away from thy holy city Jerusalem.

But we may compare this passage with Ezra 9.14. This prayer is a conventional literary form, and in such a prayer a reference to the

---

[1] See Montgomery, op. cit., in loc.

divine wrath in the prophetic tradition would be expected. It is significant that only in this prayer in Daniel is the divine name used, another concession to tradition, perhaps.[1]

APOCALYPTIC WRATH

Our study of the impersonal conception of the wrath has brought us to the very latest book on the Old Testament. But we must notice that, parallel with this impersonal treatment of the divine wrath, there grew up an apocalyptic school of writers, and in them the wrath of God is often associated with the last things. Indeed, as we have seen, in Daniel the apocalyptic and impersonal conceptions meet. In the latest parts of the Book of Isaiah we find an eschatological idea of the wrath. Settling the date of any non-Isaianic portion of the first thirty-nine chapters of Isaiah is a most difficult and precarious task, but there seems to be general agreement that some chapters of Isaiah 1—39 date from after the Exile, and that those parts with apocalyptic features date from well after the Exile. Isa. 13 seems to be such a passage[2]: in verse 9 of this chapter "the day of the Lord" is referred to, which in verses 10–11 appears to be a world judgement:

The day of the Lord cometh, cruel with wrath and fierce anger.

The day is to be a day of punishment for the Gentiles only. The whole passage has a note of violence, even ruthlessness, that is quite remarkable, e.g. 13.13:

In the wrath of the Lord of hosts and in the day of his fierce anger.

One editor[3] comments: "By the outbreak of Jehovah's wrath the material universe is shaken to its foundations." The wrath seems to be direct here, as in the very earliest passages, but we must not press the language too literally. Another passage, Isa. 30.27–33, could be called very anthropopathic:[4]

---

[1] For other prayers of penitence see Neh. 9.5 f.; Jer. 14.7–9,19–22; Baruch 1.15—3.8.
[2] Gray would date this passage as early as 550 B.C., but its apocalyptic tone seems to belong to a later date.   [3] Skinner (Cambridge Bible, 1900), in loc.
[4] Skinner (ibid.) thinks this passage post-Isaianic. Wade (ed., Westminster Commentary, London 1907, in loc.) quotes Duhm in favour of its Isaianic authorship and Cheyne as against it. In this passage wrath is direct and not mediated by natural events; also Jahveh "comes from afar" (verse 27). In the prophet Isaiah's work Jahveh is in the midst of Israel. Both these details tell against Isaiah's authorship. In Kittel's *Th. Wort. d. N.T.*, sub art. ὀργή, this passage is explained as based on the meaning of זעם as "cursing"; but this is equally anthropomorphic.

His lips are full of indignation,
and his tongue is as a burning fire.

Similarly 33.14 and 34.2 give us further examples of the vivid, unrestrained language used about the divine wrath in apocalyptic prophecies. 33.14 runs:

Who among us shall dwell with the devouring fire?
Who among us shall dwell with everlasting burnings?

And chapter 34, after speaking in verse 2 of the Lord's "indignation and fury" against the Gentiles, goes on to give a terrifying description of blood, slaughter, and corpses. Finally, at the very end of the Book of Isaiah we have in chapters 65 and 66 what seems to be an apocalyptic passage;[1] 66.14,15 runs:

[The Lord] will have indignation against his enemies . . . to render his anger with fury, and his rebuke with flames of fire.

The next verse describes a vivid theophany in which God personally slays those who have sinned against him, probably the ungodly in Israel rather than the Gentiles.

The apocalyptic conception of the divine wrath may represent a reaction against the cold, impersonal view of the Chronicler. As such, its more direct and personal terms seem to be in some respects a reversion to a more primitive idea of the wrath. But apocalyptic writers are much more sensitive to the justice and the moral nature of the divine wrath than are earlier writers. As we shall see, the writers of the New Testament made use of both the apocalyptic and the impersonal conceptions of the divine wrath, though the former was more modified by them than was the latter.

THE CUP OF WRATH

Throughout the Old Testament there occurs one figure or metaphor for the divine wrath which is so striking that it merits separate treatment; this is the figure of the cup of Jahveh's wrath. It is impossible to say with certainty how or when this figure originated in Hebrew

---

[1] There seems some reason for dating this passage at *c.* 350 B.C.: the possible reference to the Samaritan Temple on Mt Gerizim in 66.1; the division between godly and ungodly; the apocalyptic tone. See Skinner, op. cit., in loc.

literature, but it seems likely that it may have first appeared in Ugaritic literature and found its way to northern Palestine about the eighth century B.C. In the Ras Shamra Texts we find references to a magic or symbolical cup of the gods. Ras Shamra is in north Syria; the texts, which are written in a Semitic language called Ugaritic, are said to date from 1400 B.C.[1] In some of these texts we have a description of the adventures of Baal and 'Anat, a male and female deity. At one time the goddess 'Anat is trying to persuade the god 'Il to build a palace for Baal. Gordon translates ('Anat V, 40):

Let us both drain his chalice
Both of us drain his cup.

The words in italic are admitted to be of doubtful meaning. The words recur in Text 51: IV, 45. The context in each case seems to be the same. The general sense appears to be: "Let us throw in our lot with Baal." A much clearer reference occurs in Text 51: III, 15. Gordon translates:

I have drunk [disgrace] from my tables,
    Scorn from a cup did I drink.

"Disgrace" is a guess by Gordon, but the sense is clear enough. The cup is used as a symbol of evil or shameful destiny. There is another more obscure reference in Text 67: I, 20:

With both my hands I shall eat *them*
    My *seven* portions from the bowl
        Or the cup that *River* mixes.

"River" is the name of a god. The cup that he mixes may mean here the destiny or rule which he imposes, but it may be meant quite literally. In Text 62: 41 Gordon translates:

Also thou shalt not eat the [bread] of *entreaty*
    Nor drink the wine of intercession.

This shows at least that wine can be used as symbolical of an unpleasant or degrading experience. Finally Krt: Text 128: II, 15 is translated as follows:

---

[1] The main authority on these is C. H. Gordon; he has published a transcription of these Texts under the title *Ugaritic Handbook* (Rome 1947). The translation is to be found in *Ugaritic Literature* (Rome 1949).

A cup he takes [in] his hand
A goblet [in the right].

A god is here giving a blessing and is perhaps using a magic wine cup with which to bless. Compare Joseph's divining cup.[1]

From these somewhat obscure references a number of interesting facts stand out. In the fifteenth century B.C. the figure of the wine cup as a symbol of destiny, especially evil destiny, was already in use. There is no evidence for any particular connection between the wine cup and the wrath of the gods, but there was no reason why the connection should not be made, and there was plenty of time between the fifteenth and the seventh century B.C. for the connection to develop. We do also get a possible reference in the last Text quoted to the myth of a magic cup in the hands of the gods. The gap between this and the earliest mention of the figure in the Old Testament is huge; but Albright tells us[2]: "There is a veritable flood of allusions to Canaanite (i.e. Phoenician) literature in Hebrew works composed between the seventh and the third century B.C." Similarly C. H. Gordon, in commenting on the parallels between the Ras Shamra Texts and the Old Testament, says that most of the parallels occur in the later strata of the Old Testament, and that this may be due to a borrowing from Canaanite sources as late as 750 B.C. or even later.[3] So it does seem quite reasonable to claim that the figure of the wine cup as a symbol for destiny, especially evil destiny, was well established in North Semitic mythology by the time that it began to appear in Old Testament literature, and that when it does first appear it is at a time when there is some evidence that Hebrew literature was under the influence of North Semitic thought and literature.

When we turn to the appearances of this figure in the Old Testament we are at once confronted with the problem of deciding which is the earliest reference. There are references in Jeremiah, Nahum, and Habakkuk, and in the Psalms, any of which might be claimed as the first in point of time. We turn to a group of references belonging to the pre-exilic period, and falling roughly within the years 620–600 B.C. We begin with Jer. 13.13:

[1] Gen. 44.2,5.
[2] Albright, *From Stone Age to Christianity* (Baltimore 1946), p. 243.
[3] *Ugaritic Handbook*, p. 201.

I will fill all the inhabitants of this land ... with drunkenness.

Drunkenness is certainly here a figure for stupefaction and helplessness, though there is no explicit reference to the cup of Jahveh's wrath.[1] Then there is an incidental reference to the figure in Nahum 3.11. The prophet says to Nineveh:

Thou also shalt be drunken, thou shalt be hid.

There seems good reason for believing that the original reading instead of "thou shalt be hid" was "thou shalt be smashed".[2] The meaning is that Nineveh is to stagger helplessly under the calamity that is to befall it. It should be noticed that this reference is allusive, as is also that in Jer. 13.13, and it implies that the hearers are already well acquainted with the figure.

We pass to a very difficult passage, Hab. 2.15,16. Recent editors seem to be more convinced of the seventh-century date of Hab. 1 and 2 than was usual a generation ago.[3] The R.V. of this passage is as follows:

Woe unto him that giveth his neighbour drink,
that addest thy venom thereto,
and makest him drunken also,
that thou mayest look on their nakedness!
Thou art filled with shame for glory:
drink thou also, and be as one uncircumcised:
the cup of the Lord's right hand shall be turned unto thee,
and foul shame shall be upon thy glory.

The text of Habakkuk is found in one of the Dead Sea Scrolls, and Hab. 2.15,16 as given there differs in several particulars from the Massoretic Text. The matter is more fully discussed in Appendix 1. The translation we adopt on the basis of the Dead Sea Scrolls text is as follows:

---

[1] *Sic* Peake (op. cit., in loc.), Duhm (ed. Jer., Tübingen and Leipzig 1910–11, in loc.), Cornhill (ed. Jer., Leipzig 1905, in loc.).

[2] Reading תִּשָּׁבְרִי for תִּשָּׁכְרִי (see Kittel, *Bibl. Heb.*, in loc.).

[3] For example, Duhm relegated Habakkuk to the time of Alexander the Great, and Wade (ed. I.C.C., Edinburgh 1911) places this passage just before the Maccabaean era. But Albright (quoted in Rowley *Studies in O.T. Prophecy*, Edinburgh 1950, p. 2) assigns Hab. 1 and 2 to the period 605–589 B.C. Prof. S. H. Hooke in a private communication supports the same view. The fact that the psalm in chap. 3 does not appear in the text of the Commentary on Habakkuk in the Dead Sea Scrolls seems fairly decisive against its being from the time of Habakkuk.

> Woe unto him that gives drink to his neighbour,
> Pouring out his venom to make him drink also,
> So that one may gaze on their nakedness.

Thus verse 15 does not contain a reference to the wrath cup at all; it is a condemnation of those who corrupt their neighbours with strong drink. The wrath cup is aptly introduced in verse 16 (which need not be altered from the R.V. translation): because such a man has corrupted his neighbour with drink, he himself will be made drunk by Jahveh, but in a different way: he will be drunk with disaster. In verse 16 the drunkenness symbolizes the condition of helpless ruin produced by the divine wrath, and the "nakedness" is the shame which accompanies it. Hence we do not really find here what the Massoretic Text would suggest, the thought of the cup of wrath belonging to an individual and being administered by him to others. Such a conception is only found twice in all the literature surveyed in this study (Zadokite Frag. 9.19–20 and Rev. 18.3), and would be foreign to the time of Habakkuk.

Ezekiel uses this figure once in Ezek. 23.31–4:

> Thou hast walked in the way of thy sister; therefore will I give her cup into thine hand. . . . Thou shalt drink of thy sister's cup, which is deep and large: thou shalt be laughed to scorn and had in derision; it containeth much. Thou shalt be filled with drunkenness and sorrow, with the cup of astonishment and desolation, with the cup of thy sister Samaria. Thou shalt even drink it and drain it out, and thou shalt gnaw the sherds thereof.

Here "gnaw the sherds thereof" is probably not original. It may be a gloss or a misreading for "drain the dregs thereof".[1] One editor comments[2]: "She drinks it down eagerly, and then finds that she is taken with wild staggering." But this is to press the figure too far. There is no choice about accepting or refusing the cup, which represents the national destiny. The staggering represents the effects of disaster. The drinking of the cup is not necessarily a conscious process at all. The depth and largeness of the cup here indicate the extent of the coming calamity. There is no specific reference to the divine wrath, though there can be no doubt that this is the wrath cup. What is drunk

---

[1] *Sic* Cooke, ed. Ezek. (I.C.C., Edinburgh 1936), in loc.
[2] Kraetzschmar, ed. Ezek. (Göttingen 1900), in loc.

is wrath, not wine. We may put with this a passage from Lamentations which seems to be nearly contemporary with Ezekiel,[1] Lam. 4.21:

> The cup shall pass through thee, thou shalt be drunken and make thyself naked.

The words are addressed to Edom: this may be the first time that we find the cup of wrath administered to a Gentile nation. The nakedness here means shameful humiliation; the wrath is not specifically referred to, and what is drunk is disaster.

So far in tracing the history of the concept of the wrath cup we have reached about the year 580 B.C. We now come to the most prominent passage in the Old Testament where the figure occurs, Isa. 51.17–23:

> ... Jerusalem, which hast drunk at the hand of the Lord the cup of his fury;
> Thou has drunken the bowl of the cup of staggering, and drained it. ...
> [Thy sons] are full of the fury of the Lord, the rebuke of thy God.
> Therefore hear now this, thou afflicted, and drunken, but not with wine ...
> Behold, I have taken out of thine hand the cup of staggering,
> Even the bowl of the cup of my fury;
> Thou shalt no more drink it again:
> And I will put it into the hand of them that afflict thee.

Most editors agree[2] that the words "of the cup" after "bowl" in each place are a gloss to explain the rare word *qubba'ath*. Here what is drunk is wrath, interpreted as a destiny of suffering and disaster. There is no question of anyone accepting or refusing it, it is to be drunk according to Jahveh's will. We are specifically told that it is *not* wine, but fury, that is drunk. Staggering undoubtedly represents the effects of disaster. As wine makes men stagger with drunkenness, so wrath makes them stagger with disaster. It is most important to notice that the divine wrath is here, as in all the previous passages, simply the will of God worked out in human (or in the case of Habakkuk, individual) history. The recipients may not even be aware that they are drinking the cup.

We pass on to two passages in the Book of Jeremiah, 25.15 and 51.7. Both of these are here assumed not to be from Jeremiah's pen,

---

[1] *Sic* Peake, op. cit., in loc.
[2] *Sic* Box and Kissane (op. cit., in loc.). Kittel (*Bibl. Heb.*, in loc.) points out that Ambrose read "*calicem ruinae bibisti*".

but from some other prophet writing towards the end of the Exile. The reasons for this assumption are given in Appendix 2. Jer. 25.15 runs:

> Take the cup of the wine of this fury at my hand, and cause all the nations, to whom I shall send thee, to drink it. And they shall drink, and reel to and fro, and be mad . . . Then I took the cup at the Lord's hand, and made all the nations to drink.

There follows a list of nations, beginning with Jerusalem. Then verse 27 continues:

> Drink ye, and be drunken, and spue . . . if they refuse to take the cup at thine hand to drink, then shalt thou say unto them . . . Ye shall surely drink.

Here the prophet delivers the cup, a new development; but it is unmistakably Jahveh's cup. Another new characteristic is that the wine is specifically mentioned. Previously the wrath itself had been the contents of the cup; we notice also that the nations may try to refuse the cup, though in vain. Madness and reeling indicate the effects of the disaster. The second passage, Jer. 51.7, runs:

> Babylon hath been a golden cup in the Lord's hand, that made all the earth drunken: the nations have drunk of her wine; therefore the nations are mad.

This passage is echoed in Rev. 17.4; consequently many editors have suggested[1] that this passage refers to the evil influence of Babylon's luxury in debasing the nations under her sway. This is certainly the meaning in Revelation (interpreting Babylon to represent Rome), but we cannot argue back from the passage in the Apocalypse to the meaning of the prophet here. John the Divine was perfectly capable of moulding the Old Testament material to suit his own purposes. The meaning here is much more reminiscent of Isa. 10.5. Babylon has been used by Jahveh as an instrument of his wrath. The madness of the people means the effects of the calamity that is to come upon them. The golden cup symbolizes the pride and glory of the conqueror, not his debasing influence.

There are two passages in the Psalms where this figure occurs in a remarkable manner. The first is Ps. 60.3:

---

[1] E.g. Peake, Cornhill, Duhm.

Thou hast made us to drink the wine of staggering.

Oesterley thinks that this phrase is derived from Isa. 51.17,[1] and therefore places this psalm in the post-exilic period. Others think it comes from shortly before the Exile. The specific mention of the wine would certainly seem to strengthen Oesterley's conjecture, but his suggestion that it refers to the effects of an earthquake is unnecessary. Staggering means simply disaster. The second passage, Ps. 75.8, runs:

> For in the hand of the Lord there is a cup, and the wine foameth;
> It is full of mixture, and he poureth out of the same:
> Surely the dregs thereof, all the wicked of the earth shall wring them out, and drink them.

F. Buhl[2] would emend "he poureth out of the same" to read "he poureth from it wrath". But we do not meet wine and wrath together as the contents of the cup. Briggs (op. cit., in loc.) would omit "in the hand of the Lord" as a gloss, but this is not necessary. The phrase "it is full of mixture" is very doubtful in the Hebrew.[3] Cheyne is so much perplexed by the passage that he emends it, and in his version cup, wine, foam, and dregs all disappear![4] The foaming of the wine no doubt shows its intoxicating quality. It is important to observe that there is no question of there being two groups of people here, the godly who drink the best part of the wine, and the wicked who only get the dregs. The reference to the dregs only means that the ungodly drain the cup to the bottom; cf. Ezek. 23.31–4.

The last passage we must examine in this context is Zech. 12.2. All modern scholars are agreed that chapters 9–14 of Zechariah are not written by the prophet who lived and worked in 520–16 B.C., but by some later prophet, probably one who lived in the Greek period. There is no agreement as to the part of the Greek period to which we should assign this prophet. This passage runs:

> Behold, I will make Jerusalem a cup of reeling unto all the people round about.

---

[1] Oesterley, op. cit., in loc. Those who call it pre-exilic are Baethgen (ed. Psalms, Göttingen 1897) and Briggs (op. cit., in loc.).

[2] In Kittel's *Bibl. Heb.*, in loc., reading חֶמֶר for חָמַר, and אַף for אַךְ.

[3] The Hebrew is מָלֵא מֶסֶךְ.

[4] Cheyne, ed. Psalms (London 1904), in loc.

POST-EXILIC DEVELOPMENTS

The phrase "cup of reeling" is unprecedented,[1] but the meaning is perfectly intelligible: Jahveh is to punish the Gentiles, using the Jews as his instrument. It is an exact parallel to Jer. 51.7. There too the cup is Jahveh's cup, even though administered by others. Oesterley in *An Introduction to the Books of the Old Testament* (London 1934, p. 424) suggests that this passage belongs to 140 B.C., just after the murder of Simon Maccabaeus. At such a juncture the declaration of God's wrath about to be visited on the Gentiles by the hand of the Jews would be most appropriate. There is indeed something of tragic irony in the fact that in a sense wholly unintended by this prophet (perhaps the last of his line) Jerusalem did become a cup in the Lord's hand. But it was the Messiah who drank it, and the wrath was upon Jerusalem, not on him.

We should take some notice also of another figure frequently used for the divine wrath in the Old Testament, the pouring out of the wrath. There is some evidence that this figure also originated in non-Israelite literature. An inscription from Zenzirh of approximately the first half of the eighth century B.C. is translated by Cooke as:

Let Hadad pour out wrath on him.[2]

We should remember that there is some evidence that North Semitic literature was influencing Israelite writers at that time. The figure first occurs in Hos. 5.10 in the Old Testament. It does not occur at all in the Pentateuch. We meet it four times in Jeremiah,[3] and it is very frequent in Ezekiel. It occurs sporadically in Nahum, Zephaniah,[4] the Psalms, Job, Chronicles, and Daniel. Only in the two passages from Nahum and Zephaniah could it be called eschatological. It is interesting that in only one passage in the Old Testament do the figures of the

---

[1] The Hebrew is רַעַל. סַף־רַעַל is a very rare word, only here as a noun. It occurs as a verb in Nahum 2.4 and there is a cognate, רְעָלָה, in Isa. 3.19 meaning a fluttering veil. The LXX of this passage, following another meaning of סַף, translates πρόθυρα σαλευόμενα (this sense of the word is found in Jud. 19.27, where the LXX tr. πρόθυρον). Bredenkampf (ed. Zech., Erlangen 1879, in loc.) actually accepts this sense and tr. "a threshold across which the people will continually pass to and fro".

[2] The Aramaic is חדד חרא ליתכה. Cooke describes this last word as "an Aph'el imperfect 3rd sing. masc. form, with a suffix of the 3rd sing f. from נְתַךְ". See G. A. Cooke, *A Text Book of North Semitic Inscriptions* (Oxford 1903), p. 158, Inscr. 61.

[3] Jer. 7.20; 10.25; 42.18; 44.6. [4] Both in post-exilic passages: Nah. 1.6; Zeph. 3.8.

wrath cup and of the pouring out of the wrath appear together, Ps. 75.8.

Our discussion of the figure of the cup of the wrath and of the pouring of the wrath, then, has led us to the conclusion that both these figures may have originated in North Semitic mythology and first appear in Hebrew literature in the eighth and seventh centuries B.C. Both come into frequent use about the time of Jeremiah, and remain largely, though not exclusively, prophetic throughout. Neither appears in any stratum of the Pentateuch. The main relevance of these two figures to our study is that they appear prominently in the Book of Revelation, where, as we have hinted, the main clue to the meaning of the divine wrath in the New Testament lies. In view of this, it is very important to notice that in the Old Testament these figures have only the very slightest connection with eschatology. The wrath cup is never eschatological; it always refers to definite events in history, not at the end of history. The other figure is only used eschatologically in two out of thirty instances. In the case of the wrath cup, what is drunk is at first the wrath (i.e. disaster); specific mention of wine comes only later. The cup is normally administered only by Jahveh, but in two instances out of eighteen it is administered by some other person or nation.[1] The source of the cup is always Jahveh, and what is drunk is always wrath, though it may sometimes be described as wine. The author of the Book of Revelation uses both these figures, though he never uses them together. An understanding of their significance in the Old Testament is therefore necessary if we are not to misrepresent the meaning of St John the Divine. But with his usual insight he adapts them to his own purpose and gives to the wrath cup at least a deeply Christian meaning.[2]

A SUMMARY OF THE CONCEPTION OF THE WRATH OF GOD IN THE OLD TESTAMENT

The wrath first appears as the direct action of Jahveh against those who have offended him; it is not necessarily moral, not necessarily

---

[1] Jer. 51.7 by Babylon; Zech. 12.2 by Jerusalem.

[2] The following is a list of places not already discussed where the wrath-cup figure occurs: Jer. 48.26; 49.12; 51.39,57 (all assumed to be not by Jeremiah); Obad. 16; Job 21.20; Ps. 11.6; 16.5.

rational, or even susceptible of explanation. It is manifested on unusual occasions, and there is nothing either impersonal or automatic about it. In Deuteronomy and writers of the Deuteronomic school it is increasingly moralized and rationalized, and approximates to the personal reaction of Jahveh to sin; but it is still not yet his reaction to all sin in all circumstances, only to specially flagrant sins, idolatry in particular. Since a frequent manifestation of the divine wrath is through defeat in battle, the Deuteronomic school gives us the beginning of the conception of wrath as a working principle in history. Up to the Exile, the divine wrath is almost always expressed against Israel rather than against her enemies. In the pre-exilic prophets, the wrath is the strong, personal, emotional reaction of God to flagrant sin. It is neither automatic nor impersonal, and is certainly not thought of as being manifested in all misfortunes (e.g. the misfortunes of Jeremiah are never attributed by him to the wrath of Jahveh). As the Exile draws nearer, the note of the divine wrath becomes increasingly insistent in prophecy. In the earliest prophets it could not be described as an outstanding feature.

From the time of the Exile onwards, two distinguishable conceptions of the wrath of God gradually emerge. On the one hand the view of the wrath towards which the Deuteronomic school was tending now becomes standardized. The Chronicler sees the wrath as an inevitable process in history, something remote, awful, automatic, and very impersonal. It is the inevitable process of sin working itself out in history. This view is also reflected in some of the later psalms, in the Book of Proverbs, and supremely in the Book of Daniel. On the other hand the prophetic conception of the wrath as Jahveh's personal reaction to sin is carried on by exilic and post-exilic prophets, but now his wrath is expressed quite as much against Gentiles as against his own people. This prophetic conception of the wrath is accepted and strongly emphasized by the later apocalyptic writers of the Old Testament (with the important exception of the author of the Book of Daniel), but they give to it an eschatological content which it did not have before. Jahveh's wrath is to be supremely manifested against the Gentiles and faithless Jews alike at the last day. Indeed in some ways the apocalyptists, with their uninhibited use of wrath-language and frequent anthropomorphic descriptions of the divine anger, would seem to be a reversion to a more primitive view of the wrath, except that they never conceive of the wrath of God as manifested in any way that is not entirely moral and rational. At the same time, in the exilic and post-exilic periods the mercy of God came to play a larger part in the minds of the writers of the Old Testament. It is the glory of Hosea that long before the Exile he realized something of the conflict between the two attributes of wrath and mercy. Most later writers seem quite content to allow the two attributes to exist side by side, reconciling them, if at all, by the belief that, though mercy towards sinners can extend very far, divine wrath must ultimately be manifested in punishment of the obstinate. Only twice after the Exile, one in "Trito-Isaiah" and once in the Psalms, is any attempt made to reconcile the two attributes. Schultz[1] in his interesting section on the wrath of God in his book on the theology of the Old Testament discusses these points, but he does not seem to distinguish the element of impersonal wrath which proved so important in the New Testament. He writes: "All through the Old Testament, the anger of God is represented as the natural excitement of the holy God, conceived as rising into passion when his holiness and honour are assailed, when his heart boils over like a burning fire." This is true enough of the prophetic tradition (though the prophets did not mix their metaphors when they spoke of the wrath), but it is much less true of the early irrational wrath, and not true at all of the wrath in Chronicles, Proverbs, and the Book of Daniel. A few pages later he adds that the notion of God restraining his wrath was a modification of the original conception, and that his mercy and anger are not opposed, but stand side by side. This again is true, but it is important to add that in three places in the Old Testament the opposition is felt, and the attempt is made—with imperfect success it is true—to reconcile them. Finally we should note that the striking figure of the cup of Jahveh's wrath is used almost exclusively by the prophetic tradition. It would seem at first sight to be inseparably joined to a very personal view of God's anger, but, as it invariably refers to God's action in history, and never to the direct, unmediated effects of the divine wrath, it is not really irreconcilable with a conception of the divine wrath as sin working out its effects in history.

---

[1] Hermann Schultz, *Old Testament Theology* (E.T., Edinburgh 1892), pp. 175, 179.

POST-EXILIC DEVELOPMENTS

The divine wrath is not very prominent in JE, the earliest parts of the Pentateuch, or in P, the latest part. It occurs very frequently in Deuteronomy and the Deuteronomic parts of the Pentateuch. This is no doubt because the Deuteronomist needed a moral principle in history, a need not felt in earlier times. It can be said with relative accuracy that up to the time of Jeremiah the divine wrath is not a prominent feature in prophecy. Ezekiel, with 43 references, emphasizes the wrath more than any other writer in the Old Testament, but this is partly due no doubt to his repetitive style. Considering the relatively small amount of B (the name given by scholars to that part of the Book of Jeremiah which they believe was edited by Baruch), the wrath can be said to be prominent there, and also in Lamentations. This is no doubt because of the proximity of all these writers to the Exile. For contemporaries as well as for subsequent writers, the Exile was *the* great example of the wrath of God. The Persian period as a whole emphasizes the wrath, especially those writers who make up "Trito-Isaiah" and the other post-exilic parts of the Book of Isaiah. This perhaps reflects the unhappy fortunes of the Jews during that period.

There are two ideas about the divine wrath which are remarkable for their rarity in the Old Testament. The first is the idea that men may be able to appease the anger of God. Such a notion is found in the earliest parts (e.g. 1 Sam. 26.19), but in later passages it only occurs when reference is made to traditional stories (e.g. Ps. 106.23,30). The term *shūbh*, "to turn" is often used of the divine wrath, but it is normally Jahveh who turns his own wrath (e.g. Ps. 85.3). The other concept which is almost wholly lacking is the thought of the divine wrath as disciplinary. It does as a matter of fact occur once, in Ps. 6.1 (verse 2 in the Hebrew):

Oh Lord, rebuke me not in thine anger,
Neither chasten me in thy hot displeasure.

On the other hand the Psalmist here does not seem to relish the Lord's discipline, for he implores him to remove his rod. In verse 5 he reminds God that no one will remember him in death, which suggests that this "chastening" may have been more punitive than disciplinary.[1] The

---

[1] An apparent exception is Ezek. 24.1–14, where it looks as if the wrath had a purging effect, especially in verse 13: "Because I have purged thee and thou wast not purged,

fact that these two concepts are so little represented in the Old Testament is all the more significant because both of them appear quite clearly in the inter-Testamental period, and both are modifications of the idea of the divine wrath which Christian theologians have often made use of under the impression that they have sound biblical backing

---

thou shalt not be purged from thy filthiness any more, till I have satisfied my fury upon thee." But the wrath here seems to be punitive and destructive; cf. especially verse 8, where the wrath is certainly punitive ("to come up to take vengeance"). The idea is that Jerusalem (the cauldron) will be competely destroyed. A remnant will indeed survive, but not in Jerusalem. Editors on the whole take this view: Toy (Polychrome Bible, London–Stuttgart–New York 1899, in loc.): "Jerusalem is beyond cleansing; there is nothing left for her but destruction." Lofthouse (Century Bible, 1907, in loc.): "Now there remains nothing but to destroy the cauldron." Cooke (op. cit., in loc.): "To purge the city Jahveh will destroy it altogether." But destruction is not discipline. Davidson alone looks on the process as disciplinary (op. cit., in loc.). He says the cauldron is "a figure for the purifying judgements continued long after the destruction of the city". It is difficult to see how a city that has been destroyed can undergo purifying judgements. The wrath destroys the city in punishment: the remnant deported to Babylon are purged.

3

THE WRATH IN THE INTER-TESTAMENTAL PERIOD

THE APOCRYPHA

JESUS BEN SIRACH shows himself in his Book of Wisdom to be on the whole a disciple of the Chronicler in his references to the divine wrath rather than of the prophetic tradition; for example, in Ecclus. 7.16 we read:

> Remember that wrath will not tarry.

Similarly 16.6 runs:

> And in a disobedient nation wrath is kindled.

The Syriac translates this as "reigneth anger".[1] A third example is 18.24:

> Think upon the wrath that shall be in the days of the end.

See finally 23.16:

> Two sorts of men multiply sins
> And the third will bring wrath.

The Hebrew is lacking here but the Greek is ἐπάξει ὀργήν; cf. Rom. 3.5. There is an interesting phrase in 5.6 and 16.11:[2]

> And say not, his compassion is great;
> He will be pacified for the multitude of my sins:
> For mercy and wrath are with him,
> And his indignation will rest upon sinners.

Here is a simple juxtaposition of the mercy and the wrath of God, with no feeling of embarrassment at a possible clash between them. Oesterley's comment is: "Mercy and wrath are the two characteristics of God on which the two prophets Hosea and Amos lay stress." This is hardly appropriate, seeing that Amos does not mention the divine

---

[1] See Oesterley, ed. Ecclesiasticus (Cambridge 1912), in loc.

[2] One is probably a gloss; Oesterley rejects the first, Lévi the second (Lévi, ed. Heb. text Ecclus., Paris 1898, in loc.).

wrath at all. It would be more accurate to say that Hosea stresses both these qualities, but feels the tension between them far more than does ben Sirach.

It is interesting that the thought of appeasing God's wrath occurs clearly in Ecclesiasticus. In 38.28 he speaks of the winds as "appeasing the wrath of him that made them".[1] In 48.10 the author is speaking of Elijah, and says that he was "recorded ... to pacify anger before it brake forth into wrath". The Greek is corrupt and the Hebrew has no word corresponding to "wrath", but it seems to be a reference to Elijah's traditional rôle as forerunner of the Messiah (see Mal. 4.5). He was "to turn the heart of the father to the children" and thus remove occasions for wrath. It is therefore unexpectedly eschatological. We should also notice a remarkable use of the word "longsuffering" in 5.4

> Say not, I sinned, and what happend unto me?
> For the Lord is longsuffering ...

If "for the Lord is longsuffering" is part of the speech of the man reprehended by ben Sirach, then "longsuffering" here has virtually the meaning of "not bearing wrath at all", as it has in some parts of the New Testament. But Oesterley takes the phrase as our author's reply, and it will therefore have the sense: "The Lord is longsuffering, but his wrath must strike in the end." In this case it is a good parallel to Luke 18.7, where the faithful are encouraged to bear the oppression of the unjust by the thought that the Lord is longsuffering, i.e. his punishment delays but comes in the end.

The Books of the Maccabees, diverse though they are in authorship and time of writing, have a certain unity of subject; moreover they all fall roughly within the first century B.C. We find that in them the notion of man being able to appease God's wrath is expressed more clearly than anywhere in the Old Testament. 1 Macc. 3.8 has the merest allusion. Judas is described as "turning away wrath from Israel". He does this by killing the ungodly. A clearer reference occurs in 2 Macc. 7.38. One of the seven martyr brothers prays that:

> In me and in my brethren thou mayest stay the wrath of the Almighty, which hath been justly brought upon our whole race.

---

[1] Lévi, without much justification, calls this verse a gloss.

THE WRATH IN THE INTER-TESTAMENTAL PERIOD

The same sentiment is expressed at about the beginning of our era[1] in 4 Macc. 9.24, though the divine wrath is not specifically named:

> That just providence which our fathers experienced became propitious to our nation.[2]

This happened through the deaths of the seven martyrs. Similarly 4 Macc. 17.22 runs:

> So that they (the martyrs) became a ransom for the sin of the nation, and through the blood of those godly men and their propitiatory death the divine providence rescued Israel, which had suffered such evils previously.[3]

Compare also 4 Macc. 6.27,28; 12.18. In all these passages we find the new conception that the death of the righteous propitiates the divine anger.

We also find in the Books of the Maccabees the impersonal character of the wrath strongly emphasized; cf. 1 Macc. 1.64:

> And there came exceeding great wrath against Israel.

This is an echo of 2 Kings 3.27. Similarly 1 Macc. 2.49 speaks of "a season of overthrow and wrath of indignation". It is remarkable that all references to the divine wrath in 1 Maccabees speak of "the wrath" unqualified. This is not so in 2 Maccabees, where the wrath is always described as God's wrath. But the conception of the author of 2 Maccabees of the divine wrath as being evinced in the Antiochene persecution, and withdrawn as soon as Israel had been sufficiently chastized, is much more like the Book of Daniel than the prophetic-apocalyptic tradition; cf. 2 Macc. 5.17:

> Not seeing that because of the sins of them that dwelt in the city, the sovereign Lord had been provoked to anger a little while, and therefore his eye was then turned away from the place.

So also 2 Macc. 7.33. This tradition of lofty and impersonal wrath is continued in 4 Maccabees, but there must arise in the case of this book

---

[1] Emmet, ed. 3 and 4 Maccabees (London 1918).
[2] ἵλεως ἡ δικάια καὶ πάτριος ἡμῶν πρόνοια τῷ ἔθνει γενηθεῖσα (my own translation).
[3] ὥσπερ ἀντίψυχον γεγονότας τῆς τοῦ ἔθνους ἁμαρτίας καὶ διὰ τοῦ αἵματος τῶν εὐσέβων ἐκείνων καὶ τοῦ ἱλαστηρίου θανάτου αὐτῶν ἡ θεία πρόνοια τὸν Ἰσραὴλ προκακωθέντα διέσωσεν (my own translation).

the question whether the impersonal element may not be rather due to a pseudo-philosophical style than to any deliberately impersonal view of the divine anger. Compare 4 Macc. 4.21:

> Divine justice, being angered at this [Jason's impious behaviour], raised up Antiochus himself to war.[1]

See also 4 Macc. 9.32:

> Oh, foulest tyrant, you shall not escape the punishment of the divine wrath.[2]

In 2 Maccabees we find the conception of the wrath as the chastening of Israel, an idea which we have only found once in the Old Testament (Ps. 6.1). Cf. 2 Macc. 6.12–14, and especially 7.33:

> And if for rebuke and chastening our living Lord hath been angered a little while, yet shall he again be reconciled with his own servants.

We shall find the idea of the divine anger as disciplinary further developed in the Book of Wisdom. It is really a bypath or *cul de sac* in the development of the doctrine of the divine wrath. Wrath which is disciplinary is not really wrath at all. The identification could only take place when the wrath had been so far associated with the effects of the wrath that the thought of the wrath as an attitude of God towards the sinner had almost disappeared. In the New Testament we shall see that this association is so fully accepted that the wrath is not thought of as an attitude of God at all. But the New Testament does not, except for an *arrière pensée* of Paul, conceive of the wrath as disciplinary.

Oesterley's argument in his *Introduction to the Books of the Apocrypha*, whereby he lays aside the doubts he had expressed in his earlier work[3] and accepts the date A.D. 40 for Wisdom, does not seem to have commended itself to other scholars, so presumably it may still be treated as a work of the first century B.C. The author of Wisdom shows a marked tendency to modify, qualify, and as far as possible explain away traditional instances of the wrath of God against Israel. On the other hand he has no hesitation in dwelling on the examples of the wrath manifested against the Gentiles; indeed in places he emphasizes the contrast; e.g. Wisd. 11.9; speaking of Israel he says:

---

[1] ἐφ' οἷς ἀγανακτήσασα ἡ θεία δίκη αὐτόν τοι τὸν Ἀντίοχον ἐπολέμησεν.
[2] οὐκ ἐκφεύξησθε, μιαρώτατε τύραννε, τὰς τῆς θείας ὀργῆς δίκας.
[3] *The Books of the Apocrypha* (London 1916).

THE WRATH IN THE INTER-TESTAMENTAL PERIOD

For when they were tried, albeit but in mercy chastened, they learned how the ungodly were tormented, being judged with wrath.

The chastening is not here identified with the wrath, but it is in 16.5. Of the fiery serpents he says:

Thy wrath continued not to the uttermost... but for admonition were they troubled for a short space.[1]

Compare also 18.20, where again the temporary nature of the wrath is stressed. Likewise 18.25 runs:

For it was enough only to make trial of the wrath.

This contrasts with 19.1:

But upon the ungodly there came unto the end indignation without mercy.

So the author of Wisdom is expressing the idea which also appears in 2 Maccabees, that the wrath, on Israel at least, is disciplinary, not retributive. In thus softening the significance of the wrath on Israel and emphasizing the wrath on the Gentiles, the author is reversing the position which we find in the earlier parts of the Bible, and indeed right up to the Exile. Nor does he show the insight of the author of Daniel, who, as we have seen, understood the Antiochene persecution as primarily an instance of God's wrath against Israel, and the final wrath to be manifested against the persecutor is only allowed to appear in the background. It is only fair to quote also Wisd. 12.2:

And, putting them [the Egyptians] in remembrance by the very things wherein they sin, dost thou admonish them,
That escaping from their wickedness they may believe in thee, O Lord.

Here even wrath against the Gentiles is thought of as paedeutic. But no doubt Gregg is right in holding that this is inconsistent with 11.9.[2]

On the whole the author of Wisdom is with the Chronicler and the writers of the Books of Maccabees rather than with the prophets and apocalyptists, in that his conception of the wrath tends to be impersonal. In 5.20 he represents God as "sharpening stern wrath for a sword". Gregg[3] compares Ezek. 21.9, but there is no mention of wrath

---

[1] οὐ μεχρὶ τέλους ἔμεινεν ἡ ὀργή σου... εἰς νουθεσίαν πρὸς ὀλίγον ἐταράχθησαν.
[2] Ed. Wisdom (Cambridge Bible, 1909).
[3] Op. cit., in loc.

there, and a better parallel is with Isa. 13.5, with its mention of "the weapons of his indignation". In this Wisdom passage the wrath is thought of as something comparable to an avenging angel. In the ensuing verses it is associated with natural forces, which are pictured as carrying out God's commands of vengeance. Compare Ecclus. 39.28–31. A similar passage is the famous one in Wisd. 18.15f., where the "all-powerful word" is pictured as leaping like a warrior down from heaven upon the Egyptians "bearing as a sharp sword thine unfeigned commandment". If we compare together these two passages (Wisd. 5.20 and 18.15,16) with Heb. 4.12,13, the description of the word "sharper than any two-edged sword", we find a striking contrast. The word in Wisdom comes as a sharp sword to execute judgement upon the Egyptians with plagues; the Word of the New Testament comes likewise from heaven, but comes to die for the ungodly, and that very dying is a judgement and in its own way a manifestation of the divine wrath. In Wisd. 11.9 (already quoted) the divine wrath is called simply ὀργή; and in 18.20 ἡ ὀργή is used without further qualification; cf. also 18.21 (τῷ θυμῷ); 18.23 (τὴν ὀργήν); 18.25 (τῆς ὀργῆς); 19.1 (ἀνελεήμων θυμός). In none of these does the phrase "wrath *of God*" appear. It is also significant that there is no verb expressing the wrath used in the book.

In Baruch 4.24 occur the words:

My children, suffer patiently the wrath that is come upon you from God.

The Greek for "suffer patiently" is μακροθυμήσατε, a remarkable use of the word. It can only mean "be patient" with no sense at all of "forebear your wrath". Moreover the readers are called upon to look on the divine wrath as something temporary which they must endure. In other places (e.g. Isa. 26.20,21) the Israelites are called upon to hide themselves from the wrath which is to fall upon others. The nearest parallel to the Baruch passage is Job 14.13, where, however, the conception is more profound than here. Baruch seems to have been written in the Roman period, but before the fall of Jerusalem.[1] It is therefore contemporary with the New Testament, but in Baruch wrath and misfortune have been so much identified that the wrath is losing its wrathful character altogether. It is the ossification of the concept of the

---

[1] See Stevenson, *Wisdom and the Apocryphal Writings* (London 1903), in loc.

divine wrath, due no doubt to ignorance of, or deliberately ignoring, the vital new insight into the wrath which was being brought by Christianity.

JEWISH APOCALYPTIC LITERATURE

The Book of Enoch (1 Enoch) is chiefly interesting from our point of view for its emphasis on the abiding wrath of God, e.g. Enoch 55.3:

> I will cause my chastisement and my wrath to abide on them.

See also 62.12:

> Because the wrath of the Lord of Spirits resteth on them.[1]

Compare also 64.4:

> And upon the flesh of men abideth thy wrath until the great day of judgement.[2]

This is both eschatological and exemplary of the abiding wrath. In some ways this concept of the abiding wrath may have prepared the way for the Pauline (and still more Johannine) conception of the wrath as a spiritual condition.

The Testaments of the Twelve Patriarchs gives us one very remarkable phrase for the wrath in Levi 6.11:

> And the wrath of God came upon them to the uttermost.

This[3] is apparently quoted by Paul in 1 Thess. 2.16.[4] The difference of context is however most striking. In the Testaments Levi is speaking of the men of Shechem, and the form that the wrath took in their case was destruction by Levi and his brothers. Paul is speaking of the Jews, who at the time that he was writing were quite unharmed in worldly estate.

In the Psalms of Solomon there is a reference to the cup of wrath which serves to link up in some respects the Old Testament with the

---

[1] Charles (ed. *The Apocrypha and Pseudepigrapha of the Old Testament*, Oxford 1913, in loc.) dates both these passages as 105–64 B.C.

[2] Charles dates this passage as belonging to the time of Judas Maccabaeus.

[3] ἔφθασεν δὲ αὐτοὺς ἡ ὀργὴ τοῦ Θεοῦ εἰς τέλος. Recently M. de Jonge has contended that the book is a Christian work using Jewish materials, so perhaps Paul is the original here. See *J.T.S.*, Oct. 1955, p. 287.

[4] He writes ἐπ' αὐτούς.

New. In 8.15 the author of the Psalms of Solomon is speaking of the Jews who allowed Pompey to enter Jerusalem in 63 B.C.:

> God mixed for them the spirit of error,
> He made them drink a cup of unmixed wine
>   So as to make them drunk.[1]

With the first line Viteau compares Isa. 29.10, a passage which has no reference to the divine wrath, but simply discusses the foolishness and stupor which has fallen upon Israel's leaders. But in the second line phrases are used that in the Old Testament invariably mean not just madness and stupidity, but dismay and disaster. As we have seen, in the Old Testament the figurative use of the "cup of wrath" always means "destiny" or "fate", usually "evil destiny". That may be the case here, and the author may be referring to the destiny of conquest and oppression which the Jews brought upon themselves in 63 B.C. But it seems more likely that the second line is parallel in sense to the first and that "drunk" refers to stupidity and madness, not disaster. In that case the author is not really referring to the divine wrath, but is using, without fully comprehending its meaning, language which in the Old Testament is always associated with the divine wrath.

The recent discoveries of the Dead Sea Scrolls in Palestine have thrown more light on the work which for the last fifty years has been known as "The Zadokite Fragment" (though some scholars today prefer to refer to it as belonging to "The Judaean Covenanters"). The actual dating of the Fragment is not certain.[2] The Fragment is noteworthy from our point of view because of its frequent and unrestrained references to the divine wrath. Perhaps this was because the Zadokites seem in some respects to have harked back to the prophetic tradition. In the relatively small Fragment there are as much as eight references to the divine anger; e.g. 3.7, speaking of the generation before the Flood, it says:

> Until his wrath was kindled against them.[3]

---

[1] ἐκέρασεν αὐτοῖς ὁ Θεὸς πνεῦμα πλανήσεως,
ἐπότισεν αὐτοῖς ποτήριον οἴνου ἀκράτου εἰς μέθην.
Viteau (in Charles, op. cit., in loc.) dates the Psalms of Solomon as approximately 50 B.C.

[2] But it is now clear that the dating of this Fragment is intimately bound up with the dating of the Dead Sea Scrolls.

[3] Schechter's tr. of the Frag. in *Documents of Jewish Sectaries*, Vol. I, Cambridge 1910, in loc.

THE WRATH IN THE INTER-TESTAMENTAL PERIOD

Unlike the writers of Genesis, the author of this document sees the Flood as an example of God's wrath. There is some evidence that the Zadokites thought of some era as "the period of the wrath", cf. 1.5.[1] But Charles[2] brackets this phrase, and Schechter translates it "at the end of the wrath". Wrath is pronounced against Israel in 9.40:

> And during this period there shall be kindled the wrath of God against Israel.

This passage refers to the coming time of the Messiah; but the Messiah is not made the instrument of the wrath, still less is there any mention of the wrath of the Messiah. For so astonishing a thought we must turn to the Christian Apocalypse. In two places there are traces of a doctrine of reprobation. 2.6 says:

> For God chose [the wicked] from the beginning of the world, and ere they were formed he knew their works.

See also 2.10: "But them he hated he made to go astray." The thought of men being preordained to sin and wickedness seems to have grown more pronounced in the inter-Testamental period. It is not a marked characteristic of New Testament thought, though, as we shall see, Paul in one place only just avoids committing himself to it.

It is very interesting that in one place the author of the Zadokite Fragment so interprets Scripture as to find in it a reference to the wine cup of Jahveh. In 9.19–20 the writer quotes Deut. 32.33:

> ... those of whom God has said:
> The venom of dragons is in their wine; and the cruel poison of asps.
> The "dragons" are the kings of the peoples, and "their wine" is their ways;
> And "the poison of asps" is the chief of the kings of Yavan,
> Who has come to execute vengeance upon them.

Now our writer can hardly be correct in seeing a reference to the wine cup of God's wrath in this quotation from one of the Songs in Deuteronomy, but what is interesting is that he apparently thinks of the "wine cup" as meaning "evil influence or destiny brought by others", not brought directly by God. This is unprecedented in the Old Testament, where the cup is always the cup of destiny sent

---

[1] בְּקֵץ חָרוֹן.   [2] Op. cit., in loc.

directly by Jahveh, though he may give it to others to administer (e.g. Babylon or Jerusalem). Here however it is nevertheless the cup of Jahveh's wrath at one remove, for the context in the Fragment shows that he is thinking of the evil influence of the kings of Yavan as the mode of Jahveh's wrath. Dupont-Sommer[1] is no doubt right in saying that these Gentile kings were the instruments of God's wrath. The parallel with Rev. 18.3 is remarkable. The angel says of Babylon:

> By the wine of the wrath of her fornication all the nations are fallen.

In this Revelation passage also (and here also alone in the New Testament) the "wine of the wrath" means the evil influence or destiny brought on others by a Gentile nation; and here also it is God's wrath at one remove.

There are no very remarkable references to the divine wrath in the Dead Sea Scrolls so far published, though references do occur, both in the Psalms of Thanksgiving[2] and in The War of the Sons of Light and the Sons of Darkness.[3] The Commentator on Habakkuk seems to take the difficult passage Hab. 2.15 as a simple reference to literal drunkenness, for he comments on this verse (which he applies to the figure whom he calls the Wicked Priest):

> He has followed the ways of drunkenness to quench his thirst. But the cup of the anger of God [this is a reference to verse 16] shall swallow him up.[4]

Jahveh's cup swallowing its victims rather than the victims swallowing the cup is indeed a bizarre idea! It shows how much by this time the

---

[1] A. Dupont-Somner, *The Dead Sea Scrolls* (Tr., Oxford 1952), p. 56.
[2] E.g. Psalm C:
   While the rope (of destruction) descended on the damned,
   and the destiny of anger on the abandoned,
   and the overflowing of Wrath on the outcasts,
   and it was the time of Fury for all Belial.
(Dupont-Sommer, op. cit., p. 73). The most diverse opinions have been expressed by scholars about the literary value of these Psalms of Thanksgiving. Dupont-Sommer (op. cit., p. 70) greatly admires their beautiful spirituality, while G. R. Driver (*The Hebrew Scrolls*, Oxford 1951, in loc.) considers them a mere catena of Old Testament passages with no originality of their own.
[3] On the ensign of one group of the Sons of Light is to be inscribed: "Wrath of God, full of anger, against Belial, and all the people of his party, without any survivors" (Dupont-Sommer, op. cit., p. 82). [4] Dupont-Sommer tr., p. 35.

THE WRATH IN THE INTER-TESTAMENTAL PERIOD

original figure of the cup of wrath had lost its freshness and had come to represent simply a synonym for "evil destiny from God".

It would be exceedingly rash to be dogmatic about the date of these newly discovered documents and the Zadokite Fragment, since eminent authorities are still very far from being agreed among themselves on this question. There are still some apparently who would connect them with the Ḳaraite movement of about A.D. 1000,[1] but on the whole the more likely period seems to be somewhere between 200 B.C. and the time of Our Lord. Rowley (op. cit., p. 64) is inclined to think that the Zadokite Sect originated about 200 B.C. and that the Habakkuk Commentary reflects the conditions of the Maccabaean Age. The Zadokite Fragment, he suggests, may have been written about 130 B.C. Dupont-Sommer argues strongly for the period of the Roman conquest about 63 B.C. (op. cit., p. 27). But he then has great difficulty in finding a suitable candidate for the Teacher of Righteousness mentioned in the Fragment, whereas Rowley's scheme seems to fit the details better: the Teacher of Righteousness is the High Priest Onias III (murdered in 171 B.C.), the Wicked Priest is Menelaus, and the Man of Scorn is Antiochus Epiphanes. The Maccabaean period therefore seems to be the most likely of all the dates suggested so far. But further deciphering of the scrolls may bring yet more light.

2 Esdras is the only book in the inter-Testamental period which attempts a solution of the problem of the mercy and the wrath of God. The subject is discussed in chapter 8, a part of what is called the Salathiel Apocalypse. Box[2] would date this Apocalypse at about A.D. 100 and Duff[3] at A.D. 90. In 8.30 the author protests:

Nor art thou angry with those who are worse than the beasts.[4]

He probably refers to the unfaithful Jews. In 8.34 a solution to the problem is suggested. He refers to Job 7.17 and comments:

What then is man that thou shouldest be angry with him,
Or his corruptible race that thou shouldest be so bitter against him?[5]

---

[1] See H. H. Rowley, *The Zadokite Fragments and the Dead Sea Scrolls* (Oxford 1952), pp. 35–7. [2] Ed. Apocalypse of Ezra in Charles, op. cit.
[3] Ed. First and Second Books of Esdras (London 1902).
[4] *Neque indigneris eis qui bestiis peius sunt.*
[5] *Quid enim est homo ut ei indigneris,*
   Aut genus corruptibile ut ita amariceris in ipso?

He goes on to suggest that those who are destroyed by the wrath of God are qualitatively less important than the righteous who are saved. This is an attempted solution to the problem, but it is not the Christian solution; indeed it was made impossible of acceptance by the success of Christianity. Only in our day, with the rise of an explicitly non-Christian doctrine of man, has the doctrine been revived that large sections of humanity are only worthy to be destroyed.

The Martyrdom of Isaiah, a Jewish work of the first century A.D.,[1] throws some more light on the interesting use of the cup-figure which we have noticed in the Psalms of Solomon. In 5.13 Isaiah is represented as saying: "For me only hath God mingled the cup." "The cup" here certainly means "destiny of suffering", but does it also mean the cup of God's wrath? On the whole it seems unlikely; nowhere in the Old Testament is it suggested that God's faithful prophets could be the objects of his wrath, and it is very unlikely that some eight hundred years after his day, when Isaiah must long ago have been accepted as one of the saints of Israel, he would be represented as suffering from God's wrath. Already about a hundred years before the publication of the Martyrdom of Isaiah the cup-figure had been used in the Psalms of Solomon to indicate probably mere misfortune or foolishness, rather than divine wrath. The use here therefore seems to be parallel to the use of "cup" in the Gospels to mean "destiny of suffering" without any necessary implication that the suffering was caused by God's wrath. In the New Testament, where the cup is thought of as the cup of wrath it is explicitly stated. Where "the cup" is used without reference to the wrath we are not necessarily to read the wrath into it. Compare Isa. 29.10 and Ps. Sol. 8.15.

The cup or wine figure appears again in 2 Baruch or the Syriac Apocalypse of Baruch, which is dated by Charles as A.D. 50–100. The reference occurs in 13.8:

> Ye who have drunk the strained wine,
> Drink ye also of its dregs,
> The judgement of the lofty one
> Who has no respect of persons.

The contrast here is between the "strained wine" which means good

---

[1] See Charles, op. cit., in loc.

fortune, and "the dregs" which means evil fortune. This is not what we find in the Old Testament, where invariably the wine simply means disaster as an expression of the divine wrath, and where drinking the dregs only means experiencing that disaster to the uttermost. But the modification of the wine-figure which we find here is in accordance with the other two uses of the figure found in the inter-Testamental period, where, as we have seen, the cup simply stands for the destiny which God decrees and not necessarily as that destiny conceived as an expression of the divine wrath. The New Testament here follows the inter-Testamental usage. This same Apocalypse shows a marked tendency to impersonalize the wrath; cf. 12.4:

> For assuredly in its own season shall the wrath wake against thee [the land of Israel], which now in longsuffering is held in as it were by reins.[1]

See also 64.4:

> And then wrath went forth from the presence of the Mighty One.

This phrase echoes 2 Chron. 19.2. It is interesting that even in apocalyptic writings, which tend on the whole to follow the prophetic tradition of wrath-language, we can find phrases that so strongly represent the wrath as impersonal.

Finally we should notice a strange conceit in a very late Jewish work, the Apocalypse of Abraham. Wicks[2] relegates it to the very end of the first century A.D. In chapter 25 of this book[3] Abraham sees "an image of jealousy", and after that a shining bronze statue. God explains that the statue is

> my wrath with which the people that is to come from thee will make me wroth.[4]

This seems to be a reversion to the very pragmatic view of the divine wrath which we first observed in Jeremiah, whereby the wrath is almost totally identified with its effects. The identification had already

---

[1] Fragments of the Greek survive: ⟨πρός σε ἡ ὀργὴ ἡ νῦν ἡ ὑπὸ τ⟩ῆς μακροθυμ⟨ι⟩ ... Brackets in Charles' text seem to indicate letters conjecturally restored.
[2] Wicks, *The Doctrine of God in Jewish Apocryphal and Apocalyptic Literature* (London 1915), p. 240.
[3] Chapters as in Bonwetsch, *Die Apokalypse Abrahams* (Leipzig 1897).
[4] I have translated from Bonwetsch's German version. The work is only extant in Old Slavonic.

been accepted in Paul's writings when the Apocalypse of Abraham was composed.

THE RABBIS

The earliest Rabbi whose sayings can be dated is probably later than either Philo or Josephus, but it seems best to deal with the divine wrath as reflected in the rabbinic tradition at this point, as the Rabbis were in certain ways continuous with the Apocalyptists, and certainly have more in common with them than they have with the Hellenizing tradition of Philo and Josephus.

Montefiore[1] points out that on the whole the Rabbis tried to modify the full effect of the crueller descriptions of God in the Old Testament, and this certainly applies to their treatment of the wrath of God. A favourite statement is that "The Lord controls his anger and is not controlled by it", e.g. Judah the Prince; and Huna II, a Palestinian Rabbi of the fourth century A.D. Judah the Prince is also recorded as saying: "I am a jealous God, but jealousy does not rule over me."[2] Another similar sentiment is "God fences wrath, but wrath does not fence him" (Genesis Rabbah).[3] Another Rabbi, Samuel ben Nahmani (Palestinian third generation)[4] makes the distinction that when God promises good things on condition of good behaviour, he keeps his promise even if the behaviour is not good. (Ps. 105.44: "He gave them lands of nations that they might keep his statutes"; they did not keep his statutes, but he gave them the lands.) On the other hand "when God swore in his wrath he did retract, for he swore to punish. For God said, I am not a mortal man to swear to punish and to exult in doing so." This is written very much in the spirit of Hos. 11, and is perhaps the nearest the Rabbis get to an attempted solution to the problem of the wrath of God: God's wrath is less pronounced than his love and is subordinate to his love. It is as far as many Christians get also, but the New Testament has a deeper word to say. Compare also these two quotations: "Is there ever anger before the Holy One, blessed be he? Yes, for there is a teaching, A God that has indignation

---

[1] C. G. Montefiore and H. Loewe, *A Rabbinic Anthology*, p. 52.
[2] Quoted in Montefiore and Loewe, op. cit., p. 54.
[3] Quoted op. cit., p. 57.
[4] Op. cit., in loc.

every day (Ps. 7.11). But how long does his anger last? A moment. And how long is a moment? The minutest fraction of time."[1] And again: "When God is angry, he says to the sinner who has provoked him, Thou hast caused me to take up a trade that is not mine."[2]

The thought of the divine wrath as disciplinary does find an echo in the Rabbis, though it is not as prominent as one might have expected, offering as it does some relief from the wrath-mercy tension. The Canticles Rabbah[3] comments on "Thou art fair, my beloved, yea pleasant" (Cant. 1.16) punning on the word for "Yea".[4] It takes it as meaning "wrath" instead of "yea" and says, speaking on behalf of Israel: "Even thy wrath which thou bringest upon me is pleasant, because thus thou causest me to return and bringest me back to virtue." In thus modifying, and to some extent explaining away, the divine wrath in the Old Testament the Rabbis are on the whole in the tradition of the Chronicler and the Hellenizers rather than of the Apocalyptists. They say perhaps as much as can be said in palliation of the sternest elements in the Old Testament conception of the wrath of God. What is most significant about the Rabbis' treatment of the wrath, however, is what they fail to say rather than what they actually say. We find among them no trace of the impersonal conception of the divine wrath, no particular connection between the divine wrath and the Messiah, and little or no serious attempt to reconcile the divine wrath with the divine love. We can say with certainty that, whatever the source of Paul's conception of the "impersonal" wrath of God, he did not derive it from his Rabbinic background.

THE HELLENIZERS

We must now turn to a group of three writers who have one thing in common: they were all concerned to present the Old Testament in a favourable light to the Graeco-Roman intellectual world. Hence we have included them all under the title of "The Hellenizers". It is interesting to see how they deal with what the Old Testament has to say about the wrath of God.

---

[1] Berakot 7a, quoted op. cit., p. 57.
[2] Tanhuma, ed. S. Büber, quoted op. cit., p. 57.
[3] Quoted op. cit., p. 93.
[4] אַף in Heb.

The first of this group is the author of the Letter to Aristeas. According to H. T. Andrews[1] it was written some time between 130 and 70 B.C., though in its present form it may be as late as A.D. 30. In the course of this letter the Egyptian king is represented as posing a number of questions to the Jewish sages who translated the Pentateuch into Greek. In para. 254 he puts two questions:

1. How can (God) be without wrath?
2. For what cause shall he be wroth?

To both these questions one of the sages answers:

> God governs the whole universe in goodwill and without any anger at all.

The sage who gave this answer must have fervently hoped that the king would not read very far in the work that had just been translated, for he would find there a very different opinion about the divine wrath! The author of the Letter to Aristeas is plainly endeavouring to present the Hebrew religion in a favourable light to the Greeks, and consequently tries to ignore so personal an attribute of God as wrath. In the above quotation "wrath" represents θυμός in Greek, and "anger" ὀργή. Our author uses them interchangeably. In view of the use of these words in Philo, Josephus, and the New Testament, this is interesting.

As we might expect from the Letter to Aristeas, we find that in Philo the wrath of God is officially denied. It was too anthropomorphic, too unlike the passionless, intellectual God of Greek philosophy which Philo so valiantly endeavours in his metaphysical works to reconcile with the Hebrew scriptures. The *locus classicus* for Philo's conception of the divine wrath is *Quod Deus Immutabilis*, para. 51 sq.[2] Commenting on the LXX of Genesis 6.7, which is ἐθυμώθην ὅτι ἐποίησα αὐτόν ("for I am angry that I have made him"), Philo says:

> Again some people hearing these words think that absolute being endures wrath and anger (θυμοῖς καὶ ὀργαῖς). But he is no way affected by any such thing.

---

[1] In Charles, op. cit., in loc. The Greek text is printed in Swete's *Introduction to the Old Testament in Greek* (2nd ed., Cambridge 1902), p. 263. I have given my own translation.
[2] πάλιν τινες τῶν εἰρημένων ἀκούσαντες ὑπολαμβάνουσι θυμοῖς καὶ ὀργαῖς χρῆσθαι τὸ ὄν. ἐστὶ δὲ οὐδένι ληπτὸν πάθει τὸ παράπαν.

How then does he explain the frequent references to the divine wrath in the Old Testament? He seems to attempt three lines of explanation. The first is that the language of wrath is used by way of accommodation to weak and foolish understandings. Thus he says in para. 52 of this passage:

> It is said for the purpose of instructing those who can be brought to their senses by no other means.

Again in para. 60 sq. of the same work he writes:

> Moses moreover dilates upon jealously, wrath, and anger (ζῆλον, θυμόν, ὀργάς) and similar anthropomorphisms ... because a terrible master is a healthy thing for ill-trained and unreflecting slaves. They tremble at his threats and menaces and even against their will receive instruction through fear. So all this class of people should learn salutary falsehoods if they cannot be brought to reason by the truth.

A little further down he adds:

> He [Moses] hoped he would be able to frustrate this sort of character, if when introducing the ultimate cause into his narrative, he were to use threats, angry language, and unappeasable wrath, and in short police methods (ἀμυντηρίοις ὅπλοις) for the punishment of the unrighteous. For only by this means is the fool instructed.

This is the excuse for the employment of the white lie hallowed by Philo's master Plato, and it is the most intellectually respectable of Philo's apologies for the wrath. But in this same passage he suggests two other reasons for the divine wrath as well. In para. 70 of this same work he suggests that perhaps God allowed Moses to write these and similar words in order to show the bad effects of wrath (θυμός) on men's minds, because even in the case of God his wrath leads to bad effects:

> So perhaps he wishes to suggest some such thought as that bad characters become so through God's anger (θυμός), but good men become good through God's grace.

This shows among other things that θυμός had a definitely bad connotation for Philo. Finally in para. 79 of this work there is an obscure and metaphysical argument founded on Ps. 75.8 to the effect that, just as we cannot bear the unadulterated vision of God, so we could not bear his unadulterated mercy, and therefore a certain amount of wrath is necessary:

> In the same way, what mortal man could bear the understanding, wisdom, knowledge, justice of God, or indeed any other of his virtues, unadulterated?

Here Aristotle rather than Plato seems to be speaking.

In the same vein as the first of these efforts to explain away the wrath from the divine nature is *De Sacrificiis Abel*, para. 96:

> For this reason we falsely attribute to God (προσαναπλάττομεν) hands, feet, movements, enmities, estrangements, alienations, fits of anger (ὀργάς), parts and passions which are not characteristics of the ultimate Cause.

So also in *De Gigantibus*, para. 17, he is commenting on Psalm 78.49:[1] ἐξαπέστειλεν εἰς αὐτοὺς ὀργὴν θυμοῦ αὐτοῦ, θυμὸν καὶ ὀργὴν καὶ θλίψιν, ἀποστολὴν δι᾽ ἀγγέλων πονηρῶν—lit: "he sent upon them his fierce anger, wrath and rage and distress, a mission of evil angels", and explains that these are evil angels who had intercourse with the daughters of men, thus ridding God of the responsibility for their wrath. Another good example of this attempt to excuse Moses for writing about the wrath of God occurs in *Quod a Deo Mittantur Somnia*,[2] para. 234 sq.:

> The narrative adapts itself to men ... and for this reason Moses attributed a face, hands, feet, a mouth, and a voice to God, and also fits of anger and rage (ὀργάς τε καὶ θυμούς): but he employs this type of language not for the sake of truth, but for the benefit of learners.

And in para. 236 he says that according to one principle found in Scripture anthropomorphisms are used for the benefit of duller minds, such as "God being vexed and showing inappeasable wrath" (ὁ Θεὸς δυσχεραίνει καὶ ἀπαραιτήτως πρὸς τὰς ὀργὰς ἔχει).

But it is only in his more metaphysical arguments that Philo is at pains to dispense with the wrath. In his homiletical moods he is more of the Hebrew and less of the Greek; and in these places we find that he does make use of the concept of God's wrath without apparently suffering any embarrassment. A clear example is *Quod a Deo Mittantur Somnia*, para. 179, Book II: addressing his soul, Philo says:

---

[1] My translation of LXX.   [2] Or *De Somniis*, I.

So, my reason, learn what a great evil is the wrath of God (ὀργὴ Θεοῦ), and how great a blessing is his favour, and do not do anything worthy of that wrath (τῶν ὀργῆς ἀξίων) to your own undoing.

This contains the suggestion (very profound in the right context) that we bring wrath on ourselves; but it does envisage very clearly the possibility of the divine wrath. Another example occurs in *De Abrahamo*, para. 41; he is speaking of the sins of the Prediluvians, and he says: "God, being very naturally vexed with them ... etc." (ὁ Θεὸς εἰκότως δυσχεράνας . . .). Here his moral sense has overcome his metaphysical convictions, and he uses the very word he has disclaimed in *Quod a Deo Mittuntur Somnia*, para. 234. A very similar passage is *De Vita Moysis*, I, para. 119:

> For they [the Egyptians] realized what was indeed the truth, that these disastrous events were caused by divine displeasure (ἐκ μηνιμάτων θείων).

Cf. Sib. Orac. III, 632; 766. More than this, in several places Philo allows the possibility of appeasing God. In *De Vita Moysis*, II, para. 147, he writes as follows:

> To sin ... is natural to every creature; to prevent the Divine Being (τὸ θεῖον) from being roused and visiting (διακινηθὲν ἐπιθεῖτο) for this sin, it is necessary to propitiate it (ἐξευμενίζεσθαι) with prayers and sacrifices.

In para. 166 of the work he says of Moses standing in the gap:

> Then this healer and appeaser (κηδέμων καὶ παραιτήτης) propitiated the great Guide (ἐξευμενισάμενος, sc. Θεόν).

Compare also *De Specialibus Legibus*, II, para. 209:

> That they may not have any experience of misfortune they mollify God and appease him with intercessions (λιπάρουσι ... καὶ ἐξευμενίζονται).

There is also one reference to provoking God. In *De Virtutibus*, paras. 171, 172, he is commenting on Num. 15.30: "But the soul that doeth aught with a high hand, the same blasphemeth the Lord." For "blasphemeth", Philo, following LXX, reads παροξύνει "provoketh". Philo's comment is (para. 174):

> Such a man might very well, as the sacred writer says, find God had become his adversary and chastiser (ἀντιδίκῳ καὶ κολάστῃ).

So he admits the possibility of provoking God.[1]

There is also to be found in Philo an interesting parallel to Paul's conception of the powers that be as διάκονοι τῆς ὀργῆς "ministers of the wrath". As we shall see when we deal with Pauls' epistles, he had a very definite conception of the wrath as a process which God permits to take place rather than personally directs, and in particular he looked on the ruler or rulers as ministers of the wrath; cf. Rom. 13.1–7. Philo does not speak of the wrath of God as being executed by such means, but he does speak of God's justice as sometimes being administered by ὑπηρέται "servants"; cf. *De Sacrificiis Abel*, para. 133; Philo is commenting on Ex. 21.13, and is comparing the accidental slayer and the Levite in whose city he may take refuge, and he says:

> So let these two servants of the divine dispensation live together as ministers of two different kinds, the Levite as minister of beneficial activity, and the unwitting slayer, a minister of punishment.

The word here for "minister" is ὑπηρέτης. His meaning becomes clearer in *De Fuga et Inventione*, para. 65:

> For it is unbecoming for God as the first and noblest Lawgiver to punish (κολάζειν), but he punishes[2] through others who are his ministers (δι' ὑπηρετούντων ἑτέρων) not his own hand.

A similar sentiment is expressed in *De Abrahamo*, para. 143, where Philo is commenting on the three angels that appeared to Abraham. He advances the theory that of the three angels, the angel which did not take part in the destruction of Sodom was ὁ πρὸς ἀλήθειαν ὤν "He who truly is". The other two were "powers" (δυνάμεις) because God

> held it fitting that he should be present to give good gifts by his own agency, but should leave the execution of the opposite of the good entirely in the hands of his potencies acting as his ministers (καθ' ὑπηρεσίαν) so that he might appear to be the cause of good only, but not directly the cause of anything evil.[3]

---

[1] Similarly in *Quod deterius potiori insidiari potest*, para. 69. Philo attributes ἀγανάκτησις to God.

[2] MS. κολάζειν, but Colson and Whitaker read κολάζει (Loeb ed., London 1929, in loc.).

[3] Colson and Whitaker's translation. All other passages are my own.

In *De Vita Moysis*, III, paras. 121, 122, he uses a supplementary word ὄργανα "instruments", to describe the function of the involuntary homicide:

> For he seems to subserve the divine judgement (θείᾳ κρίσει ὑπηρετῆσαι) ... since God uses involuntary homicides ... as ministers of punishment (ὑπηρέταις κολάσεως) ... as if he were employing suitable tools (ὄργανα ἐπιτήδεια) for execution (τιμωρίαν).

A little farther on (para. 129) he speaks of the homicide as

> one who with his hands is the minister of Justice (ὑπηρετήσαντα), that arbiter of human affairs.

And in para. 136 he actually makes the homicide a minister of Nature: τοῖς τῆς φύσεως ὑπηρετῆσαι βουλήμασιν. A final example, and perhaps the closest parallel to Paul, comes from *De Providentia*, Frg. 2, para. 39[1]; Philo is saying that God uses tyrants to purge and clean cities:

> The Guardian of the great Cosmopolis sets tyrants over cities like public executioners (δημίους κοινούς).

And in para. 41 he adds that God also uses pestilences as his ministers (ὑπηρέταις). Now it seems probable that Philo's motive in advancing this theory of God as using persons and things as his agents in punishment was his Hellenic conception of God; so human an activity as punishment should not, he felt, be directly attributed to God. Paul, on the other hand, worked out his theory of the ministers of the wrath and of the impersonal nature of the wrath, because he felt that the revelation of God's love for mankind in Jesus Christ made it inappropriate to speak of God as being angry, or as directly moving his anger against men. Starting from rather different premises, Philo and Paul arrived at much the same conclusion on this particular point. As they were roughly contemporaries, we cannot say that Paul had not read Philo's works, though there is no real evidence of Paul's having borrowed his theory of the wrath from Philo. It does, however, help us to understand the evolution of Paul's doctrine of the wrath when we see a somewhat similar doctrine evolved in Philo, whose circumstances and principles, though certainly not identical with Paul's, yet did include

---

[1] Quoted in Eusebius, *Praep. Evang.* VIII, 14, 386–99.

the necessity for reconciling the Hebrew conception of God with a different set of principles. Those principles in Philo's case came from Greek philosophy, especially Platonism. In Paul's case the necessity was to reconcile the Hebrew conception of God with what was for Paul a new and startling set of facts, the life, death, and resurrection of Jesus of Nazareth.

Philo's vocabulary in those places where he does allow the wrath of God is varied and literary. He uses ὀργή three times; μήνιμα once; ἀγανάκτησις twice (in the same passage); δυσχεραίνω once; χαλεπαίνω once; and παροξύνειν once. It is very interesting that he never uses θυμός unequivocally for the wrath. For him, with his Platonic background θυμός had an unpleasant savour about it; cf. *Legum Allegoria*, III, para. 115, where he calls one part of the soul θυμικόν and associates it with anger in a bad sense; a little later (paras. 123, 124) he says:

> And in addition to its other characteristics θυμός has this quality, falsehood.

The nearest he gets to predicting it of God is in the passage already considered, *Quod Deus Immutabilis*, para. 70, where he suggests that if θυμός could be allowed in God, it would only be for the purpose of showing what a bad effect it produces. This avoidance of the use of θυμός becomes significant in view of the rarity of its appearance in the New Testament also.

Philo's conception of the wrath is interesting, because it appears in his works as a sort of plumb line which shows the extent to which he was prepared to depart from a truly Hebraic conception of God in the interest of his metaphysical convictions; and that departure is not as great as one might imagine if one concentrated purely on his metaphysical system. On the other hand the very fact that Philo did feel constrained to explain away the wrath to some extent is in itself an indication that the wrath did present a problem to anyone who was not content simply with Judaism as it had developed up to the time of our Lord's appearance on earth. In that sense, Philo is a good *Preparatio Evangelica*. He prepares one for the fact that the wrath in the New Testament is not a relatively simple and straightforward concept as it is in the Old Testament.

Josephus was no metaphysician, and we find in his works that he has no embarrassment at all in describing the anger of God and God as angry. Seeing that the *Archaeologia* is in fact a popular exposition of Jewish history for Gentile readers, it would have been impossible for Josephus not to have declared his conception of the wrath, which plays so definite a part in Old Testament history. Accordingly we find early on in his history that where the sacred books say God was angry, Josephus says so too without any hesitation; thus in *Archaeologia*, I (50)[1] God in Eden is described as angry (ὀργισθείς) with the serpent. Indeed so familiar is he with the concept of the divine wrath, that in several places he uses wrath language to explain an incident which in the Old Testament is narrated without a specific reference to the Wrath: e.g. *Arch.* IV, (130), Balaam's plan for seducing the young men of Israel is summed up on the words:

For by this means God would be angry with them (ὀργισθήσεσθαι).

Similarly in the two outstanding instances of irrational wrath in I Samuel, the men of Beth-Shemesh and the death of Uzzah, Josephus uses wrath language not to be found in the text (*Arch.* VI, 167):

The wrath and anger of God (ὀργή καὶ χόλος) visited seventy men of the village of Beth-Shemesh; it struck them down dead because, though they were not worthy to touch the ark (for they were not priests), they approached it.

One notices of course Josephus' rationalizing of the wrath here; he adapts the excuse which the Chronicler found for Uzzah's death: a layman daring to touch consecrated things. See also *Arch.* VII (81); when he comes to deal with Uzzah's death he says that Uzzah died, through the wrath of God (ὀργή), because not being a priest he touched the Ark. We can say of Josephus what can be said of the Chronicler: it is not wrath that embarrasses him but irrational wrath. Another example of Josephus using wrath-language where there is no explicit reference to it in the Old Testament, is in his account of David's adultery with Bathsheba. In *Arch.* VII (147) he says God felt anger towards David on this account, and in (151) describes Nathan as "laying bare the wrath of God". And, in (321) and (328) similar language is used about David's sin in connection with the census.[2]

---

[1] All references are from S. A. Naber, ed. *Josephus Opera Omnia* (Leipzig 1888).
[2] ὀργή is used in all these instances.

Here indeed Josephus shows himself almost naïf about the wrath, for he says quite simply that God was wroth with David because of the census, without making any suggestion as to why this should arouse divine wrath.

On the other hand, there is one place where he does feel constrained to explain away, or at least to justify the manifestation of the divine wrath in the wilderness period. In *Arch.* III (315), he represents Moses as explaining to the people that their forty years sojourn in the wilderness was not through any arbitrary wrath of God:

> God was not instigated by caprice to manifest some sort of human anger (ὀργήν) against them; but rather adjudged them guilty after due deliberation (γνώμη καταψηφισάμενον).

This does show a real fear of anthropomorphism such as we are more familiar with in Philo. The contrast here is between ὀργή, a human passion, and γνώμη, considered as characteristic of divine judgement. Once more we find Josephus concerned, not to explain away the wrath, but to represent it as just and dignified. He stands in the tradition of the Chronicler. He gives us two examples of his own interpretation of more or less contemporary events in which he sees the wrath of God. The first is rather amusing. In *Arch.* XV (299), speaking of Herod the Great's reign, he says:

> In that year, which was the thirteenth of Herod's reign, the most terrible disasters afflicted the land—either because God was angry (μηνίσαντος), or else because such disasters recur at regular intervals.

Here the devout Jew and the Greek scientist meet and agree to differ! He is more of a Jew when he says in the *Bellum Judaicum*, VII (328), speaking of the sufferings of the Jews:

> For if God had been favourable or even only mildly offended with us (μετρίως ἀπηχθημένος) he would not have permitted so great a slaughter of men to take place.

In vocabulary Josephus is extremely varied, showing his literary superiority to most of the Septuagint. ὀργή is his favourite word; he uses it eleven times. μῆνις occurs three times, and μηνίζω once; for the rest he uses the following words once each: ἀγανακτῶ; ὀργίζομαι; παροξύνομαι; χόλος; ἄχθομαι; ἀπάχθομαι. He uses τὸ θεῖον for

God in connection with the wrath twice. One instance is *Arch.* III (321); illustrating from a contemporary incident how strictly the Jewish priests obeyed the law, he says:

> [Each priest] feared the law and that wrath (ὀργή) which the Divine Being always exhibits against trespasses, even secret ones.

The other place is *Arch.* V (132):

> The Divine Being, provoked by these actions (παροξυνθέν) ... etc.

We may guess that his use of τὸ θεῖον in these places was, half unconsciously perhaps, intended to mitigate for the Gentile readers the un-Hellenic notions of God being angry or provoked to anger. Most interesting of all is his avoidance of the word θυμός for the divine wrath; in a writer such as Josephus who took some pains with his style, this is certainly significant. Combined with the fact that Philo also avoids using it for the divine wrath, it seems to show fairly surely that θυμός had an emotional and human connotation that was at least less prominent in ὀργή.[1]

If we attempt to sum up the development of the conception of the divine wrath in the inter-Testamental period, we may say that the two strains of thought about the wrath which we observed by the end of the Old Testament period are continued in the inter-Testamental period. The Apocalyptists, with their strong, personal, eschatological concept of the wrath, are the heirs of the Prophets in this respect. But they do not always show the Prophets' restraint in speaking about the wrath, so that in certain respects the Apocalyptic literature represents a reversion in the development of the wrath conception. On the other hand, some of the Apocalyptists are obviously conscious of the danger of anthropomorphism, and therefore tend to use impersonal language (e.g. 2 Baruch). The tradition of the Chronicler, however, is mainly

---

[1] There is an illuminating passage in *Bell. Jud.* II (135). He describes the Essenes as ὀργῆς ταμίαι δίκαιοι, θυμοῦ καθεκτικοί. One might be tempted, on the analogy for example of 2 Thess. 2.7, where ὁ κατέχων means "he that restrains", to tr. καθεκτικοί as "restraining". In that case there would be a contrast between ὀργή and θυμός: "just administrators of wrath, but suppressing extreme anger". Liddell and Scott (1925 ed.) give the sense of "able to hold in", quoting Aristotle's *Problemata* 33.15,4: καθεκτικὸς τοῦ πνεύματος as opposed to προετικός, which means "emitting easily". It is therefore a possible sense of καθεκτικός here; see also Moulton and Milligan, *Vocabulary of the Greek N.T.*, sub κατέχω: κρόνος ὁ κατέχων τὸν θυμὸν ... τῶν ἀνθρώπων.

sustained by the writers of the various books of the Maccabees. After that we can trace it in Philo, with whose marked Hellenic background this impersonal strain fitted in well. In the Rabbis this impersonal treatment is quite absent, though they are far more conscious of the dangers of anthropomorphism than are many of the Apocalyptists. Indeed in this respect, they almost touch hands with the Hellenizers. Of the Hellenizers, especially Philo, it may be said that, though their motives were primarily to make the Old Testament palatable to Greek readers, their treatment of the wrath is at best a witness to the fact that it did present a problem, and the fact that Paul's treatment of that problem, though not identical with theirs, can nevertheless be compared with theirs, can go some way in justifying their attempt to solve the problem, even though we cannot accept their solution.

In the inter-Testamental period two new, or almost new conceptions arise. The first is the idea that the divine wrath can be propitiated, especially by the death of the innocent. This is not unparalleled in the Old Testament, but it is not at all prominent there. In the Maccabaean books the idea occurs in several places, in most of which the death of the innocent is the method of propitiation (an altogether new idea, not found at all in the Old Testament). This notion of propitiation of the wrath is found also, strangely enough, in Philo. One other new idea is the conception of the wrath as discipline: this is almost never found in the Old Testament. It first occurs in 2 Maccabees, is prominent in Wisdom, occurs also in the Apocalyptic Literature, and is echoed in the Rabbis. It is fundamentally an attempt to avoid the cutting edge of the wrath as manifested against Israel. Wrath that is discipline is not really wrath at all.

The wrath-cup figure undergoes a modification during this period. In the Old Testament the cup always stands for evil fortune; but in the three instances of the employment of this figure which we meet in this period the cup means simply "destiny", and the nature of the destiny has to be specifically mentioned as well. As a result the wrath-connotation of the Cup is weakened, so that in some cases (e.g. the Martyrdom of Isaiah) it disappears altogether. This is in fact what we find in the New Testament, whose writers in this respect are heirs of the Apocalyptists rather than of the Old Testament direct.

On the whole, the problem created by the conflict between the

THE WRATH IN THE INTER-TESTAMENTAL PERIOD

mercy and the love of God is not very deeply appreciated in this period; we must look to parts of the Old Testament for a profounder understanding of it. As in the Old Testament, so here, there is no sign at all of any particular connection between the Messiah and the wrath, though, as many of the Apocalyptists are chiefly concerned with the last things, we do sometimes find that the days of wrath are also the days of the Messiah (e.g. Book of Enoch). But for the Apocalyptists as for the authors of the Old Testament, "the wrath of the Lamb" would be a completely novel concept.

4

THE WRATH IN PAUL'S WRITINGS

WHEN we enter the New Testament, our first impression is that the wrath of God plays a very insignificant part in it. The writers of the New Testament were primarily concerned with the love, and not with the judgement, of God. Hence there is a temptation to try to dismiss the comparatively few references to the divine wrath in the New Testament as mere residual traces of an Old Testament outlook, and to suggest that the concept of the wrath of God in the New Testament has no real connection with the new knowledge of God in Jesus Christ with which the writers of the New Testament were primarily concerned. But a closer inspection of the references to wrath and judgement in the New Testament gives a different impression. We find that New Testament writers were aware of both the impersonal and the prophetic-apocalyptic conceptions of the wrath which we find in the Old Testament, and that they accepted and used them in their writings. But at the same time, with their keen apprehension of the love of God revealed supremely in the Cross of Christ, they felt that judgement and wrath, far from being outmoded attributes of God, were themselves in a sense revealed, explained, and profoundly modified by that all-important event. So that the concept of the divine wrath does not by any means gradually fade away in the course of the New Testament's composition, like the rite of circumcision for instance, but remains as the reverse side of the divine love and in some sense its complement; and in the last book of the New Testament it plays a most significant part, and is fully related to the Cross of Jesus Christ as part of the revelation which the New Testament records.

It is in St Paul's epistles more than in any other part of the New Testament, with the exception of Revelation, that we find a conception of the wrath of God explicitly stated. Indeed, at first sight it would seem that a study of the wrath of God in the New Testament might confine itself to St Paul's epistles and the Apocalypse; but reason is shown later on to believe that much the same conception of the wrath as Paul entertained lies behind the other books in the New Testament.

Paul, at any rate, gave more thought to the meaning of the wrath than did, for example, the Synoptists. The most striking feature of his conception of the wrath has been pointed out by C. H. Dodd in his commentary on Romans. Dodd remarks that the divine wrath as depicted by Paul is very impersonal in its operation; it does not seem to be an emotion attributed to God, but is rather " the effect of human sin ... an inevitable process of cause and effect in a moral universe".[1] As such, wrath is not of course purely eschatological in Paul; on the contrary he frequently surprises us by pointing to contemporary examples of the operation of the wrath. On the other hand, Paul does not eschew the eschatological aspect of the wrath; in several places wrath is plainly eschatological, and he does not seem to be at all embarrassed by the difference between contemporary wrath and wrath to come. The truth is no doubt that he did not clearly distinguish between them. Wrath was a process already operating, peculiarly manifested through the coming of the New Dispensation, ultimately to be fully revealed and consummated. But there can be little doubt that for Paul the impersonal character of the wrath was important; it relieved him of the necessity of attributing wrath directly to God, it transformed the wrath from an attribute of God into the name for a process which sinners bring upon themselves. That process was one which operates according to the moral laws of the universe; that is why it can be called the wrath of God. But God is never described as angry, and no verb describing anger is ever used of him by St Paul, or any writer of the New Testament.

In 1 Thess. 1.10, Paul refers to our Lord as "Jesus which delivereth us from the wrath to come". This is certainly eschatological wrath, but it is interesting to notice the contrast with a passage like Isa. 26.20f. In the Old Testament passage the godly are called upon to hide from the wrath that is to come on the ungodly. In this passage Christians are being rescued (ῥυόμενον) from the wrath that is now coming (ἐρχομένης). The thought is not of hiding from some future catastrophe, but of escaping out of (ἐκ τῆς) a process that is already beginning. In 1 Thess. 2.16, the wrath is more clearly realized: it is the famous passage about the Jews. Paul, having enumerated all their sins,

---

[1] Dodd, ed. Romans (Moffatt Commentary, London 1932), pp. 20-4.

such as slaying the Lord and the prophets and persecuting Christians, says that the end of this wickedness is ἐς τὸ ἀναπληρῶσαι τὰς ἁμαρτίας πάντοτε: "to fill up their sins alway". And he adds the significant comment: ἔφθασεν δὲ ἐπ' αὐτοὺς ἡ ὀργὴ ἐς τέλος: "but the wrath is come upon them to the uttermost". The statement has puzzled editors greatly: the Tübingen school hailed it as an indication that this epistle was written after the fall of Jerusalem, and therefore Paul was not the author of it. Milligan[1] comments: "In what exactly this 'end' consisted is not easy to determine." A recent writer, Tasker,[2] would interpret it as a prophetic perfect. The thing has so nearly happened that it is spoken of as being in the past. But Tasker himself repudiates this explanation of ἀποκαλύπτεται in Rom. 1.18,[3] so what will not pass for a present tense will hardly do for a perfect. Similarly R. F. Fuller in *The Mission and Achievement of Jesus*,[4] in discussing the use of ἔφθασεν in this passage, writes: "He is using the familiar prophetic device of speaking of a future event as though it were already present. The certainty of the event is so overwhelming, the signs of its impendingness so sure, that it is said to have occurred or to be occurring already." This is Tasker's argument, and it seems to be unconvincing in view of the phrase "to the uttermost". That is not a phrase which one uses of an event which has not yet taken place, no matter how certain one is that it will take place. Besides, both the letters to the Thessalonians were written in some sense to persuade the Thessalonians that the signs of the end had not yet appeared. It hardly seems appropriate in such a context to speak of something yet future as if it had already happened because the signs of its imminence were so sure. The truth is that Paul means exactly what he says: the wrath has come upon them to the uttermost. The fact that the Jews were outwardly prosperous when he wrote makes no difference to this fact. To be under, or in, the wrath is primarily a spiritual condition or process, and Paul uses ἐς τέλος "to the uttermost", because they have committed the greatest of all possible sins, they have slain the Lord Jesus. The conception of the Wrath as a process is brought out clearly by his

---

[1] Milligan, ed. 1 and 2 Thessalonians (London 1908), in loc.
[2] Tasker, *The Biblical Doctrine of the Wrath of God* (London 1951), pp. 43–4.
[3] Op cit., in loc.
[4] Fuller, *The Mission and Achievement of Jesus* (London 1954), p. 26.

using here the phrase ἐς τὸ ἀναπληρῶσαι αὐτῶν τὰς ἁμαρτίας πάντοτε: "to fill up their sins always". Compare with this passage Rev. 18.24:

> καὶ ἐν αὐτῇ αἷμα προφητῶν καὶ ἁγίων εὑρέθη, καὶ πάντων τῶν ἐσφαγμένων ἐπὶ τῆς γῆς. And in her was found the blood of prophets and of saints and of all that have been slain upon the earth.

There as here, the wrath is a process in history which is openly declared and consummated, rather than executed or inflicted, in the last days. Editors, in looking for some outstanding event in history to explain this passage, are still thinking in pre-Christian terms; their explanations would better suit the passage in Test. XII Patriarchs, Levi 6. 11, from which this phrase may be quoted. There the wrath is expressed in the destruction of the men of Shechem by Levi. Here it is expressed in the single fact that the Jews have crucified the Messiah. Notice also in both I Thess. 1.10 and 2.16 the extremely impersonal nature of the wrath. The same note occurs in 1 Thess. 5.9, where Paul says: ὅτι οὐκ ἔθετο ἡμᾶς ὁ Θεὸς εἰς ὀργὴν ἀλλὰ εἰς περιποίησιν σωτηρίας.

For God appointed us not unto wrath, but unto the obtaining of salvation.

The ὀργή is here looked on as the end of the process, but it is made to correspond with the περιποίησιν σωτηρίας, and just as that salvation is not a purely future event, but is anticipated in the present experience of Christians, so the ὀργή is not entirely something in the future, but is a process to be consummated, a process which has already begun, and is already revealed to faith.

In 2 Thess. 1.3–10, we find a very eschatological description of the judgement of God. The Lord Jesus will come and punish those who have been persecuting the Thessalonian Christians. It is plainly something that is to take place in the future; but even here we have indications that judgement is a process. In verse 5 Paul describes the faith of the Thessalonians in their afflictions as ἔνδειγμα τῆς δικαίας κρίσεως τοῦ Θεοῦ, "a manifest token of the righteous judgement of God". Something is already happening, and it points forward to a greater happening in the future; Paul claims that Christians can by faith trace the course of God's judgement in history. The Book of Revelation might almost be called a commentary on this passage. Indeed in Rev. 6.16, we have an echo of the same passage (Isa.

2.10) which Paul seems to have in mind here: "Hide thee in the dust from before the terror of the Lord and from before the glory of his majesty." Both New Testament writers are striving to express what the judgement of God in Christ means, but on the whole John the Divine is the more profound, as he speaks with astonishing boldness of the "wrath of the Lamb" (Rev. 6.17). In Revelation the judgement is more closely connected with the Cross and more obviously expressed in history; Paul here seems to relegate it mostly to the end of history, but 1 Thess. 2.16 reminds us that for Paul the end had already begun.

Another remarkable parallel with Revelation is provided by 2 Thess. 2.1–12, where Paul describes the Man of Sin. In Revelation the description of the rival dispensations of God and of Satan is well known: the Satanic Trinity of the Dragon, the Beast, and the False Prophet is set up in rivalry to the true Trinity; and the parallel between the two dispensations is drawn out in some detail. Here also a rival Satanic dispensation is looked for. In 2.3 the man of sin ἀποκαλυφθῇ, "is revealed", in the same way as the Son is to be "revealed" (see also verses 6, 8). In verse 7 we find there is a μυστήριον τῆς ἀδικίας, "a mystery of lawlessness", just as there is a μυστήριον of Christ; what is more, like the wrath or the salvation of Christ, it is already at work; ἤδη ἐνεργεῖται. This lawless one like Christ is to have a παρουσία, a coming; he does great signs and wonders (verse 9; cf. Mark 13.22 and Synoptic parallels); his adherents show faith in him (verse 11, εἰς τὸ πιστεῦσαι αὐτοὺς τῷ ψεύδει). There is even a possibility of a Satanic spirit; though the word πνεῦμα is not used. God sends them ἐνεργείαν τῆς πλάνης, "a working of error" in verse 11. This may be an echo of 1 Kings 22.21, where the Lord sends a lying spirit to deceive Ahab. Finally with the phrase εὐδοκήσαντες τῇ ἀδικίᾳ, "have pleasure in unrighteousness", compare the welcome accorded to the Beast in Rev. 13.4 following. It is interesting to observe how much more effective is the manner in which the author of Revelation treats the Antichrist theme. He interprets the myth in terms of a contemporary situation, the persecution of the Christian Church at the hands of the Roman Empire. Thus he uses myth as it should be used, to give a picture of the impact of the transcendent on the temporal. John is more effective because he expresses his myth in contemporary terms: the Man of Sin was already on the stage of history, he believed; his eschatology is realized. Paul still sees it as in the future; his theology of the last things was not as fully in focus with the contemporary situation as was John's. But we must remember that this is one of the earliest of Paul's writings; his later epistles show a more deeply considered eschatology. Both writers, however, express the same conviction that in certain respects the divine dispensation revealed in Christ shows as it were the groundwork of the universe, a pattern to which all other dispensations, true or false, must in some way conform; there must be a Father, and a Son (according to Milligan[1] the ἄνομος in 2 Thess. is not Satan but his emissary), perhaps a Spirit, certainly a revelation, and a mystery that demands faith. In this respect Milligan is misleading when he says *à propos* 2 Thess. 2.3: "The word ἀποκάλυψις is placed in mocking counterpart to the ἀποκάλυψις of the Lord Jesus himself." There is no hint of mockery, either here or in Revelation. It is a serious rivalry (ἀντικείμενος, verse 4), albeit a fraudulent one, which must dance to the tune that God has played because ultimately the pattern of all things is his, not Satan's. Note therefore finally the emphasis running all through both the accounts of the Satanic dispensation on the fact that it is permitted by God; in 2 Thess. 2.11 it is God who sends the ἐνεργείαν τῆς πλάνης; and in Rev. 13 the word ἐδόθη, "there was given", occurs like a refrain throughout. The operation of the Satanic dispensation is of the same nature as the operation of the wrath; it is something which God permits but does not directly inspire.

In Galatians we are only concerned with one passage, 3.7–22, but it is one that is so difficult, and yet so important to an understanding of Paul's conception of the relation between Law and Wrath that we must spend some time on it. The kernel of the passage is 3.13:

Χριστὸς ἡμᾶς ἐξηγόρασεν ἐκ τῆς κατάρας τοῦ νόμου γενόμενος ὑπὲρ ἡμῶν κατάρα ὅτι γέγραπται, Ἐπικατάρατος πᾶς ὁ κρεμάμενος ἐπὶ ξύλου.
Christ redeemed us from the curse of the law, having become a curse for us: for it is written, cursed is every one that hangeth on a tree.

From the earliest times there have not been lacking commentators who took this to mean that Christ bore the curse, and therefore the wrath of God. For example, Luther, commenting on these very words, says:

[1] Op. cit. in 2 Thess. 2.4.

"Christ being made a curse for us (that is, a sinner under the wrath of God) ..."[1] Similarly a modern theologian, Duncan, insists that the curse here is not only the curse of the Law but also the curse of God, because the Law "does have for Paul an essential place in his providential order".[2] This is an appalling conclusion; but the evidence seems on the whole to be against it. As Lightfoot points out,[3] in the passage from which Paul is quoting in Deuteronomy the curse is called "a curse of God" (Deut. 21.23); Paul has omitted the words ὑπὸ Θεοῦ found in the LXX, though he calls it "a curse of the law". This conclusion is accepted by Burton,[4] who believes that Paul is distinguishing between what is of God and what is of the Law. Both these editors maintain, however, that all Paul means here is that Christ accepted the consequences of our sins, and that hanging on a tree was one of these consequences and therefore could be described as a curse on the strength of Deut. 21.23. But this seems to be putting the cart before the horse; a man is not accursed because he hangs on a tree. He hangs upon a tree because he is accursed. Driver in his commentary on the passage in Deuteronomy confirms this.[5] The hanging on a tree, he says, was a sign that God's curse rested upon the man hanging for his crime.

It seems more likely therefore that Paul is maintaining that Christ really was under a curse, the curse of the Law, because he, being the Righteous One, did not live by the Law, but by faith. The hanging on a tree was just the outward and visible sign that he had come under this curse. But by his resurrection he broke the power of this curse, and showed that it could be conquered. That we all come under the curse of the Law is the theme of Romans. If we adopt this interpretation Gal. 3.10,11 is seen in its right context. It could be said of Christ that he did not "continue in all things that are written in the book of the Law", not because he broke the Law but because he transcended it. He did not "live by the Law" (cf. v. 12 here), he lived by faith. Thus in verse 22 of this passage ἐκ πίστεως Ἰησοῦ Χριστοῦ is not just

---

[1] Luther, ed. Galatians (tr. Middleton, London 1940), in loc.
[2] Duncan, ed. Galatians (Moffatt Commentary, London 1934), in loc.
[3] Lightfoot, ed. Galatians (London 1881), in loc.
[4] Burton, ed. Galatians (I.C.C., Edinburgh 1921), in loc.
[5] Driver, ed. Deuteronomy (Edinburgh 1902).

"faith in Jesus Christ", but "the faith of Jesus Christ", the same faith as Jesus Christ showed. Compare with this John 7.49: "But this multitude which knoweth not the Law are accursed"; they are accursed because they believed (ἐπίστευσε is used in John 7.48) in a Messiah who came from Galilee. Lightfoot, in commenting on Gal. 3.19,20, agrees that Paul is here disparaging the Law at the expense of the promise. The promise was direct and absolute from God; the Law was mediated by both angels (Midrash) and Moses.[1]

This reference to the indirect relation of the Law to God brings out the bearing which this passage has on St. Paul's conception of the wrath. The Law-sphere, according to St Paul, is the sphere of wrath, and *vice versa*. Wrath works according to Law; like the Law, it is something less than personal, and hence not admitting of faith. Like the Law, "it came in because of sin", and hence, like the Law, it is in a sense of God, but of God at one remove; it is something within God's providence, but at the same time something which Christ transcended. Indeed verses 7–8 of chapter 6 of this very epistle give us a good example of the nature of the wrath; it works according to an exact Law of δράσαντι παθεῖν (we might almost call it *karma*), from which there is no escaping except by faith. This connection between the Law and the wrath lies behind all Paul's references to both these subjects, and indeed, as is indicated later on, behind most of what the New Testament has to say about judgement. In this sense, no doubt, the "curse" here could be called "the wrath of God"; it was wrath to all who tried to live by the Law and failed. We all come under the curse of the Law; we must have been under it for Christ to have "brought us from under it" (3.13). In this respect Duncan[2] is mistaken in maintaining that "the curse" here only applies to the Jews. Just as Paul uses "the Law" primarily for the Jewish Law, but also broadens it out to include all attempts at living by a moral code, so the curse stands both for the curse invoked in Deuteronomy, and for the curse that falls on all who try to live by works.[3] But when Christ came under the curse because

---

[1] Dr Sydney Cave: in *The Doctrine of the Work of Christ* (reprinted London 1947), pp. 44 f., comes to very much these conclusions about this passage.

[2] Op. cit., in loc.

[3] Cf. Gal 3.22 with 2 Cor. 5.21; there Christ becomes ἁμαρτία. In Gal. 3.13 he becomes κατάρα; therefore we are shut up under the κατάρα.

he would not "live by the Law" it proved not to be the curse of God; he transcended it, and broke its power. So also when Christ bears the consequences of our sins, which in a sinner would be the wrath, they prove not to be the wrath, and the cup which in the Old Testament is the cup of Jahveh's wrath proves, when drunk by the Messiah, to be a cup of blessing.

In 1 Cor. 5.12,13 Paul draws an interesting distinction between the judgement of "them that are within" and "them that are without".[1] The judgement on those outside is going on all the time by the unrelenting process of history; from this process Christians escape through faith in Christ. Judgement inside the Church is therefore nothing more than that process of self-knowledge and confession of sin that any Christian should practice.

In 1 Cor. 10 we have an intensely interesting passage, for in it Paul first of all discusses instances of the wrath in Old Testament times, and then goes on to envisage the possibility of Christians provoking Christ. In verses 1–13 he cites several instances of the Israelites having been slain in the wilderness for their sins, all of which are described in the Old Testament as instances of the wrath of God, and he tells the Corinthian Christians to take warning, implying that a like fate may befall them. There is nothing to be wondered at in this: the attitude of the writers of the New Testament to the Old Testament was that of the orthodox Jews of their day, and hence if the Old Testament recorded an event as having taken place because of the wrath of God they would accept it without question. The author of the Epistle to the Hebrews adopts the same attitude; see the discussion of Heb. 3.7—4.13. Even in the later parts of the Old Testament, as we have seen, writers such as the Chronicler accepted traditional instances of the Wrath without question, even though they might be embarrassed by the way in which the wrath was recorded as expressing itself. The reason which Paul gives for these instances of wrath in the Old Testament is that the people were ἐπιθυμητὰς κακῶν, "they lusted after evil things": (verse 6). The "evil things" after which the Israelites lusted are recorded in Num. 11.4 as being "flesh, fish, cucumber, melons, leeks, onions, garlick", but Paul no doubt saw in this incident primarily a

---

[1] Evans, ed. 1 Corinthians (Clarendon Bible, Oxford 1930), in loc.

refusing of the supernatural food (manna) and a lusting for natural things. He draws the moral that Christians should not desert the Eucharist for the feasts of the mystery religions, or try to keep both going at once. Even in the case of Israel in the wilderness the crime for which they died was no doubt in his view not just desiring leeks instead of manna, but deliberately rejecting the highest spiritual good which they knew. This goes some way towards mitigating Paul's unqualified acceptance of a very severe, and even arbitrary, manifestation of wrath in the Old Testament. Whether Paul thought that the Corinthian Christians, if they failed to take warning by these Old Testament examples, would meet with the same kind of fate, or whether, because the benefits they were receiving were spiritual, he thought that their punishment would be spiritual also, we cannot say. But in view of 1 Cor. 5.5; 11.30, we cannot rule out the possibility that Paul thought the punishment even of those "upon whom the ends of the ages are come" might be physical.

Then in verse 22 we find the striking quotation from Deut. 32.21: ἢ παραζηλοῦμεν τὸν Κύριον; "Or do we provoke the Lord to jealousy?" This sentence is unique in the New Testament. Nowhere else is it suggested that it is possible for Christians to "provoke the Lord".[1] There can be no doubt that "the Lord" here is Christ. Editors seem to take this verse very calmly, not realizing apparently how very remarkable it is. Godet[2] is content to point out that it is Christ who is provoked. Goudge comments[3]: "There is no love without jealousy, when the claims of love are put at nought", a statement which begs the whole question of the doctrine of the wrath in the New Testament. Robertson and Plummer in the I.C.C. Commentary,[4] and Moffatt,[5] in his own series, find no difficulty in the conception. It is possible that the complacency of the commentators is accounted for by their thinking that παραζηλῶ could be equated with ἐκπειράζω, and "tempting God" is quite a common thought in the New Testament. But in fact

---

[1] See the discussion of the "provocation" language used in Hebrews in the chapter on that epistle.

[2] Ed. 1 Corinthians (tr. Cusin, Edinburgh 1887), in loc.

[3] Ed. 1 Corinthians (Westminster Commentary, London 1903), in loc.

[4] Robertson and Plummer, ed. 1 Corinthians (Edinburgh 1911), in loc.

[5] Moffatt, ed. 1 Corinthians (London 1938), in loc.

the two ideas are separate.¹ The same root, πειράζειν, is used in Acts 5.9 of tempting the Holy Spirit. Foakes-Jackson and Kirsopp Lake² in their commentary on this passage remark that the notion of tempting God seems primitive and anthropomorphic. It seems likely that what they really object to is the idea of provoking God, which does not occur in the Acts passage. Tempting God means in fact treating God as if he were something less than personal; Satan, in urging our Lord to throw himself from the temple, was treating God as an automatic safety device; Ananias and Sapphira were treating him as someone less than wise and holy. So παραζηλοῦμεν remains unique.³

There can be no escaping the conclusion that in this chapter Paul is not at his most profound with respect to the wrath, though it is significant that he does not actually use the word "wrath" throughout. There is, however, one piece of evidence that modifies the somewhat Old Testament quality of his teaching here. In verses 11 to 13 Paul suggests that the dangers into which the Corinthian Christians have fallen (despising the Eucharist as the Israelites despised the manna) may have been a temptation for them (πειρασμός). Hence the punishment, whatever form it may take, would be in the nature of a disciplinary punishment. The whole process whereby some of them have fallen into the same sort of sins as those which the Israelites committed in the wilderness and are being punished for them, is thought of as a temptation. So perhaps the punishment (conceived of as divine wrath in the Old Testament parallel) may have a disciplinary character. The church in Corinth is being disciplined but not destroyed. The passage

---

¹ The two words correspond to different verbs in the Old Testament. παραζηλοῦμεν here stand for the Hiph'il of כעס, which we have met in the Old Testament part of this study; this is the only place in the New Testament where כעס of God appears in translation. ζῆλος and cognates are freely used by Paul elsewhere, but with four exceptions, always of men. The exceptions are: Rom. 10.19; 11.11; 11.14, where παραζηλῶ is used of God provoking the Jews to jealousy (in a quotation from the Old Testament); and 2 Cor. 11.2: ζηλῶ γὰρ ὑμᾶς Θεοῦ ζήλῳ, where it is used of the yearning love of God, with no wrath content. It occurs in John 2.17, in a quotation from the Psalms applied to Christ, but without any wrath connotation. All other instances in the New Testament are of human jealousy, except Heb. 10.27, which is so difficult as to require separate treatment, in Chapter 6. "Tempting" God is a quite different conception. πειράζειν or ἐκπειράζειν is a translation, not of כעס, but of נסה, as in Deut. 6.16, quoted by our Lord in Matt. 4.7.

² Ed. Acts (London 1933), in loc.

³ Stumpff (art. ζῆλος in Th. Wörterbuch d. N.T., Stuttgart 1933) agrees with this interpretation of ζῆλος here.

in 5.5 agrees with this, where Paul hands the offender over to Satan, that his spirit may be saved in the day of the Lord. Even this suggestion, that wrath may be disciplinary, is unique in the New Testament. It reminds one of Wisdom's treatment of wrath, where traditional instances of divine wrath on Israel are explained as disciplinary. In the same way, Paul may be seeking to tone down for Christians the severity of the divine wrath as manifested in the traditional examples in the Old Testament.

In 11.19: "For there must be also heresies among you, that they which are approved may be made manifest among you", we have a hint of how judgement operates, not as a sentence inflicted from outside, but as a self-operating process. The same notion seems to appear in verses 31 and 32 of this chapter. There are three kinds of judgement here: the self-judgement in confession of sin by Christians who live by faith (ἑαυτοὺς διεκρίνομεν); the judgement inflicted by God, perhaps from outside by sickness, etc., on Christians who should be, but are not, living by faith (κρινόμενοι ὑπὸ τοῦ Κυρίου); this is definitely disciplinary in character (παιδευόμεθα); thirdly, the judgement which non-Christians suffer, which is not disciplinary but penal, and is executed by the impersonal moral laws working themselves out in history (σὺν τῷ κόσμῳ κατακριθῶμεν—note the κατα—implying final judgement). Goudge[1] takes κατακριθῶμεν of the last day. One cannot be too confident about this; there are plenty of instances in Paul's writings of judgement on non-Christians described as operating at the time he was writing: cf. κρίνει in 5.13.

In 2 Corinthians 2.15,16 there is a passage which throws much light on Paul's conception of judgement. Paul's life of service is "a sweet savour of Christ unto God, in them that are being saved (τοῖς σωζομένοις) and in them that are perishing (τοῖς ἀπολλυμένοις)". Notice the present participles here: the process is now going on: "to the one a savour from death unto death (ἐκ θανάτου εἰς θάνατον) to the other a savour from life unto life (ἐκ ζωῆς εἰς ζωήν). ἐκ θανάτου εἰς θάνατον here means that those who do not believe are already in a state of spiritual death because they do not believe, and are destined for final and eternal death when the present process is consummated. The fact of Christ's triumphant death and resurrection, reproduced in Paul's

[1] Op. cit., in loc.

life, is itself the judgement. We might compare with this the use in Revelation of "the Lamb" to mean the eternal and always contemporary significance of Christ's death. The judgement here is also apprehended by faith.

In 2 Cor. 5.20—6.10 occurs a passage very like Gal. 3.13 and therefore presenting the same difficulties of interpretation. The problem is verse 21:

τὸν μὴ γνόντα ἁμαρτίαν ὑπὲρ ἡμῶν ἁμαρτίαν ἐποίησεν, ἵνα ἡμεῖς γενώμεθα δικαιοσύνη Θεοῦ ἐν αὐτῷ. Him who knew no sin he made to be sin on our behalf; that we might become the righteousness of God in him.

Augustine would have translated ἁμαρτία here either as "sin-offering" or as "human nature with its liability to sin". Both are linguistically impossible; Paul's word for the latter concept is σάρξ anyway. Goudge[1] makes the suggestion that ἁμαρτία here means "consequences of sin", and he finds a distinction in meaning between ἐποίησεν used here of Christ's being made sin and γενώμεθα of our becoming righteousness. He became sin, he suggests, in a less profound and intimate way than the way in which we become righteousness and hence the difference in the verbs. But this suggestion is refuted by a comparison with Gal. 3.13, where it is said that Christ was γενόμενος ὑπὲρ ἡμῶν κατάρα, "becoming a curse for us", a phrase which is surely on a level with the one under discussion here. Plummer[2] would leave the phrase simply as a paradox which we cannot understand: "He [Paul] could be so near to a substitutionary view of the Atonement without accepting it." He goes on to expound the Old Testament quotation in 6.2 as one which Paul applies to himself. Paul, like the prophet, has a message for the Gentiles, has experienced a time of discouragement, and is now helped by God. But this is to detach the Old Testament quotation too much from the main theological argument of 5.20,21, and to make it a mere illustration, an Old Testament parallel to Paul's experience in his ministry. Besides, nowhere in all his writings does Paul ever interpret the second persons singular in Old Testament quotations as applying to himself. For figures of his quotations from the Psalter, see the discussion on Rom. 15.3, where Sanday and Headlam adopt the same interpretation

[1] Ed. 2 Corinthians (Westminster Commentary, London 1927), in loc.
[2] Ed. 2 Corinthians (I.C.C., Edinburgh 1915), in loc.

as Plummer does here.[1] Strachan[2] commenting on 2 Cor. 5.21, contends that the wrath of God is as personal in the New Testament as is his love, and therefore it is quite as appropriate to say that Christ "was made sin", as to say that we "become righteousness". "His wrath", he says, "and his love are alike his word . . ." The wrath is "the active manifestation of his essential incapacity to be morally indifferent", and he points out, quite rightly, that the wrath is revealed quite as much as the love is (e.g. Rom. 1.18). But it is just the "active manifestation of the wrath" that we miss in the New Testament (except Revelation) as contrasted with the Old Testament. The fact that God is never described as angry, far less as being "wrath" in the same way as we read "God is love", is surely of the utmost significance here. The outstanding characteristic of the wrath in the New Testament is its indirect, impersonal nature. This is true even of the wrath in Revelation, if the arguments advanced in chapter 7 are sound. In this context it is useful to recall the Johannine description of judgement: Christ did not come to judge, though judgement is one result of his coming. In the same way, Christ came to reveal not the wrath but the love of God, though the revelation of the wrath is one result or by-product of his coming.

It would seem therefore that the most satisfying interpretation of this difficult passage is along the same lines as those attempted in the discussion of Gal. 3.13. What Paul means is that Christ became sin *according to the Law*, just as he became a curse *according to the Law*. The righteousness which we thereby receive is a righteousness of faith, a righteousness which transcends the Law. So God himself now deals

---

[1] See pp. 99 f. The figures for Paul's quotations of Old Testament passages containing the second person singular from all other books of the Old Testament are as follows: total number of quotations excluding repetitions, 15; of these 4 are quite straightforward, requiring no mystical explanation; e.g. God to Pharoah (Rom. 9.17); God to Abraham (Rom. 9.7). 5 are moral commands applicable to the Old or the New Israel (e.g. Rom. 7.8: οὐκ ἐπιθυμήσεις; Eph. 6.2: τίμα τὸν πατέρα σου); 5 are instances of God addressing the Jews or Old Testament characters or the Messiah, but quoted as applying in Pauls' day to the Christian Church, (e.g. Gal. 4.27: εὐφρανθῆτι στεῖρα ἡ οὐ τίκτουσα; Rom. 10.8: ἐγγύς σου τὸ ῥῆμά ἐστιν). One is the quotation under discussion. The nearest that Paul gets to applying an Old Testament quotation to himself is Phil. 1.19: τοῦτό μοι ἀποβήσεται εἰς σωτηρίαν from Job 13.16 in LXX; and Phil. 2.16: ἐς κένον ἐκοπίασα from Isa. 49.4. But these are both first persons singular, and cannot outweigh the overwhelming weight of the evidence of the other quotations that Paul does not apply second persons singular in the Old Testament to himself.

[2] Ed. 2 Corinthians (Moffatt Commentary, London 1935), in loc.

with us not on a legal basis. By having sent his Son to live according to faith, not according to Law, God has himself come under the judgement of the Law, which, as we have seen, demands that all should live by it, or else be condemned by it. As Paul says in verse 17 of this chapter: "The old things [the legal dispensation] have passed away." God no longer reckons trespasses (verse 19); he no longer deals with us as a judge; he has become an ambassador instead; he entreats us (verse 20). That we might receive this new supra-legal righteousness, he permitted his Son to undergo the condemnation of the Law, to be reckoned a sinner by the Law in just the same way as we are reckoned righteous by him. If we follow this interpretation, the quotation from Isa. 49.8 fits in very well. It is God addressing the Church who speaks and says: "I have made you accepted, not by asking you to keep the Law (I have transcended and broken that in Christ), but by sheer grace." The "acceptable time", the "day of salvation", the "helping", all point to the action of God in grace contrasted with the static and ineffective Law. By Christ's being made sin, then, Paul meant primarily Christ's accepting the condemnation of the Law, as in Gal. 3.13; but in the background is also the wider thought that he accepted the consequences of our sins, which were after all the fruits of that moral law for all men which Paul often signifies by the word "Law". In any other, these consequences would be wrath, curse, and sin, but in Christ they were not God's wrath, God's curse, or sin denounced by God as such, but were turned into blessing and victory by him. Thus Paul can speak of Christ being both curse and sin because these words can be thought of as belonging to the Law and not to God. He does not say Christ was made wrath, because, for all Paul's efforts to conceive it as impersonal and indirect, wrath is a personal word, and needs a person to give it meaning. To speak of "the wrath of the Law" would not be significant.

Finally in 13.1–10, there is a very illuminating passage concerning the nature of God's power. That power is based on human weakness voluntarily accepted in Christ. Goudge[1] here well remarks that spiritual power cannot be misused; it only turns against him who misuses it and becomes judgement. Notice ἑαυτοὺς πειράζετε ...

---

[1] Op. cit., in loc., à propos 13.8.

ἑαυτοὺς δοκιμάζετε, "Try your own selves... prove your own selves', in verse 5: this is the self-criticism of Christians who are within the sphere of grace, and have passed out of the sphere of God's judgement. Moreover, the opposite to being in Christ here is to be ἀδόκιμος—a negative word, describing one who has failed a test and is therefore shown up to be unfit, rather than one who has experienced a positive judgement. Throughout the New Testament, judgement is a process of showing up, which culminates, it is true, in the last days, but is emphatically not a passing of judgement only taking place at the end. In this connection Paul's use of δόκιμος and ἀδόκιμος is significant; he has a fondness for the words, no doubt because they expressed that *indirect* judgement which was certainly a part of his belief. He uses δόκιμος five times, assuming that 2 Tim. 2.15 is not Pauline. Of these, two (Rom. 16.10; 1 Cor. 11.19) definitely bear the suggestion of "self-proved to be faithful", and another (2 Cor. 10.18) might well bear that sense. The man whom the Lord commends is δόκιμος; but surely the Lord's way of commending or approving a man is to let him prove himself. ἀδόκιμος is used also five times by Paul. In all five places (Rom. 1.28; 1 Cor. 9.27; 2 Cor. 13.5,6,7) it has the meaning of "shown up to be unfaithful or sinful", not "rejected as unfaithful", i.e. it implies a process of judgement which consists primarily in the judgement we pass on ourselves by our conduct. Thus the word is obviously suitable for the large element of realized judgement which we find in St Paul's thought.

It is in Romans that Paul's conception of the wrath comes out more clearly, and in this epistle there are more explicit references to the wrath than in all the rest of Pauls' epistles put together. The very first reference is most significant. We find in Rom. 1.18–32 what we might almost call a handbook to the working of the wrath. Paul describes the wrath as it is working itself out in the contemporary Graeco-Roman world. For this process he uses the word ἀποκαλύπτεται: he writes:

ἀποκαλύπτεται γὰρ ὀργὴ τοῦ Θεοῦ ἀπ' οὐρανοῦ ἐπὶ πᾶσαν ἀσέβειαν καὶ ἀδικίαν ἀνθρώπων. For the wrath of God is revealed from heaven against all ungodliness and unrighteousness of men.

Sanday and Headlam[1] do their best to render the present tense as if it

[1] Ed. Romans (I.C.C., Edinburgh 1907), in loc.

was a future, saying that it refers mainly to the approaching end. Of the word ὀργή they remark that it is in the Old Testament specially connected with the Covenant, a statement whose inaccuracy has already been pointed out. They go on to say that in the prophets ὀργή is connected with the day of the Lord, another statement of great inaccuracy; in so far as it is true at all, it is only true of the later prophets, and not even of all of them. From these premisses it is not surprising that their conclusion is also precarious: "Hence the use in the New Testament seems to be mainly, if not altogether, eschatological." They refer to 2 Thess. 2.16 which would seem to be a very obvious exception to their rule, but they explain it away by saying: "The state of the Jews seems to Paul to be only a foretaste of the final woes." To describe the words "has come upon them to the uttermost" as expressing only a foretaste of what is to come seems something of a *meiosis*, to say the least of it. Tasker in his little book already quoted interprests ἀποκαλύπτεται in a different way. He rejects the idea that it is a "prophetic present", i.e. that it really refers to the future; he also refuses to accept the conclusion that it refers to the conditions of the Roman Empire in Paul's day only. He would take it as a "frequentative present", meaning "is continually being revealed", and he goes on to say that the divine wrath is permanent and unwavering, unlike human wrath. He quotes Lactantius *De Ira Dei* to support his conception of the wrath, but it is significant that he does not quote any Old Testament reference illustrating this contrast between the unchanging divine wrath and capricious human wrath. The fact is that such a contrast does not occur anywhere in the Bible or inter-Testamental literature.[1] Moreover, Tasker seems to ignore the parallel which verse 18 offers to verse 17. In verse 17 we read:

δικαιοσύνη γὰρ Θεοῦ ἐν αὐτῷ ⟨sc. εὐαγγελίῳ⟩ ἀποκαλύπτεται ἐκ πίστεως εἰς πίστιν. For therein [in the gospel] is revealed a righteousness of God by faith unto faith.

Verse 18 is connected to this one by a γάρ, so we can hardly fail to understand ἀποκαλύπτεται in the same sense in both verses. The first ἀποκαλύπτεται must mean: "is now being revealed under the Christian dispensation", so we can hardly take ἀποκαλύπτεται in

---

[1] Op. cit., in loc. The only exception is Josephus, *Arch.* III [315]; see p. 64.

verse 18 as meaning: "is continually being revealed". The meaning must surely be that just as the righteousness of God is now revealed to faith, so the wrath of God is now revealed by the Christian dispensation, to faith—a thought which we have already encountered in Paul (cf. 2 Cor. 2.15,16 and comment in loc.). It is not that the wrath has only begun to operate in the Christian dispensation; it has been operating ever since the Fall (Tasker is right in this). In verse 24 God παρέδωκεν, "gave them up"; the process has already been in operation some time in the Roman Empire; but the advent, death, and resurrection of the Messiah has now revealed that wrath. In the same way, Paul would no doubt have claimed that the righteousness of faith was also in some sense to be had, or at least to be apprehended, in the Old Testament dispensation, but it was fully revealed in Christ. Tasker would take ἀπ' οὐρανοῦ "from heaven", in verse 18 to signify: "it is universal in scope", but it seems more satisfactory to take it as definitely connecting the revelation of the wrath with the Incarnation.

Throughout this exposition of the operation of the wrath we find Paul using language which suggests that he viewed the wrath essentially, not as something directly inflicted by God, but as something which men bring on themselves. Thus in verse 24 God παρέδωκεν αὐτούς . . . εἰς ἀκαθαρσίαν, "gave them up to their own hearts' lusts, and let them follow their own imaginations". It was something they brought on themselves; God allows the wrath; he does not inflict it. Similarly in verse 27, the words τὴν ἀντιμισθίαν ἣν ἔδει τῆς πλάνης αὐτῶν ἐν ἑαυτοῖς ἀπολαμβάνοντες, "receiving in themselves that recompense of their error which was due", continue in this strain. It is ἐν ἑαυτοῖς, "in themselves", not something imposed from outside. On verse 27 Sanday and Headlam comment that the phenomena described in this verse are "a proof of God's displeasure". This is inaccurate: they *are* God's displeasure; wrath in the New Testament is not an emotion or attribute of God, but the effects of sin. Dodd[1] well remarks: "The 'reprobate mind' is the Nemesis of sin: the revelation of the wrath."

We pass on to 2.1–16, a passage which is remarkable for its em-

---

[1] Ed. Romans (London 1932), in loc.

phasis on the eschatological characteristics of the wrath, as contrasted with the passage we have just been considering. Dodd suggests that it is an early address originally delivered by Paul to a Jewish audience and incorporated in his letter to the Romans. Its resemblance to 2 Thess. 1.6ff., also an early work, seems to confirm this. In this Romans passage the emphasis is certainly on the wrath which is yet to be revealed; Dodd, however, comments: "The difference between the revelation of wrath in chapter 1, where it is a process observable in the facts of pagan civilization, and the day of wrath here... is smaller than it appears to be." The phrase in verse 5: ἐν ἡμέρᾳ ὀργῆς καὶ ἀποκαλύψεως τῆς δικαιοκρισίας τοῦ Θεοῦ, "in the day of wrath and revelation of the righteous judgement of God", tends to confirm this. It is a revelation perhaps rather than an execution. But on the other hand, the words θησαυρίζεις, "treasurest up", and ἡμέρᾳ ὀργῆς, "day of wrath", would seem to fix the wrath very definitely in the future, even though we may still be permitted to think of it as a process.

The vocabulary which Paul uses to describe this ἡμέρα ὀργῆς is interesting, and prompts the question; how exactly did Paul envisage this ὀργή as being manifested? Verses 8 and 9 give us four words to describe the fate of sinners; they are ὀργή, θυμός, θλίψις, στενοχωρία. In this respect verse 8 is unique in the New Testament outside Revelation. Nowhere else, outside Revelation, is θυμός used for the wrath of God. As will be indicated in chapter 7, the author of Revelation's use of θυμός is entirely peculiar to himself. Sanday and Headlam say that θυμός is the manifestation of the wrath, ὀργή the settled feeling. As far as Biblical evidence goes, this statement has little foundation. In the LXX ὀργή and θυμός are used absolutely interchangeably for any and every manifestation of the wrath, and no such distinction can possibly be maintained there (see Appendix 3). In the New Testament, θυμός and cognates are often used of human anger, always of culpable human anger, e.g. Luke 4.28: the congregation in the synagogue at Nazareth ἐπλήσθησαν πάντες θυμοῦ. Similarly in 2 Cor. 12.20, the Corinthian Christians are warned against ἔρις, ζῆλος, θυμοί (which probably here means "bursts of anger"). So also Matt. 2.16 says of Herod: ἐθυμώθη λίαν. Hence Lightfoot's definition of the two words is at least nearer the truth as far as human anger is concerned;

he says[1] that ὀργή denotes settled hatred, θυμός "a tumultuous outburst of passion". We have already seen that both Philo and Josephus deliberately avoid using the word for divine anger, and there can be no doubt whatever that θυμός had an anthropomorphic, emotional flavour which made the writers of the New Testament avoid it.[2] Why then does Paul use it here, and nowhere else? It probably slipped in with ὀργή because he was quoting the Old Testament. The most likely passage is Psalm 78.49 (77 in LXX): ἐξαπέστειλεν εἰς αὐτοὺς ὀργὴν θυμοῦ αὐτοῦ, θυμὸν καὶ ὀργὴν καὶ θλίψιν, "He sent upon them his fierce anger, wrath and rage and distress."[3] He was no doubt quoting from memory, not perhaps even consciously. But considering the frequency of the conjunction of ὀργή and θυμός in the Old Testament, we cannot tell with certainty which passage exactly Paul was echoing.

Θλίψις (verse 9) is a neutral word. There is the θλίψις, a testing-time, of the Synoptic apocalypses, and the μεγάλη θλίψις of Revelation. It is *the* New Testament word for the trials and persecutions which Christians undergo; Paul himself uses it in this sense frequently and in this epistle, e.g. 5.3; 8.35; 12.12. In two other places in the New Testament is θλίψις used of the punitive action of God. One is 2 Thess. 1.6: ἀνταποδοῦναι τοῖς θλίβουσιν ὑμῖν θλίψιν, "to recompense affliction to them that afflict you", a passage which, as we have noted, is very like this one in being also eschatological. The other passage is Rev. 2.22, where, because Jezebel and her friends have not repented, Christ throws them (or is about to throw them) εἰς θλίψιν μεγάλην, "unto great tribulation". This is not eschatological, and there is a hint of the θλίψις being disciplinary, for (Rev. 2.23) by this action the churches will know that Christ is "he which searcheth the reins and hearts". Moreover, in Rev. 2.10, it is Satan that sends tribulation, where it is certainly disciplinary. θλίψις is used of mental anguish in 2 Cor. 2.4. In fact θλίψις is normally very much bound up with events in history, and only here and 2 Thess. 1.6 is it connected

---

[1] Lightfoot, ed. Colossians (London 1892), p. 212.
[2] Büchsel, art. θυμός in the *Th. Wörterbuch d. N.T.*, maintains there is no difference between ὀργή and θυμός in the New Testament, but he has not considered the evidence given here.
[3] Compare Philo's euhemerization of this passage in *De Gigantibus*, para. 17, p. 284.

with final punishment. We may guess perhaps that Paul used it here without stopping to reflect on its implications. As we have seen above, it may be an Old Testament echo. στενοχωρία is used, as Sanday and Headlam point out, in 2 Cor. 4.8 of "pressed on every side (θλιβόμενοι) yet not straitened (στενοχωρούμενοι)". Again in Rom. 8.35 neither θλίψις nor στενοχωρία nor διωγμός will separate us from the love of God in Christ. It seems to mean very largely mental anguish, not unlike the λύπη which "worketh death" of 2 Cor. 7.10. As such it is quite appropriate for describing the sufferings of the lost. It is curious that the love of God in Christ is described in Rom. 8.35 as coming to us in spite of both θλίψις and στενοχωρία but in 2 Cor. 4.8 we are θλιβόμενοι but not στενοχωρούμενοι. στενοχωρία seems to mean being overcome or overtaken by circumstances; θλίψις is just being harried by circumstances, and usually circumstances in the form of human agency. We may fairly conclude that this is an early passage incorporated into Romans, that Paul when he wrote it had no very clear idea as to how the punitive suffering was to be inflicted in the day of wrath, and that as his theology matured his conception of wrath and punishment showed a more realized eschatology even within the Epistle to the Romans itself.

We now meet with four references requiring less detailed attention. In 3.5b, Paul asks

> μὴ ἄδικος ὁ Θεὸς ὁ ἐπιφέρων τὴν ὀργήν; Is God unrighteous who visiteth with wrath?

Dodd translates this, "brings retribution on us". It seems on the whole not to be eschatological; Paul is arguing about the present relation of God to man, and says in verse 5a:

> But if our unrighteousness commendeth the righteousness of God, what shall we say? Is God unrighteous because he brings wrath to bear on us? [last sentence not R.V. translation].

Then he goes on to argue that God has put all men under sin (verse 9). Hence the point here is that God must not be called unrighteous just because he has brought all men under sin. So ὀργή here is probably realized wrath, the Law-wrath sphere in which all are before they are justified by faith. The next passage is 4.15:

ὁ γὰρ νόμος ὀργὴν ἐργάζεται· οὗ δὲ οὐκ ἔστιν νόμος, οὐδὲ παράβασις. For the law worketh wrath; but where there is no law, neither is there transgression.

Here are law and wrath explicitly associated; compare with this the statement in 1 John 3.4 that ἡ ἁμαρτία ἐστὶν ἡ ἀνομία, "sin is lawlessness". Paul might almost have said ἁμαρτία ἐστὶν νόμος, but his meaning is much the same as John's, that sin and law are inextricably connected. Sanday and Headlam suggest that Paul is here saying that God never intended the Law at all. It would seem more satisfactory to say that the Law-wrath system exists as an inevitable background in a moral universe, but God has prepared a better way (foreshadowed indeed in the promise to Abraham). Note how extraordinarily impersonal the wrath is here — anything but the generous emotion which we meet in the eighth-century prophets. The subject matter of this verse is the theme of all great Greek tragedies, and is not part of God's revelation in Christ. Through sin, the man who honestly tries to obey God's laws as he sees them is as much caught up in the Law-wrath process as the man who goes ahead and breaks the known laws of God, because the very effort to obey the rules is an act of the autonomous moral reason, and God did not create the moral reason to be autonomous. The third passage is 5.9:

πολλῷ οὖν μᾶλλον δικαιωθέντες νῦν ἐν τῷ αἵματι αὐτοῦ σωθησόμεθα δι' αὐτοῦ ἀπὸ τῆς ὀργῆς. Much more then, being now justified by his blood, shall we be saved from the wrath through him [R.V. inserts "of God" after wrath, not in the Greek text].

ὀργή here cannot possibly be an attribute or attitude of God, otherwise we have the unhappy picture of a suffering Son saving us from an angry Father; we are rather saved from the process of wrath which will culminate in the last day. The ὀργή here is still future, but 4.15 reminds us that it is present also, for the νόμος works ὀργή all the time. Sanday and Headlam here discuss at some length how God can first be angry with men then be reconciled. Once the wrath is seen to be not an attitude or attribute of God but a condition of sin, such discussion is rendered unnecessary. Dodd comments here: "that the wrath does not mean 'an act and attitude of God'." *À propos* of 5.17 Barth[1] well points out that the reign of death and sin is also the realm of wrath.

[1] Barth, ed. Romans (tr. Hoskyns, Oxford 1933), in loc.

THE WRATH OF THE LAMB

The next passage that demands consideration is one of the most difficult in the book, 9.14-33, where Paul goes nearer to a doctrine of reprobation than he does anywhere else. The key passage is verse 22:

εἰ δὲ θέλων ὁ Θεὸς ἐνδείξασθαι τὴν ὀργὴν καὶ γνωρίσαι τὸ δυνατὸν αὐτοῦ ἤνεγκεν ἐν πολλῇ μακροθυμίᾳ σκεύη ὀργῆς κατηρτισμένα εἰς ἀπώλειαν, καὶ ἵνα γνωρίσῃ τὸν πλοῦτον τῆς δόξης αὐτοῦ ἐπὶ σκεύη ἐλέους ἃ προητοίμασεν εἰς δόξαν . . . κτλ. What if God, willing to show his wrath, and to make his favour known, endured with much longsuffering vessels of wrath fitted unto destruction, and that he might make known the riches of his glory upon vessels of mercy, which he afore prepared unto glory, etc.

Editors have given this passage all possible latitude: Sanday and Headlam very truly emphasize that God is not represented as preparing the σκεύη ὀργῆς in the way he is described as preparing the σκεύη ἐλέους. Dodd adds that God is at least shown to be a forbearing God, and that the whole dispensation had as its motive the ultimate salvation of both Jews and Gentiles. But the fact remains that Paul has written the appalling phrase: σκεύη ὀργῆς κατηρτισμένα εἰς ἀπώλειαν, "vessels of wrath fitted unto destruction". It is possible, however, that Paul did not necessarily mean by this phrase merely "*recipients* of wrath prepared for destruction". May he not also have meant "*instruments* of wrath forged for destruction"? The phrase σκεύη ὀργῆς appears in two passages in the LXX: one is Isa. 13.5 and the other Jer. 50.25 (27.25 in LXX). In both these places the Hebrew is $k^e l\bar{e}y\ za'am$ and the meaning is certainly "weapons of wrath".[1] The use by Paul of the words ἐνδείξασθαι τὴν ὀργὴν καὶ γνωρίσαι τὸ δυνατὸν αὐτοῦ "to show his wrath and to make his power known", tends to support this meaning of "instrument" rather than "recipient". It is significant that Tasker,[2] who manifests otherwise no tendency to mitigate the severity of this phrase, in commenting on verse 17, describes Pharoah as an *instrument* of the wrath. If God showed his wrath upon Pharoah, it was not merely gratuitous, but with an object, i.e. in order to warn others or to encourage the Israelites. So God may use some as instruments of his wrath. Indeed one might say that this is the purpose of the wrath process, that is, to show what happens when men disobey God's laws

---

[1] Cf. also Rom. 13.4: ἔκδικος εἰς ὀργήν, a construction which tells strongly on the side of the "instrumental" interpretation.

[2] Op. cit., p. 21.

and to show that the world is God's not man's. In this connection μακροθυμία, "longsuffering", is quite in order; it will mean that he does not punish instruments of wrath like Pharaoh immediately or directly, but lets them carry out their own will, and thus forward the process of wrath; cf. Luke 18.7, for μακροθυμεῖν meaning "to be slow to punish those who ought to be punished". Of course, if σκεύη ὀργῆς is to be taken as meaning "the instruments of wrath forged for destruction [of others besides themselves]" quite as much as "recipients of wrath doomed to destruction", in verse 23 σκεύη ἐλέους must mean "instruments of mercy, which he hath prepared that others besides themselves may be glorified". But this is quite appropriate for, as he argues in this very epistle, both the faithful remnant of Jews has been the means of evangelizing the Gentiles, and the accession of the Gentiles themselves is to be ultimately (at least such is Paul's hope) the means of bringing in the unbelieving Jews.[1]

We can therefore claim that in this passage Paul is thinking of unbelievers in some sense at least as instruments of wrath, bringing destruction to those who are with them caught up in the wrath process. The use of the word κατηρτισμένα is significant; he does not say by whom they were κατηρτισμένα, because he does not like to say that wrath is the *direct* action of God. It is the impersonal process which

---

[1] If we look at the figurative use of σκεῦος in the rest of the New Testament we find that there is certainly evidence to support the interpretation of the word here as primarily "instrument". It is used in a literal sense of "pot, tackle, furniture", etc., 14 times; figuratively 8 times. Of these 8, 5 come from Paul. There are 3 in this passage; the first εἰς τίμην σκεῦος (verse 2), with the implied εἰς ἀτιμίαν (σκεῦος), must surely mean vessels for an honourable or dishonourable use, cf. Wisd. 13.11. In 1 Thess. 4.4: τὸ ἑαυτοῦ σκεῦος. This could be translated either way, but the body is thought of by Paul as primarily the instrument of the spirit. The other reference is 2 Cor. 4.7: ἐν ὀστρακίνοις σκεύεσιν. Here certainly the meaning "vessel" is predominant. Thus the evidence in Paul is inconclusive. Of the other three figurative uses in the New Testament, one comes from 2 Tim. 2.20,21. The author of 2 Timothy has not rightly understood Rom. 9.14 f. on which his passage is modelled; but on the whole the meaning seems to be instrumental. These are to be "used for an honourable or dishonourable purpose". The second passage occurs in Acts 9.15: σκεῦος ἐκλογῆς μοί ἐστιν. Grammatically this is not instrumental; it means "an object of choice", but hermeneutically it is instrumental, "a chosen instrument"; the sentence goes on with the words τοῦ βαστάσαι τὸ ὄνομα which gives the purpose for which the σκεῦος was chosen. By analogy in 9.21 σκεύη ὀργῆς ought to mean "instruments of wrath forged for destruction". The third occurrence outside Paul is 1 Peter 3.7: ὡς ἀσθενεστέρῳ σκεύει referring to woman; here it is certainly not instrumental.

he has permitted. The σκεύη ὀργῆς are recipients of wrath in the sense that they are involved in this process, a process which by the moral law of cause and effect goes on involving mankind in itself, generation after generation, and therefore they are also, and perhaps primarily, instruments of wrath. After all, Pharaoh was much more an instrument than a recipient of wrath; he suffered much less than the Egyptians who were (not innocently according to Wisdom at least) involved in the consequences of his opposition to God. Once we see the wrath as an impersonal process, the sting of Paul's apparent doctrine of double predestination is removed. There can be no question of a personal decree of God predestining anyone to destruction.

In 11.22 Paul draws a comparison between the severity (ἀποτομία) and the goodness (χρηστότης) of God. This at first sight looks like the contrast between the wrath and the love of God which we have met in such places as Hos. 11 and Ps. 85. But in fact the words used bear out the significance of the wrath as we have seen it in the rest of this Epistle. ἀποτομία does not mean "harshness" or "undue punishment", it means demanding exactly what the law requires. Moulton and Milligan (*Vocab. of the Gk. N.T.*, s.v. ἀποτομία) quote several examples from the papyri; on one of the examples they comment: "The word does not suggest straining at a statute, but simply exacting its provisions to the full." Thus the contrast here is between the Jews, who try to attain to righteousness by the law, and hence can only apprehend the "uttermost farthing" which the wrath exacts, and the Gentiles, who have abandoned the legal approach, and are thus able to apprehend God's mercy.

Rom. 12.19 offers a most remarkable example of the impersonal wrath:

> μὴ ἑαυτοὺς ἐκδικοῦντες, ἀγαπητοί, ἀλλὰ δότε τόπον τῇ ὀργῇ. γέγραπται γάρ Ἐμοὶ ἐκδίκησις, ἐγὼ ἀνταποδώσω, λέγει Κύριος. Avenge not yourselves, beloved, but give place unto wrath: for it is written, Vengeance belongeth unto me: I will recompense, saith the Lord.

The reference to the wrath here is so impersonal that many have taken it for human wrath[1]; but a careful study of the passage shows that here

---

[1] Cf. the A. V. translation, "to give place unto wrath"; R.V. marg. gives "the wrath of God". The point was well made by E. H. Blakeney in a letter to *The Guardian*, 4 Aug. 1950, but his comparison with Lactantius is misleading, see p. 84.

ἡ ὀργή can mean nothing but the divine wrath. Thus it is taken by Sanday and Headlam and thus by Dodd; in fact it is à propos this passage that Dodd makes his well-known comment: "The Wrath ... is the principle of retribution inherent in a moral universe." Tasker (op. cit., p. 46) insists that in this passage the wrath must be eschatological, because of Deut. 32.35 being quoted immediately afterwards, and that, he claims, is an eschatological passage. But in fact Deut. 32.35 is nothing of the sort. The passage occurs in the Song of Moses, which, as we have seen, is much too early to contain eschatological wrath. The passage continues:

> For the day of their calamity is at hand, and the things that are to come upon them shall make haste.

This only indicates that Jahveh will some day punish Israel's enemies; it might be called "a day of the Lord". Nor can it safely be claimed that Paul thought that it did refer to the Last Days. This would infer that Paul was looking forward to the Last Days when God would directly punish the enemies of Christ and of Christians. If so, it is most incongruous that he should go on in verse 20 to urge them to feed their enemies. Also why does he say δότε τόπον, "give place", which suggests making way for a process that is happening now, not a waiting for something that is to happen in the future? E. H. Blakeney, in the letter referred to above, well translates δότε τόπον as "let God's wrath do its work". "Vengeance is mine" means, says St Paul, a present process, with which Christians are not to interfere, but rather show all possible love to those who are implicated in it, in the hope of redeeming them from it.

In 13.1–7 the divine wrath is presented in a new aspect, as exhibited in the activities of the "powers that be". ὀργή is used twice here. In verse 4 the rule is described as

> Θεοῦ γὰρ διάκονός ἐστιν, ἔκδικος εἰς ὀργὴν τῷ τὸ κακὸν πράσσοντι. For he is a minister of God, an avenger for wrath to him that doeth evil.

He continues:

> διὸ ἀνάγκη ὑποτάσσεσθαι, οὐ μόνον διὰ τὴν ὀργὴν, ἀλλὰ καὶ διὰ τὴν συνείδησιν. Wherefore you must needs be in subjection, not only because of the wrath, but also for conscience sake.

Here surely none who has studied the way in which Paul uses ὀργή will dispute that ὀργή is used in an impersonal and non-eschatological sense. The rule is part of God's divine economy whereby sin brings suffering; cf. verse 2: ἑαυτοῖς κρίμα λήμψονται "shall receive judgement to themselves". It is very interesting that Paul apparently makes no distinction between the various agents through whom the wrath operates. We can distinguish perhaps three categories: the first is what we would call "natural agencies", such as disease. Of these an example can be found in Rom. 1.27: καὶ τὴν ἀντιμισθίαν ἣν ἔδει τῆς πλάνης αὐτῶν ἐν ἑαυτοῖς ἀπολαμβάνοντες, "and receiving in themselves that recompense of their error which was due", which seems to refer to the physical effects of unnatural intercourse. Perhaps also some of the plagues in Revelation are examples of this sort of agency. The second category consists of unconscious or semi-conscious operations and reactions of the human mind or conscience. Of this we have an instance in Rom. 1.21: ἀλλὰ ἐματαιώθησαν ἐν τοῖς διαλογισμοῖς αὐτῶν, καὶ ἐσκοτίσθη ἡ ἀσύνετος αὐτῶν καρδία, "but became vain in their reasonings, and their senseless heart was darkened". Here also may we put the wrath that has come upon the Jews to the uttermost in 1 Thess. 2.16; it is a spiritual condition, but it is manifested in a psychological condition. The third category consists of direct human agency; the passage under consideration gives us an instance of this. Non-Christian rulers, punishing on principle, are the instruments of the wrath. It is not here exactly an instance of "Ho, Assyrian, the rod of mine anger", for the Assyrian was not acting on principle, which meant, in Paul's day at least, in the name of some divine sanction. The Assyrian was acting simply in the interests of his own aggrandisement and was under the impression that he was the arbiter of his own destiny. The Roman ruler was acting consciously in the name of justice, though, like the Assyrian, he was unaware that he was the instrument of God's wrath. In this category also we must place all expressions of the wrath by human agency, especially in wars and political action. The long catalogue of sins in Rom. 1.29–32 belongs here also. But it is in Revelation especially that this category of wrath comes to the fore. It should be emphasized that these distinctions are not made by Paul, but are merely helpful in elucidating his thought. The fact that Paul does not in any way distinguish between these three agents of the wrath is itself significant. It would seem to indicate that in his view the coercive power of government was something belonging to the natural order. The State is the realm of law and wrath; the Church that of grace and love. But of course this law and wrath are not independent, but are themselves the instruments of ultimate love. These considerations alone should give pause to those who would apply the teaching of the Sermon on the Mount directly to political or international affairs. The comments of Oscar Cullmann[1] on this passage are relevant: "The apostle is anxious to explain how it is that the members of the Church themselves ought to obey the law *despite this* [i.e. despite the fact that the State does the opposite to what the Church does, exacts punishment]. We must understand in its context the positive command of submission to the State in the light of the background design (*arrière-plan*) which is wholly negative.... Although the State applies a principle which is opposed to the fundamental Christian law, the law of love, we must *all the same* obey it.... It is the duty of this minister to accomplish the divine vengeance and to execute the just judgement of the wrath of God. The Christian knows that this divine vengeance is founded in the divine love of Jesus Christ." Cullmann here well draws out the contrast between the sphere of wrath and the sphere of grace. Paul tells the Roman Christians that they must obey the authorities, not only because to disobey them is to be involved in the wrath-process, but also "for conscience sake" (verse 5). This is the enlightened Christian conscience, not the mind and conscience that is the helpless victim of moral and psychological laws under the realm of wrath. That this law-grace, wrath-love contrast is in Paul's mind is further shown by his juxtaposition of the two in verses 9–10. With this whole passage also compare 1 Cor. 5.13; 11.27–32.

Commentators have often contrasted Paul's attitude towards the rulers of the Roman Empire as expressed here with that of the author of Revelation. The contrast is certainly striking, but as far as the fundamental conceptions underlying Paul's and John's theology of the wrath are concerned, there is no great difference. For John the Divine also the rulers of the Roman Empire were σκεύη ὀργῆς, cf. Rev.

---

[1] *Christ et le Temps* (Neuchâtel and Paris 1947), p. 144 (my translation).

14.8; 18.3. Rome was in the end to fall by the hand of the kings from the East, and therein was to be seen her drinking of the cup of the wrath of God (Rev. 16.19). Both the rulers of the Roman Empire who consciously punish crime in the name of justice, and nations and kings who attack that Empire in their lust for power, are instruments of the wrath. Unredeemed history is the sphere of its manifestation. How Tasker can maintain[1] that the wrath in Rom. 13 is eschatological it is difficult to understand.

It would hardly seem necessary to discuss the view maintained by some that "the powers that be" referred to here are not Roman rulers but discarnate intelligences akin to the "world rulers of this darkness" of Eph. 6.12 (τὰς ἐξουσίας occurs in the previous phrase there). But as this view has found some modern support perhaps reason should be shown for rejecting it. In the first place, Paul's other references to "world rulers" suggest that he would hardly invite the Roman Christians to obey such powers, but rather to reject them. Secondly, immediately after referring to "the powers that be" in Rom. 13.1–5 he speaks about paying tribute (verse 6). This hardly fits a context of angelic powers, nor does his reference in verse 4 to these powers bearing the sword, while both these details suit well a discussion of the relation of Christians to the Roman government. Thirdly, the passage in 1 Pet. 2.13,14 which appears to deal with the same subject can only refer to Roman rulers, for they are described as being "an ordinance of man" and the ensuing phrases refer specifically to the king and governors. The author of 1 Peter uses the same word (ἐκδίκησις; Paul uses ἔκδικος) to describe the function of the king, etc. as Paul uses to describe that of the "powers that be". If the function is the same it is likely that the functionary is the same. An alternative is to suggest that the author of 1 Peter mistook Paul's meaning, or else that he is making a completely independent observation. But neither of these is a convincing hypothesis. Compare also Titus 3.1:

> ὑπομίμνησκε αὐτοὺς ἀρχαῖς ἐξουσίαις ὑποτάσσεσθαι, πειθαρχεῖν. Put them in mind also to be in subjection to rulers, to authorities, to be obedient.

It might be maintained that these are superhuman powers also, but the word πειθαρχεῖν does not suit such an idea. One could imagine people

[1] Op. cit., p. 46.

submitting to a destiny imposed by some superhuman power, but one can only *obey* a command. Paul can hardly be accused of conceiving these discarnate intelligences as issuing commands to be obeyed. Hence the author of the Pastorals is a witness against this view, and it must be conceded that if Paul really had been referring to discarnate intelligences in Rom. 13.1–7, it is more likely that the author of the Pastorals would have realized it, since he lived in a mental atmosphere in which such an idea would not be strange, than that it should have been left to modern scholars to discover, whose mental atmosphere is so totally different.

The two last passages that we have been considering, Rom. 12.19 and 13.1–7, are unique in the New Testament in one respect. Nowhere else is divine punishment explicitly connected with the wrath. Divine punishment is mentioned only eleven times in the New Testament: once in Matthew, twice in Hebrews, once in 2 Peter, twice in Revelation, and five times in Paul.[1] It is used of the state of the damned after death only twice, Matt. 25.46: κόλασις αἰώνιος, "eternal punishment", and 2 Pet. 2.9: ἀδίκους εἰς ἡμέραν κρίσεως κολαζομένους τηρεῖν, "to keep the unrighteous under punishment unto the day of judgement". It is perhaps significant that neither passage is very early. It seems that the writers of the New Testament as a whole did not like to speak of divine punishment much and did not like overtly to associate wrath with punishment. This is not because the two were not associated in their minds; on the contrary, as we have seen, wrath *is* punishment, not the divine emotion which prompts or accompanies punishment. But to associate divine wrath with punishment too explicitly would be to run the risk of giving just the impression that they wished to avoid, the suggestion that divine wrath is some divine affection or attribute which accompanies punishment. And it is surely significant that in both the places where Paul does explicitly associate divine wrath and divine punishment, that wrath and punishment are manifested not in the direct action of God, but in an indirect historical process.

The words which Paul uses to describe this ministerial function of the rulers are startlingly ecclesiastical to our minds: they are διάκονοι

[1] The vocabulary is: κόλασις and cognates twice; τιμωρία once; ἔκδικος and cognates eight times.

in verse 4, and λειτουργοί in verse 6. Similarly we find the rulers in 1 Pet. 2.14 described as δι' αὐτοῦ ⟨sc. Θεοῦ⟩ πεμπομένοις εἰς ἐκδίκησιν κακοποιῶν, "sent by him for vengeance on evil-doers". Might they not almost be called ἀπόστολοι, despite the absence of the crucial word? As a matter of fact his use here of πέμπω rather than ἀποστέλλω probably has significance. It indicates the difference between the unwitting agent and the apostle, between the indirect and the direct action of God. Again we should not be too much astonished by Paul's use of διάκονος or λειτουργός here; the words had not yet acquired the technical flavour which they have for us.[1] Philo, as we have seen, is fond of the word ὑπηρέτης to describe an office very similar to this one. But ὑπηρέτης is used twice in the New Testament to describe Christian ministry: Acts 26.16 and 1 Cor. 4.1. Hence we cannot in this Romans passage imagine that Paul in using διάκονος and λειτουργός was attributing an office to the rulers that had any connection with the new dispensation. Theirs was the service of the wrath.

Finally, there is one more passage in Romans where Christ is described as accepting the consequences of men's sins in a manner reminiscent of Gal. 3.13 and 2 Cor. 5.21. The passage is Rom. 15.3:

> καὶ γὰρ ὁ Χριστὸς οὐχ ἑαυτῷ ἤρεσεν, ἀλλά, καθὼς γέγραπται οἱ ὀνειδισμοὶ τῶν ὀνειδιζόντων σε ἐπέπεσαν ἐπ' ἐμέ. For Christ also pleased not himself; but as it is written, The reproaches of them that reproached thee fell upon me.

The quotation is from Ps. 69.9b. The question arises: to whom does it refer? Sanday and Headlam say that it refers to mankind. Dodd on the other hand explains the σε as referring, apparently, to God the Father. Christ accepted the enmity of the enemies of God. Neither rendering is very easy; the first because it gives an interpretation of σε in the Psalms which is very unlike what we normally expect in the New Testament, the second because it is difficult to see when exactly, in the life of our Lord, God the Father was reproached by his enemies. St Paul may be thinking of the mockery on the Cross; cf. Matt. 27.43: "He trusted in God: let him deliver him now if he desireth him." But the two other Synoptists represent all the reproaches as falling on

---

[1] Incidentally, Paul's use of λειτουργός for the Emperor Claudius and his subordinates here should warn us against interpreting λειτουργός in Rom. 15.16 in an exclusively sacramental sense.

Christ, not on God the Father. An examination of every instance of a quotation of the Psalms in the New Testament in which the second person singular occurs weighs conclusively against Sanday and Headlam's interpretation.[1] The results are as follows: not counting duplicates (whether two or three writers quoting the same passage or one writer quoting it more than once), quotations from the Psalms which include the second person singular occur in the New Testament twenty-one times. Of these twenty-one passages, in *six* the Father is represented as addressing the Son (four in Hebrews and one in the Synoptics, one in Acts). In *seven* the Son is represented as addressing the Father (two in Hebrews and in Matthew–Mark, one in Luke, one in John, one in Acts, one in Romans). The Johannine quotation is very relevant to our purpose here as it is a quotation from Psalm 69.9a: "The zeal of thine house hath eaten me up", quoted in John 2.17. There can be no doubt that σοῦ in that quotation refers to God the Father. Equally relevant is the quotation in Romans; it comes six verses after the verse under discussion, Rom. 15.9. Ps.18.49: "Wherefore I will praise thee among the Gentiles", etc., is apparently attributed to the Son, addressing the Father. There seems to be no other possible subject for "I". Sanday and Headlam agree that Christ is speaking. In *one* passage the Psalmist is represented as addressing the Messiah. This is Matt. 4.6: "He shall give his angels charge concerning thee," etc., a quotation from Ps. 91.11,12. Admittedly this quotation is made by Satan, but it is not repudiated by Christ (Luke 4.10 is a duplicate). In *two* quotations the Psalmist is represented as addressing the Father (Romans once, Hebrews once). In *four* passages Israel, or the Church or the martyrs, or an angel address the Father (one in Romans, three in Revelation). The Revelation passages must be mentioned for the sake of completeness, but they are not really relevant to this passage. They are not direct quotations from the Psalms, but rather extracts from the Psalms worked into various utterances; hence they do not necessarily give us the author's interpretation of the Psalm which he quotes.[2] The last quotation is the passage in question, Rom. 15.3.

---

[1] For an examination of the 2nd person sing. in New Testament quotations from the rest of the Old Testament, see p. 81.

[2] For a discussion of John the Divine's peculiar treatment of the Old Testament see Preston and Hanson, *The Revelation of John the Divine* (2nd ed., London 1951), pp. 34 f.

This examination shows then that, in every other quotation from the Psalms in the New Testament, where the second person singular occurs it is understood as applying either to the Father or the Son. Moreover in Romans itself (the only Pauline epistle in which such quotations occur) there are three other quotations of the second persons singular in the Psalms (3.4; 8.36; 15.9), in all of which the Father is represented as the person addressed. There can be no doubt therefore that Sanday and Headlam are wrong and Dodd is right. The σε in Rom. 15.3 refers to the Father. We must then understand the verse as saying that Christ bore the consequences of men's enmity to God. Because they were enemies to God, they crucified Christ. The quotation is not entirely appropriate, because the Psalmist must be thinking of scoffers who openly mocked God. The men who crucified Christ thought that they were pleasing God in doing so. But this difference between the Old Testament situation and the New Testament application only serves to emphasize one of the underlying themes of the New Testament, the hidden Messiah. In crucifying Jesus the Jews were really trying to do away with God: cf. 1 Cor. 2.7,8; see also Heb. 11.26 and 1 Pet. 4.14, where the reproaches that men level against God's chosen are described as being "the reproach of Christ" or as being reviled in Christ's name. Just as in these cases men in reviling the elect were really reviling Christ, so in Rom. 15.3 it is said that men in reviling Christ during his life on earth were really reviling God. The passage is a little reminiscent of 1 Cor. 4.11–13, where the apostles, like Christ, are described as bearing the consequences of men's sins. If we put this Romans passage together with the two quoted above (Heb. 11.26 and 1 Pet. 4.14), we have a picture of first Christ, and then the members of his body, bearing the consequences of men's sins—the opprobrium and insult and even violence caused by their reproaches. In the case of those who were not under grace but under law, this would be an instance of the wrath. Insult would provoke counter-insult, and so the process would go on. But in Christ consequences of sin are not wrath, but are turned to blessing and transcended by his sacrificial love; and so it may be for Christians too, as Paul reminds his readers in verses 1 and 2 of this passage.[1]

---

[1] The substance of this discussion of Rom. 15.3 has already appeared in *Hermathena*, No. LXXIII, May 1949 (Dublin and London), pp. 68 f.

In Phil. 1.28, there occurs a passage which is very reminiscent of 2 Cor. 2.15,16. In both passages judgement is seen as a process to be apprehended by faith. Here Paul says that the firmness of the Philippian Christians is αὐτοῖς ⟨sc. τοῖς ἀντικειμένοις⟩ ἔνδειξις ἀπωλείας, ὑμῶν δὲ σωτηρίας, "which is for them [the adversaries] an evident token of perdition, but of your salvation" Here is a continuing process; the ἀπώλεια was as much already apprehended as was the σωτηρία. The same idea is expressed in Phil. 3.19: ὧν τὸ τέλος ἀπώλεια, "whose end is perdition". Lightfoot[1] well compares Rom. 6.21; 2 Cor. 11.15; and Heb. 6.8. In all these the idea of a continuing process is implied. Just as Paul could describe those who have not been justified as "dead in their sins" and yet say that their end was death, so those whose end is ἀπώλεια are already being destroyed.

In Col. 1.21, the word ἐχθρούς occurs to describe the condition of Christians before they accepted Christianity. Lightfoot points out that this means "enemies" not "hateful". Things may be hateful to God (cf. the use of βδέλυγμα in the Synoptics) but persons never. They are ἐχθροὺς τῇ διανοίᾳ i.e. it is their own will and mind that have made them enemies. The action does not come from God's side. There is a spiritual condition which they have brought on themselves. Similarly in Col. 2.13,14 we find Paul describing the law-system in such a way as to show that it is identical with the wrath-system. Just because the Law was there, wrath was there also; the Law meant that the conscience made an attempt to obey, and on failing, became involved in the system of wrath. And yet "the Law is holy and good", the wrath is the wrath of God. As long as there was nothing but the Law, sin increased, God's moral laws continued to operate, the "principalities and powers" exercised their authority. Then came Christ; he entered into the whole process; he voluntarily accepted the consequences of other men's sins, the wrath which was no wrath in his case. But at the same time he both fulfilled and transcended the law. All these things together led to the Cross. It was because of his relation to the law that he was crucified. Hence the Cross, where Paul describes him as "nailing" the obligations of the Law, was the supreme point where the worst consequences of sin (the execution of the innocent Messiah) had the most glorious

---

[1] Ed. Philippians (London 1890), in loc.

result, and wrath is turned into its true end, love. One can observe perhaps a tendency in these three epistles to supplement the working of the wrath by referring to the activity of the power of darkness. Was this perhaps because Paul felt that the wrath-principle was too impersonal to explain the apparently purposive nature of the evil which he met with in the course of his ministry?

Col. 3.6 and Eph. 5.6 ought to be taken together. The Colossians passage runs:

δι' ἃ ἔρχεται ἡ ὀργὴ τοῦ Θεοῦ. For which things' sake cometh the wrath of God.

(The better reading leaves out the phrase "upon the sons of disobedience" here.) And the Ephesians passage is:

διὰ ταῦτα γὰρ ἔρχεται ἡ ὀργὴ τοῦ Θεοῦ ἐπὶ τοὺς υἱοὺς τῆς ἀπειθείας. For because of these things' sake cometh the wrath of God upon the sons of disobedience.

In each of these cases ἔρχεται seems to be present rather than future. δι' ἅ and διὰ ταῦτα means here not exactly "because of these things", but rather "through them"; by the operation of these sins we find ourselves under the wrath. Compare Heb. 2.10; Rev. 4.11; and Moulton and Milligan, *The Vocabulary of the Greek New Testament* (London 1930) sub διά. διὰ τὸ ὕδωρ and διοικονομήθη τὰ πάντα διὰ σέ from the Papyri are both uses akin to what is suggested here. Abbott[1] remarks *à propos* Eph. 5.6 that wrath is not to be limited to God's judgements, nor to the Last Judgement: "The wrath of God will be manifested then, but it exists now." If this means that it is operating now, then the statement is quite true; but if it means that the wrath exists in the mind of God as an emotion or an attitude, it is very far from the New Testament conception of the wrath. The spiritual condition described in these two passages is not exactly that of being τέκνα φύσει ὀργῆς "by nature children of wrath", as in Eph. 2.3, for that describes the condition of those who have not accepted Christianity. These two passages refer to the danger of Christians falling back again into the wrath-process from which they have been redeemed by Christ. On the whole in these two places the absolute impersonality of the

---

T. K. Abbott, ed. Ephesians (I.C.C., Edinburgh), in loc.

wrath is less emphasized than in Romans, for the wrath is ἡ ὀργὴ τοῦ Θεοῦ not just ἡ ὀργή (though ὀργή occurs unqualified in Eph. 2.3). But the way in which the wrath is spoken of is entirely in accord with the New Testament conception of the wrath. If Paul had been capable of saying that God could be angry, here surely was the place to say it: "Do not do these things, or God will be angry with you." Instead of that, he speaks of the wrath coming. Nowhere else perhaps in the New Testament is the determination not to speak of God as angry more clear.[1]

In Eph. 2.3 we come upon a phrase that has given much concern to scholars. Paul, describing the state of his readers before conversion, says:

καὶ ἤμεθα τέκνα φύσει ὀργῆς ὡς οἱ λοιποί. And we were by nature children of wrath, even as the rest.

Similar phrases occur in the inter-Testamental period; cf. Apocalypse of Moses 3.2: ὀργῆς υἱός; Sibylline Oracles 3.309f.: θυμοῦ τέκνα. In the Apocalypse of Moses the phrase refers to Cain after the murder of Abel. It has therefore no predestinarian meaning, but simply implies that he has incurred the divine wrath for his crime. In the Sibylline Oracles "objects of wrath" is no doubt an adequate translation. But in the Ephesians passage a permanent condition which comes φύσει, "by nature" is plainly intended; it is the possibility that Paul believed some people to be born into or under the wrath that causes editors concern. Abbott[2] holds that the phrase does not mean "objects of God's wrath", but "worthy of God's wrath", on the analogy of "sons of death" in 1 Sam. 26.16. He cannot contemplate the possibility of God both loving men (as Paul declares he does in verse 4) and being angry with them at the same time. This is very true, but Abbott is assuming that to speak of "the wrath of God" is the same thing as to say God is angry. Armitage Robinson[3] is ready to accept the translation "objects of God's wrath", but he would take φύσει in contrast to χάριτι, and

---

[1] In the present state of the subject, the Pauline authorship of Ephesians must be treated as an open question; it is called Pauline here, but even if it should not be Paul's, the Continuator had sufficient understanding of Paul's thought for his conception of the wrath to be treated as one with Paul's.

[2] Op. cit., in loc.

[3] Armitage Robinson, ed. Ephesians (London 1907), in loc.

translate it as "in ourselves". He emphasizes that there is no suggestion of the sin and death which are involved in Adam's disobedience but that all this language simply refers to actual transgressions, "a conversation in the lusts of the flesh". If so, it is indeed remarkable that Paul should use these three words ἁμαρτία, "sin" (verse 1), νεκρούς, literally "corpses" (verse 1), ἀπειθεία, "disobedience" (verse 2) to describe the condition of non-Christians. F. R. Tennant[1] agrees with Armitage Robinson about the meaning of φύσει, saying that it means only the natural condition before conversion and does not refer to any doctrine of inherited depravity. The latest author to comment on this phrase, Tasker,[2] will have no half-measures: "But the word φύσις should refer to what is innate or ingrained, and not to something which is due to a defect caused by particular conditions or circumstances.... They are inevitably involved in behaviour which renders them the objects of the divine wrath." And he quotes with approval Knox's translation: "God's displeasure is their birthright." This is in fact an unsatisfactory translation, first because it is not ὀργὴ τοῦ Θεοῦ here, and the absence of qualification adds to the impersonal nature of the wrath; and second because "displeasure" suggests at once a personal feeling in God, which ὀργή in the particular sense used by Paul is very far from expressing.

The truth is that as long as you look on the wrath of God as an emotion or attribute of God, you will have ultimately to translate τέκνα φύσει ὀργῆς as "objects of God's wrath"[3] and you must then face the perplexing question of how God can be angry with, and love, men at the same time. Most editors solve this, as Hosea did, by simply saying that is how it is; e.g. Gore[4] comments: "He [God] resents the perversion, the spoiling of His own handiwork in us. He cannot tolerate uncleanness, rebellion, unbelief." "God resents" is not a phrase which is found anywhere in the New Testament and the essence of the Incarnation and the Death of the Son of God is that he did tolerate these things in his own body. Once, however, it is realized

---

[1] F. R. Tennant, *The Sources of the Doctrine of the Fall and Original Sin* (Cambridge 1903), in loc.   [2] Op. cit., p. 16.

[3] Abbot's suggestion of "worthy of God's wrath" is surely refuted by the occurrence of ὀργή in Col. 3.6, and Eph. 5.6.

[4] Ed. Ephesians (London 1909), in loc., p. 96.

that for Paul, as for nearly all the writers of the New Testament, wrath is not an affection of God but a condition of unregenerate man, the phrase τέκνα φύσει ὀργῆς becomes perfectly simple. Paul has already described the unconverted as "dead", in verse 1, a spiritual condition, τέκνα φύσει ὀργῆς simply elaborates this description. φύσις belongs to God; he made it, and so those who are involved in the process of the wrath are so by nature. There is no difficulty whatever in saying that God loves those who are involved in the wrath-process; on the contrary it has the very highest significance. He loved us so much that he saved us from the condition which we brought on ourselves by our disobedience to his laws. We are not "objects of wrath" but "involved in wrath". Wrath is the process of this world into which we were born, and from which we need to be born out again (συνεζωοποίησεν, verse 5). Unless, in fact, you understand the impersonal nature of the wrath in the New Testament, you are constantly stumbling over the question of guilt: "Was it really fair? Were they really deserving of all that wrath?" Now it is remarkable that Paul does not seem to be much concerned about the question of guilt. He does speak in Rom. 3.19 of the whole world as ὑπόδικος, which the R.V. translates "brought under judgement"; cf. also 1 Cor. 11.27; but this Romans passage is one where Paul is urging that the whole world has fallen short of God's glory by its attempt to live by law. It is not a place where exact merits and demerits are discussed. Too much emphasis on guilt by itself leads back to the Law, and ultimately to the Hindu conception of *karma*. The wrath was not for him a condition of people being condemned by God, it was a process in which men were involved and which carried them farther and farther away from God. It was an existential, not a theoretical problem, and Christ's salvation, which took them out of the sphere of law and wrath, was equally real.

Eph. 2.14–16 must be quoted in full, as it contains implicit in it the attitude to the law which we have observed most markedly in Romans:

αὐτὸς γάρ ἐστιν ἡ εἰρήνη ἡμῶν ὁ ποιήσας τὰ ἀμφότερα ἓν καὶ τὸ μεσότοιχον τοῦ φραγμοῦ λύσας, τὴν ἔχθραν, ἐν τῇ σαρκὶ αὐτοῦ, τὸν νόμον τῶν ἐντολῶν ἐν δόγμασιν καταργήσας, ἵνα τοὺς δύο κτίσῃ ἐν αὐτῷ εἰς ἕνα καινὸν ἄνθρωπον ποιῶν εἰρήνην ἵνα ἀποκαταλλάξῃ τοὺς ἀμφοτέρους ἐν ἑνὶ σώματι τῷ Θεῷ διὰ τοῦ σταυροῦ, ἀποκτείνας τὴν ἔχθραν ἐν αὐτῷ. For he is our peace, who made both one, and brake down the middle wall of partition, having abolished in his flesh the enmity, even the law of commandments contained in ordinances; that he might create in himself of the twain one new man, so making peace; and might reconcile them both in one body unto God through the cross, having slain the enmity thereby.

We are chiefly concerned with the first few phrases here, especially from ὁ ποιήσας τὰ ἀμφότερα ἕν, "who made both one", to δόγμασιν καταργήσας, "contained in ordinances". Both Abbott and Armitage Robinson assume that τὴν ἔχθραν in this phrase qualifies τὸ μεσότοιχον, and is simply an explanatory word added to clarify the meaning of τὸ μεσότοιχον. Abbott goes so far as to say,[1] "Indeed it may be added that κατηργήσας is not a verb appropriate to ἔχθραν", and therefore he concludes that the only object to καταργήσας is τὸν νόμον. This linguistic argument is surely refuted by 1 Cor. 15.26: ἔσχατος ἐχθρὸς καταργεῖται ὁ θάνατος, "The last enemy that shall be abolished is death." There is therefore no reason at all linguistically and syntactically why ἔχθραν should not be the object of καταργήσας here, and τὸν νόμον etc. be the explanatory phrase in apposition to it. If it were pointed thus it would be plain: τὸν μεσότοιχον τοῦ φραγμοῦ λύσας, τὴν ἔχθραν ἐν τῇ σαρκὶ αὐτοῦ (τὸν νόμον τῶν ἐντόλων ἐν δόγμασιν) καταργήσας, "having broken down the middle wall of partition, having abolished in his flesh the enmity (i.e. the law of commandments contained in ordinances)"—my own translation. This is confirmed by the fact that in verse 14 Paul speaks of Christ as: ἀποκτείνας τὴν ἔχθραν ἐν αὐτῷ ⟨sc. σταυρῷ⟩. Thus σταυρῷ would here correspond to ἐν τῇ σαρκὶ αὐτοῦ above. Chrysostom and Oecumenius take ἔχθραν in verse 14 as the object of κατηργήσας. What Paul is saying here is that Christ's act of redemption of Jew and Gentile had two "moments". He removed the wall of partition between them, which was the Mosaic Law. But that was not enough; merely to abrogate the Law would be to put both in a state of alienation from God. He also removed the ἔχθρα or enmity *to God* caused by the Jews' efforts to live by the Law and the Gentiles' efforts to live by their own law. To reconcile a mutual enmity would not have been enough; Jew and Gentile would still have been enemies to God. He reconciled both together to God by "slaying" the enmity which the Law created.

[1] Op. cit., p. 62.

Hence both Jews and Gentiles are now on the same footing, as reconciled sinners. As a matter of fact, Paul never uses ἔχθρα or cognates of enmity between Jew and Gentile, but very frequently of the enmity of men to God (e.g. Rom. 8.7; 5.10; 11.28; Phil. 3.18, where it is ἐχθροὶ τοῦ σταυροῦ τοῦ Χριστοῦ "enemies of the cross of Christ"; Col. 1.21). If he had wanted to express enmity between man and man, Jew and Gentile, we might have expected him to use ἐναντίος; cf. 1 Thess. 2.15, where he describes the Jews as πᾶσιν ἀνθρώποις ἐναντίων, "contrary to all men".

Both Abbott and Armitage Robinson assume that the way in which Christ abolished the enmity between Jew and Gentile was simply to remove the yoke of the Law. Hence there was thereafter no difference between Jew and Gentile; both could obey God "in the Spirit", freed from "external ordinances".[1] But this is to leave out a step. The way Christ reconciled Jew and Gentile was to put them both under judgement and hence to open up to them a way of approach to God through faith in Christ, not through moral obligation primarily. He effected this by himself undergoing the "curse of the Law", i.e. accepting the condemnation of those who condemned him because he came to fulfil and transcend the Law, not to live by it. Hence he showed "in his own flesh" that the effort to live by the Law ended in the most appalling enmity to God manifested in the murder of the Messiah. The removal of this enmity meant the removal of the Law as a way of life, a system of "commandments contained in ordinances". Abbott and Armitage Robinson see the Law just as a barrier between Jew and Gentile which Christ transcended and removed by his teaching and example. They do not see it as the thing which was instrumental in putting Christ to death, and the final proof of the equality of Jew and Gentile before God. Armitage Robinson does however qualify his former interpretation by saying[2]: "It is noteworthy that, as the Apostle proceeds, the hostility between Jew and Gentile has been gradually put into the background. The reconciliation of which he speaks is the reconciliation of both to God, even more than of each to the other." It seems rather that this latter thought has been predominant from the beginning. Gore has a truer appreciation of the passage when he says[3]: "These [ordinances

---

[1] Armitage Robinson, op. cit., p. 64.   [2] Op. cit., p. 66.
[3] Op. cit., p. 107.

of the Law] ... had no other function than to awaken and deepen the sense of sin which they were powerless to overcome. Thus it was that Christ, in breaking down one partition, had broken down the other also."

Two final passages in Ephesians call for attention. The first is 4.18,19:

> Being darkened in their understanding, alienated from the life of God because of the ignorance that is in them, because of the hardening of their heart; who, being past feeling, gave themselves up to lasciviousness, to work all uncleanness with greediness.

We notice the self-imposed, voluntary characteristics of this description of the wrath-condition. Nowhere is it suggested that God "alienated" them, or even that he hardened their hearts. And we notice especially ἑαυτοὺς παρέδωκαν, "gave themselves up", in verse 19, reminiscent of Rom. 1.24,26,28, where it is Θεὸς παρέδωκεν, "God gave them up". The meaning is the same, but in Ephesians the process is realized even more clearly to be a voluntary, self-imposed one.

The other passage is the famous description of the Christian's armour in 6.10–20. As many scholars have pointed out, it is founded on Isa. 59.17, and may perhaps have been influenced by Wisd. 5.18, where God avenges the righteous; cf. especially Wisd. 5.20: "His severe wrath (ἀπότομος ὀργή) shall he sharpen for a sword, and the world shall fight with him against the unwise." In Isaiah the armour was that which God had used against his enemies, and the same thought is expressed in Wisdom. It is most significant that in each case Paul has changed the passage so as to use it as a description of the Christian defending himself against his spiritual enemies. God's way of attack is now revealed to be the sufferings of his Church in Christ. It does seem as if in later life Paul gave the kingdom of evil a larger place in his thoughts. In his theology of the atonement in Romans there is a remarkable absence of any reference to the devil. Was this modification due to the modification of his expectation of the Parousia? Since the powers of evil were not, it appeared, to be given that full scope which was expected on the very eve of the Parousia—not yet a while anyway—it was all the more necessary to warn Christians of their present activity. Their relation to the wrath is simply as agents in the spiritual and moral realm. The man involved in the wrath was under the power of sin.

THE WRATH IN PAUL'S WRITINGS

We should now be in a position to attempt an answer to the question: Whence did Paul derive his conception of the wrath? Thirty years ago the origin would have been looked for in the mystery religions. To-day one would naturally turn to the Rabbis. In fact, neither of these sources can give us any help in answering our question. Undoubtedly the primary source of his conception of the wrath was his overwhelming experience of the love of God in Christ. A God whose love could go to such amazing lengths could not be described as "angry" or "provoked", or as "resenting". And yet there was such a thing as the wrath. Not only was it an irremovable element in the Old Testament, but it did correspond to something in Paul's experience. Some people, most of the people in the world indeed, were really perishing because they had abandoned God. So there had to be some sort of a doctrine of the wrath. Here one element in the Old Testament conception of the wrath came to Paul's aid. As we have seen, one school of thought in the Old Testament, especially the Chronicler and Daniel, emphasized very much the remote, awful, majestic, impersonal, and almost automatic side of the divine wrath, and this conception is not entirely absent from the Apocalyptists, though on the whole the more personal, eschatological strain prevails. Here then was a conception of the wrath that was surely compatible with a God whose love was his chief and determining characteristic. The wrath was not an emotion or attribute of God, it was simply a word for what happened to those who broke God's moral laws. It was in fact the "principle of retribution in a moral universe". Paul must of course have been helped to come to this conclusion by the intensely pragmatic and concrete (and therefore Hebraic) treatment of the wrath in every part of the Old Testament. Even in the fiercest passages of the prophets the wrath is first and foremost the effects of the wrath. It is "poured out", it is visible, it comes, it goes. Modern scholars, perhaps because of the psychology-laden atmosphere which we breathe, have not always remembered this; and time and again confusion has been caused by their tacitly assuming that when Paul uses the word ὀργή he must be predicating something of God's mind, while in fact he is describing a condition of men. But it must be added that Paul himself in the formation of his conception of the wrath perhaps owed something to the mental atmosphere of his age. Of course the picture popular in some

THE WRATH OF THE LAMB

quarters a generation ago of Paul as an unscrupulous Hellenizer of an originally Hebraic gospel is nonsense. But he did work, increasingly perhaps, in a world where the mental furniture of most educated men would derive ultimately from Greek philosophy. We have seen that the three Hellenizers all had to make some accommodation in order to fit the notion of the wrath into their scheme of things. Paul's conception of the wrath was not theirs, certainly, but an impersonal wrath, operating on the principle of δράσαντι παθεῖν, was certainly more suited to the philosophical climate of the Graeco-Roman world than the strong personal wrath of for instance the Book of Enoch or the Sibylline Oracles. It must also be said that Paul's conception of the wrath, though more carefully elaborated by him than by any other writer in the New Testament except St John the Divine, is not peculiar to him. Its fundamental presuppositions can also be traced in the rest of the New Testament.

We might therefore summarize Paul's conception of the wrath as follows: the wrath of God is wholly impersonal and does not describe an attitude of God but a condition of men; in its realized aspect it works generally through the moral or historical process, and even in its eschatological aspect is as much a revealing as an execution. ὀργή is used by Paul from the beginning for both realized and eschatological wrath, though the eschatological aspect recedes in his latest works. The realized wrath is at first directed against individuals or groups, but later includes all who do not believe. The sphere of the wrath is also the sphere of law, sin, and curse; it is a process as much as a condition, a condition which Paul comes ultimately to predicate of all who do not believe. This law and its accompanying wrath have been ordained of God, but the wrath is not directly applied by him (with certain possible exceptions). It is a self-operating process. The wrath is never to be propitiated, appeased, or satisfied. It abides, and we are rescued from it by Christ. Christ never endured the wrath, but by his self-offering through faith culminating in his death he submitted to it in its aspect as the consequences of men's sin; transcended it, and thereby proved the law, the principle whereby it worked, ineffective. He thus opened a way whereby through faith men can escape the curse of the law, which is the working of the wrath. The Cross is therefore in one aspect the revelation of the wrath, but only as a by-product of the revelation of salvation. But the same process that saves the faithful shows the condemnation of the unfaithful. Faith is needed to perceive the wrath as well as the love of God. Paul definitely avoids a doctrine of reprobation, though some of his arguments were leading him in that direction. He uses ὀργή eighteen times for the wrath of God, and θυμός once, but probably in an early passage and possibly in a quotation from the Old Testament. ζῆλος is used of God once, but not in a wrath-connotation. παραζηλῶ is used once of the possibility of provoking Christ.

5

JUDGEMENT IN THE SYNOPTIC GOSPELS AND ACTS

THE ὀργὴ τοῦ Θεοῦ as such is only mentioned twice in the Synoptic Gospels, and not at all in Acts. The first of the two places in the Gospels is Luke 3.7: John the Baptist, says to his hearers:

> τίς ὑπέδειξεν ὑμῖν φυγεῖν ἀπὸ τῆς μελλούσης ὀργῆς; Who warned you to flee from the wrath to come?

Plummer[1] citing Romans 1.18 says this refers to the penalties of the last day. We have already seen that in Rom. 1.18 the ὀργή is contemporary, not eschatological, and we must remember here that it is John the Baptist who is speaking, and he is still a subject of the old dispensation. Hence τῆς μελλούσης ὀργῆς, "the wrath to come", refers to the coming of the Messiah; it cannot have any suggestion of a Parousia in the sense of a Second Coming. John was still looking at things in a foreshortened way; there was one coming, that was all, and that coming was to be in its way a revelation of wrath. The other reference is also in Luke's Gospel: Luke 21.23. In Luke's version of our Lord's apocalyptic discourse over against the Temple he represents him as saying:

> ἔσται γὰρ ἀνάγκη μεγάλη ἐπὶ τῆς γῆς καὶ ὀργὴ τῷ λαῷ τούτῳ. For there shall be great distress upon the land, and wrath unto this people.

Now this is fairly certainly a reference to the Fall of Jerusalem. Neither Matthew nor Mark uses this phrase in his apocalypse. As such, the ὀργή is worked out in history, like the ὀργή and θυμός in the Book of Revelation, and hence is not eschatological, but is akin to the ὀργή of Rom. 1.18. It is not as purely a spiritual condition like the ὀργή of 1 Thess. 2.16, but it is not on the other hand the wholly eschatological ὀργή of Rom. 2.5. It is also extremely significant that in both these references the ὀργή is unqualified, and therefore extremely impersonal. The ὀργή of Luke's Gospel is the ὀργή of Paul's epistles.

[1] Ed. Luke (I.C.C., Edinburgh 1901), in loc.

On the other hand in two, and possibly three, places in Mark's Gospel our Lord is described as evincing anger. The first is Mark 3.5:

περιβλεψάμενος αὐτοὺς μετ' ὀργῆς. He looked round about on them with anger.

The occasion was in a synagogue, when the Pharisees were watching him to see if he would heal on the Sabbath. Mark adds: συνλυπούμενος ἐπὶ τῇ πωρώσει τῆς καρδίας αὐτῶν, "being grieved at the hardening of their heart". In this version of this incident Luke (6.6–11) omits μετ' ὀργῆς and adds that the Pharisees were filled with madness. The First Gospel (12.9–14) omits both these details. The second example is Mark 10.14:

ἰδὼν δὲ ὁ Ἰησοῦς ἠγανάκτησεν. But when Jesus saw it, he was moved with indignation.

This was when the disciples rebuked the mothers who brought their children to Jesus. Matthew (19.13–15), simply omits ἠγανάκτησεν. Luke also omits it (18.15–17). A third possible instance occurs in Mark 1.41: Here Westcott and Hort's text reads:

καὶ σπλαγχισθεὶς ἐκτείνας τὴν χεῖρα αὐτοῦ ἥψατο. And being moved with compassion, he stretched forth his hand and touched him.

But Codex Bezae, three old Latin MSS., and Ephraem's commentary on Tatian's Diatessaron read ὀργισθείς for σπλαγχνισθείς. If ὀργισθείς is right, Jesus is angry because the leper whom he is about to cure has doubted his willingness to heal by saying (verse 40): ἐὰν θέλῃς δύνασαί με καθαρίσαι, "If thou wilt, thou canst make me clean". In this case the argument "*difficilior lectio melior*" must have much weight, because the tendency would be to change ὀργισθείς, and it is not easy to see why anyone should want to make a change the other way.[1] But Tasker[2] in discussing the reading, concludes that ὀργισθείς cannot be regarded as certain. In the same passage Tasker argues very emphatically that these two, and possibly three, instances of our Lord's showing anger mean that we must be ready to attribute anger to God,

---

[1] Matt. 8.2–4 and Luke 5.12–16 entirely omit any reference to our Lord showing any emotion in their account of this incident, a slight evidence in favour of ὀργισθείς; the word may have embarrassed them in a way that σπλαγχνισθείς would not.

[2] Op. cit., pp. 30–1.

as Jesus was the full revelation of God's character. In the first place we may observe that this argument did not appeal to Luke. He speaks of "the wrath" in two places, but it can hardly be doubted that he avoids attributing anger to Jesus. This is not to suggest that Mark was wrong in doing so; far from it. There can be little doubt that Mark in describing our Lord as angry was more accurate than the other two Synoptists. But it does show that Mark's picture of our Lord exhibiting the human emotion of anger is something quite different from Luke's use of the word ὀργή, and that Luke's conception of ὀργή is not just the emotion of anger subsisting in the divine nature. In the second place, one cannot argue directly from the fact that our Lord showed certain human emotions to the conclusion that those emotions must be attributable to God the Father. *That there must be something corresponding to them* in the divine nature is certainly true. For example, our Lord is several times described as weeping; that does not mean that we can describe God as weeping, or even as sorrowful. Something in the divine nature certainly corresponds to our Lord's human emotion exhibited on several occasions in tears, some aspect, some depth of love or eternal will to self-giving. But you cannot argue *tout simplement* from the fact that Jesus was sometimes angry to the fact that God is angry. The New Testament in the most remarkable way refrains from describing God as angry, though his wrath occurs on several occasions, even outside Paul's epistles. What corresponds to Jesus being angry is indeed the wrath of God, the arrangements which God has made whereby sin brings its own consequences with compound interest *ad infinitum*. But the wrath of God is a very different thing from God's being angry.

Although the explicit references to the wrath in the Synoptic Gospels and Acts are very few indeed, clear traces can be found of a conception of the sin–wrath–law process such as appears in St Paul. An interesting example occurs in Mark 4.12 and the Matthew parallel. Here our Lord says that to those who are without, all is done in parables:

> ἵνα βλέποντες βλέπωσιν καὶ μὴ ἴδωσιν, καὶ ἀκούοντες ἀκούσωσιν καὶ μὴ συνίωσιν, μή ποτε ἐπιστρέψωσιν καὶ ἀφέθῃ αὐτοῖς. That seeing they may see and not perceive; and hearing they may hear and not understand; lest haply they should turn again and it should be forgiven them.

JUDGEMENT IN THE SYNOPTIC GOSPELS AND ACTS

Luke in his version of this *logion* (8.10) retains the ἵνα. Matthew (13.13f.) phrases it differently; he writes ὅτι βλέποντες etc., not ἵνα; and he adds in verse 14:

καὶ ἀναπληροῦται αὐτοῖς ἡ προφητεία Ἡσαΐου ἡ λέγουσα· ἀκοῇ ἀκούσετε καὶ οὐ μὴ συνῆτε ... κτλ. And unto them is fulfilled the prophecy of Isaiah, which saith, By hearing ye shall hear, and shall in no wise understand ...

But he adds a much more extended quotation from Isaiah 6 in verse 15:

ἐπαχύνθη γὰρ ἡ καρδία τοῦ λαοῦ τούτου,
καὶ τοῖς ὠσὶν βαρέως ἤκουσαν,
καὶ τοὺς ὀφθαλμοὺς αὐτῶν ἐκάμμυσαν·
μή ποτε ἴδωσιν τοῖς ὀφθάλμοις,
καὶ τοῖς ὠσὶν ἀκούσωσιν ... κτλ.

For this people's heart is waxen gross,
And their ears are full of hearing,
And their eyes they have closed.
Lest haply they should perceive with their eyes,
And hear with their ears ...

Most editors of the various Synoptic Gospels have commented on the ἵνα with which Mark and Luke begin their quotation, since it gives the strange impression that Jesus deliberately spoke in parables so that those outside should not understand and be saved. Thus Swete[1] says that the parabolic form of the teaching finally conveys the judgement of God: "It was intended to fulfil the sentence of judicial blindness pronounced on those who will not see." On the other hand, Plummer[2] commenting on Luke explains the phrase ἵνα βλέποντες μὴ βλέπωσιν as meaning that what the unsympathetic hear without understanding they remember because of its impressive form. McNeile[3] commenting on Matt. 13.13f. suggests among other reasons that ἵνα in two of the Synoptic quotations is equivalent to ὥστε. Allen[4] also commenting on Matthew says that his changing the ἵνα of the other two Synoptists to ὅτι is deliberate: "He found the notion of purpose intolerable." Some of these comments seem rather to explain away than to explain these

---

[1] Ed. Mark (London 1898), in loc.
[2] Ed. Luke (I.C.C., Edinburgh 1901), in loc.
[3] Ed. Matthew (London 1915), in loc.
[4] Ed. Matthew (I.C.C., 3rd ed., Edinburgh 1902).

passages. Allen is surely mistaken in imagining that the author of the First Gospel wished to avoid the notion of purpose in giving the quotation from Isaiah, since he introduces it himself in Matt. 13.15, where he quotes: μή ποτε ἴδωσιν τοῖς ὀφθαλμοῖς κτλ., "lest haply they should perceive..." etc. What Matthew[1] has done, however, is to put the whole quotation in such a way as to show clearly that this process of blindness to which the quotation refers is self-induced. His objection is not to the connection of the parabolic technique with blindness, but to the suggestion in Mark and Luke that our Lord deliberately caused this blindness by his parables. The true explanation of all these passages is surely that indicated by Swete, and not Plummer's. The parabolic form is a sign for faith, and is therefore, in the case of those who will not accept it, what St Paul would call an ἔνδειξις ἀπωλείας, "an evident token of perdition": Phil. 1.28. Compare also 1 Cor. 1.18: ὁ λόγος γὰρ τοῦ σταυροῦ τοῖς μὲν ἀπολλυμένοις μωρία ἐστίν, "For the word of the cross is to them that are perishing foolishness." It is not God or Christ who has shut their eyes, it is they themselves. The parable merely shows up their πώρωσις. Behind the use of these quotations, therefore, by all three Synoptists, is the conception of unbelief as the result of a self-induced process of sin. McNeile, despite his apparent desire to avoid the purposive element in these quotations, seems to realize the self-induced character of the process implied here, for he adds (op. cit., p. 190): "All except my disciples have rendered themselves morally incapable of grasping the truth; their own action has produced their punishment." The author of the First Gospel further manifests a rather deeper understanding of this self-imposed judgement by his use of the phrase: ἀναπληροῦται αὐτοῖς ἡ προφητεία, "and unto them is fulfilled the prophecy". Plummer[2] points out that this is a unique word in the Gospels. It is used instead of the more usual πληροῦσθαι. He does not, however, seem to realize its significance; it implies a process. Compare with this 1 Thess. 2.16: εἰς τὸ ἀναπληρῶσαι αὐτῶν τὰς ἁμαρτίας πάντοτε, "to fill up their sins alway". The conception is of the sin–law–wrath process working itself out. It is perhaps significant that Mark after

---

[1] Of course the use of "Matthew" for the author of the First Gospel does not indicate the opinion that it was written by the apostle Matthew.

[2] Ed. Matthew (London 1909), in loc.

giving our Lord's explanation of the parable, adds: "There is nothing hid that shall not be revealed." The process of wrath–sin–judgement is at work, and the activities of the Messiah serve to show it up.

T. W. Manson in *The Teaching of Jesus* (Cambridge 1935, 2nd ed., pp. 75f.) has a considerable discussion of this passage. His general conclusions support the view taken here that the quotation from Isaiah indicates the parables are to be understood as a sign of judgement; e.g. Manson says on p. 76: "The parable is in practice a test; and the response of a man to it is what determines whether he shall ever get beyond it to the secret of the Kingdom." Again on p. 79, he writes: "The purpose of parables is not to harden the hearts of the hearers, but ... it is the hardness of the hearts of the hearers that defeats the purpose of the parables." On the other hand, like McNeile and Allen, he cannot accept Mark's use of ἵνα, which suggests that the hardening of the hearts was purposely sent by God. He makes the ingenious suggestion that ἵνα is a mistranslation of an Aramaic particle which can be used to introduce either a final or a relative clause. He suggests that our Lord was quoting the Aramaic Targum on Isa. 6, which includes this particle at this point in the quotation, and that it has been mistranslated in the Greek as ἵνα, whereas the correct translation would be οἵ. If this is the right explanation, it is important to note that it makes no difference to the interpretation of the significance of the parable defended in this work. Manson's own words make this clear. But one may well ask: Why is this explanation necessary at all? Neither Matthew nor Luke thought it necessary to remove the idea of purpose, as we have seen. Manson supports his argument by the suggestion on p. 78 that if Mark had wanted to suggest the idea of purpose he could have quoted from Isa. 6.9, the words: "Make the heart of this people fat, etc.", a passage which brings out the notion of purpose more clearly than the passage he does quote. But Manson has apparently overlooked the significant fact that Matthew does quote this very passage from Isa. 6.9 as noted above (Matt. 13.15); but the version he quotes is not purposive in form at all; it is all cast in the past tense: ἐπαχύνθη γὰρ ἡ καρδία etc. We may therefore be allowed to conjecture that if our Lord did not quote the M.T. of the words from Isa. 6.9 which he is recorded as quoting in Mark, he would not be likely to quote the M.T. either of the words from that passage which occur in Matthew but not in Mark. In fact Manson has recourse to the Targums to defend his interpretation of the passage which Mark omits. In short, the passage on whose omission in Mark he lays so much stress probably fails to support his argument, as the form in which it is quoted by Matthew has omitted the notion of purpose. Another point against this explaining away the ἵνα in Mark is that John, who cannot be suspected of the purely editorial attitude towards Mark which we may justly read into Matthew and Luke, also quotes Isa. 6.9,10, and quotes it in a form in which the notion of purpose is strongly emphasized (John 12.40). It is, therefore, extremely precarious to try to eliminate the notion of purpose from this quotation, seeing that in the best texts of the Gospels which we have it is present in all four evangelists. But once it is realized that the notion of purpose is thought of as belonging not to the direct action of God, but to the impersonal self-operating action of the wrath or judgement, the real sting of the objection which modern editors feel to this ἵνα is removed.

A similar conception underlies the use of the word μαρτύριον in the Synoptic Gospels. For example in Mark 6.11 Jesus is instructing the disciples in how they are to behave when he sends them out two by two, and tells them that if there is any place that will not receive them they are to shake the dust of that place off their feet εἰς μαρτύριον αὐτοῖς, "for a testimony unto them". It is to be a visible sign of the process of judgement that is going on all the time. The Son of Man comes for judgement as well as for salvation. Mark uses the same phrase again in 13.9 in his "Little Apocalypse", where he says that the disciples must stand before rulers and kings εἰς μαρτύριον αὐτοῖς, "for a testimony unto them". This is the witness which is a sign of the process of judgement taking place. If we compare Matt. 10.18 and Luke 21.13 we shall see that, whereas Luke takes this coming event as a testimony in favour of the disciples, Matthew sees it as both a witness against the Jews and an opportunity for witness to the Gentiles. Mark sees it as a witness against the Jews. So if the same event can be interpreted in Mark as a witness against the Jews and in Luke as a witness in favour of the disciples, there seems no reason why Matthew should not take it as a witness against the Jews and also as an opportunity for the Gentiles to hear the Gospel.[1] It is in fact precisely what St Paul is

---

[1] McNeile (op. cit., in loc.) accepts this interpretation.

expressing in 2 Cor. 2.15,16, where he describes his life of service as "a savour of death unto death" to them that are perishing and to them that are being saved "a savour of life unto life". Another word, ἐπισκοπή, seems to be used by Luke in the same double sense as μαρτύριον. Our Lord lamenting over the folly of Jerusalem says (Luke 19.44):

> ἀνθ' ὧν οὐκ ἔγνως τὸν καιρὸν τῆς ἐπισκοπῆς σου. Because thou knewest not the time of thy visitation.

Plummer[1] appears to be anxious to tie this word down to one of its two senses, for he says that it is "a neutral term, and may imply either blessing or punishment. In the sense of visiting with punishment it does not occur in the New Testament." But the "visitation" here is quite as much a visitation of punishment as of blessing. The quality, in fact, does not lie in the visitation, but in the reaction of those visited. Plummer is perhaps making ultimately the same error as those who would see the divine wrath as something in God's mind and not something in man's condition. The word occurs with exactly the same connotation in 1 Peter 2.12, where Christians are exhorted to good conduct in order that Gentiles may glorify God ἐν ἡμέρᾳ ἐπισκοπῆς, "in the day of visitation". The reference here is surely eschatological, and the "day of visitation" will be a blessing to the faithful and a judgement to the unfaithful. The phrase occurs in Isa. 10.3: "What will ye do in the day of visitation[2] and in the desolation which shall come from far?" Here certainly it seems to mean "punishment" rather than "blessing".

There are also traces of the law-wrath process in the parables, often discernible in the comments of the Synoptists themselves on the parables. A good example is the parable of the Wicked Husbandmen. It is interesting that all the Synoptists apparently see the judgement of the Jews implied at the end of this parable as taking place in history rather than at the end of history. Mark, who cannot have the fall of Jerusalem in mind, represents our Lord as saying (12.9):

> ἐλεύσεται καὶ ἀπολέσει τοὺς γεωργούς. He will come and destroy the husbandmen.

---

[1] Op. cit. (ed. Luke), in loc.
[2] LXX translates τῇ ἡμέρᾳ τῆς ἐπισκοπῆς.

Matt. 21.41 represents the crowd as answering:

> κακοὺς κακῶς ἀπολέσει αὐτούς. He will miserably destroy those miserable men.

Luke writes (20.16):

> ἐλεύσεται καὶ ἀπολέσει τοὺς γεωργούς. He will come and destroy these husbandmen,

and he and Matthew add an interesting quotation:

> πᾶς ὁ πεσὼν ἐπ' ἐκεῖνον τὸν λίθον συνθλασθήσεται· ἐφ' ὃν δ' ἂν πέσῃ, λικμήσει αὐτόν. Everyone that falleth on that stone shall be broken to pieces; but on whomsoever it shall fall, it will scatter him as dust.

Plummer identifies this as a combination of Isa. 8.14 and Dan. 2.34,35,44. There can be little doubt that, by the use of this quotation, Luke and Matthew mean to identify this smashing and destruction with the fall of Jerusalem. Thus the destruction brought by the advent of the Messiah on those who reject him is not a direct eschatological punishment, but something that is worked out in the course of history; and the Isaiah quotation implies that it may be one which they bring upon themselves. In two other parables also the nature of the state of unbelief as a law-process becomes very clear. One is Matt. 18.23-35, the parable of the Unmerciful Servant. Our Lord's comment at the end here is (v.34):

> ὁ κύριος αὐτοῦ παρέδωκεν αὐτὸν τοῖς βασανισταῖς ἕως οὗ ἀποδῷ πᾶν τὸ ὀφειλόμενον αὐτῷ. And his lord ... delivered him to the tormentors, till he should pay all that was due.

Then comes the comment:

> οὕτως καὶ ὁ πατήρ μου ὁ οὐράνιος ποιήσει ὑμῖν ἐὰν μὴ ἀφῆτε ἕκαστος τῷ ἀδελφῷ αὐτοῦ ἀπὸ τῶν καρδιῶν ὑμῶν. So shall also my heavenly Father do unto you, if ye forgive not every one his brother from your hearts.

This might at first sight seem to be a not very enlightened comment of the evangelist himself, but, though the phraseology is no doubt of Matthew, the thought may well be that of our Lord. It is an expression of the dreadful destructive power of the wrath, the sphere in which those live who do not accept God's free grace. They must accept the reign of law which exacts "to the uttermost farthing". The attribution of this process directly to God is probably the evangelist's addition. But there is no reason why the process itself should not have been in our Lord's mind as he uttered this parable. Similarly the parable of the talents as told by Matthew and Luke (Matt. 25.14–30; Luke 19.12–27) is an excellent exemplification of the nature of the wrath. The Lord is kind and even generous to the least sign of a response to his commands, but to those who act towards him on a legal basis (ἴδε ἔχεις τὸ σόν Matt. 25.25: "Lo, thou hast thine own") he is stern. Those who will not accept God's love must accept the alternative of a legal retributive process which they bring upon themselves. The ordinary laws of interest or the ordinary laws of nature serve as examples. In each case it is the Lord in the parable who is represented as the exactor or the stern judge. But this does not mean that these qualities are to be directly attributed to God. They are parables, intended to illustrate one point only, not allegories. This is the mistake which Tasker seems to make,[1] when he argues from the fact that characters representing God in our Lord's parables are sometimes described as angry to the conclusion that therefore God is conceived as being angry. For instance in Matt. 22.7, the king who made the wedding feast is described as ὀργισθείς, "wroth", and likewise in Luke 14.21 we read τότε ὀργισθεὶς ὁ δεσπότης, "then the master of the house being angry"; another example comes from the parable quoted above, the parable of the unmerciful servant (Matt. 18.34) where the verse runs: καὶ ὀργισθεὶς ὁ κύριος, "but his lord was wroth". But in fact to say the king or the lord "represents God" in these parables is misleading. The whole story illustrates one aspect of God's approach to men. Neither the king nor the lord is intended as a complete picture of all God's characteristics. If we were to proceed on the assumption that any figure in a parable who seems to correspond to God actually gives us a picture of God, we would have to say that God was an unrighteous judge and a master who praises an embezzling steward. We cannot argue from the fact that these figures in the parables are described as angry to the conclusion that the evangelist intended to represent God as angry. There *is* a corresponding element in the divine economy; it is the process of sin and law to which unbelievers consign themselves. There are several

[1] Op. cit., pp. 28, 29.

other places in our Lord's teaching also where we can glimpse the law–wrath process in the background. One occurs in the passage common to Luke and Matthew where our Lord speaks of the blood of all the righteous who were ever slain since Abel, saying that it will be required of this generation (Luke 11.49–51; Matt. 23.35, 36). Here we see with remarkable clearness this process of judgement unfolding itself, and here it actually culminates in the Cross. The sending of the prophets culminated in the sending of the Son; the killing of the Son was the judgement. So the sending of the Son can be described as being for the purpose of exacting the blood of all the righteous slain from the time of the murder of Abel. The death of the Son was the climax which consummated the judgement. Luke 11.51 and Matt. 23.36 both emphasize that this blood will be exacted from "this generation". Plummer suggests that the primary reference is to the fall of Jerusalem; no doubt this coloured the phraseology of these two evangelists, but for them to put into the mouth of Jesus represented as speaking in A.D. 30, a prophecy about "this generation" which was only fulfilled forty years later seems to be straining likelihood too far. "This generation", or some phrase corresponding to it, must go back to a source before A.D. 70. "This generation" means in fact in that context the generation that witnessed the crucifixion. The arrival of the Messiah consummates the judgement, and the judgement is visible on the Cross.[1] The legal background of judgement also appears in Luke 12.58; Matt. 5.25: "Be reconciled with thine adversary whiles thou art in the way." The alternative is waiting in prison till the uttermost farthing is paid. Luke gives this saying a slightly eschatological context by 12.56:

τὸν καιρὸν δὲ τοῦτον πῶς οὐ δοκιμάζετε; How is it that ye know not how to interpret this time?

The meaning when our Lord uttered it was no doubt: "Accept the love of God while it is offered now. If not, there only remains the way of wrath where you are your own exactor (πράκτωρ, v.58)." Allen,[2] commenting on Matthew's presentation of this *logion* (5.26), suggests that the reference to "the uttermost farthing" is only an example of Matthew's legalist tendency. But, as we have seen, the same phrase

---

[1] See also p. 128.
[2] Op. cit., in loc.

occurs in Luke, and it illustrates rather the contrast between the love of God which we may accept now, and the wrath process which goes on punishing to the uttermost.

Two other places concern us here, one in Matthew and one in Luke. In Matt. 12.20, Isa. 42.1–4 is quoted in order to illustrate Christ's quiet and bloodless conquest of mankind. The quotation follows a Greek text which represents neither M.T. nor LXX as we know it. McNeile[1] suggests that Matthew is following an Aramaic collection of *testimonia* which was translated from a Hebrew recension of the Hebrew unknown to us. But, in view of the arguments adduced by Kahle,[2] we cannot be at all dogmatic about what text the N.T. writers used of the LXX. Anyway the quotation as Matthew cites it in verse 20 runs: ἕως ἂν ἐκβάλῃ εἰς νῖκος τὴν κρίσιν, "till he send forth judgement unto victory", which seems to mean: "till he bring judgement to a victorious conclusion." The earlier part of the quotation emphasizes the quiet activity of the Servant of the Lord, who will not break the bruised reed or quench the smoking flax; so Matthew seems to be suggesting that the judgement of Christ (καὶ κρίσιν τοῖς ἔθνεσιν ἀπαγγελεῖ, "And he shall declare judgement to the Gentiles") works quietly and in an unseen fashion until it is openly manifested in the accession of the Gentiles and the rejection of the Jews. Judgement here is a quiet, bloodless process, very like the spiritual condition which is described as judgement in 1 Thess. 2.16. The second passage is Luke 18.1–8: the parable of the Unjust Judge. At the end our Lord says (verse 7):

> ὁ δὲ Θεὸς οὐ μὴ ποιήσει τὴν ἐκδίκησιν τῶν ἐκλεκτῶν αὐτοῦ τῶν βοώντων αὐτῷ ἡμέρας καὶ νυκτός, καὶ μακροθυμεῖ ἐπ' αὐτοῖς; And shall not God avenge his elect, which cry to him day and night, and he is long-suffering over them?

This is followed up by the statement:

> I say unto you, that he will avenge them speedily. Howbeit, when the Son of man cometh, shall he find faith on the earth?

The meaning of μακροθυμεῖ is curious here. Plummer insists rightly that αὐτοῖς must be the elect, not the persecutors. In that case,

---
[1] Op. cit., in loc.
[2] Kahle, *The Cairo Geniza* (London 1947), p. 165.

μακροθυμεῖ here means "to be slow or patient" in vindicating the righteous. But it must have its full meaning of "retaining wrath *for a time*", because the next verse makes it clear that there is quite soon to be a term to that patience. When the Son of Man comes, the θυμός will be manifested and the righteous vindicated. But, when that happens, will he find faith on the earth; i.e. will people have faith to recognize (literally "the faith that recognizes"—τὴν πίστιν) this event as ἐκδίκησις? Will they know the θυμός when they see it? Now, if this is the right interpretation of the argument, our Lord when he uttered this parable must have been thinking of only one Parousia, and that a Parousia which it would require faith to recognize. The faithful can hardly be expected to wait for a *second* coming. Hence it seems that in this case the vindication of the righteous and the term to the μακροθυμία of God must be found in the death and resurrection of Christ, an event which it requires faith to interpret as judgement and vindication. In fact the meaning of this parable fits in well with the quotation from Isaiah cited above from Matthew. Judgement is a process which culminates in the death and resurrection of the Messiah, not necessarily in a great assize at the last day.

There is a remarkable link with the Apocalypse in Luke 23.30,31. Jesus, on his way to the Cross, quotes Hos. 10.8: "Then shall they begin to say to the mountains, Fall on us, etc." The same passage is quoted in Rev. 6.16 in connection with the manifestation of the wrath of God and of the Lamb. Jesus in the Luke passage adds the proverb; "For if they do these things in the green tree, what shall be done in the dry?" The sense here is: "If the Jews display such passionate determination in rejecting the true Messiah, how appalling will their self-destruction be when they accept a false one!" In its context in Luke it must refer to the events of A.D. 70, but of course there is no reason at all why Jesus himself should not have foreseen the dreadful fate of a people that rejects a true, and abandons itself to a false, Messiah. The interesting point here is that the conduct of the Jews is seen as a process, and as a process of self-judgement. Whether the reference be to the fall of Jerusalem or to some other less definite form of political self-destruction, it is a process of judgement, and it is something they do. And when they do it they will be appalled at their own folly (verse 30). In Hosea the phrase is used in connection with destruc-

JUDGEMENT IN THE SYNOPTIC GOSPELS AND ACTS

tion from God; in the Apocalypse it is used in connection with the wrath of the Lamb. Both these meanings are implicit in Luke, and that wrath and that destruction are the same as that which we meet with in St Paul's epistles, a process carried out in history and one self-imposed, not directly inflicted by God.

Finally we should observe an interesting parallel between Matt. 23 and Rev. 9.12f. In Matt. 23 we have our Lord's terrible denunciation of the Pharisees. Plummer[1] points out that the words οὐαὶ ὑμῖν, "woe unto you", occur seven times in this chapter, and compares the Seven Thunders of the Apocalypse. He has not, however noticed that we do find "the Woes" spoken of in the Apocalypse. The last three of the Seven Trumpets are also described as "woes" (Rev. 9.12; 11.14). They are first, the opening of the abyss, and consequent scourge of locusts; second, the horsemen from the Euphrates; and third, apparently, the Beast, who makes his first official appearance in 13.1. Now in Matthew's "woe" passage, the last "woe" occurs in 23.29, and it refers to the murder of the Messiah by which they "fill up the measure of their fathers who killed the prophets". Thus in Matthew the crowning "woe" is the murder of the Christ, and in Revelation the crowning "woe" is the appearance of the Anti-Christ. We have the same conception underlying both; both represent judgement as something being worked out in history as well as at the end of history, and both show judgement and sin coinciding in one great end-event. What our Lord had in mind in his denunciation of the Pharisees was the Cross as the crowning judgement. What was implied in the Rival Dispensation of Satan in the Apocalypse is discussed in our last chapter.

The use of the word "cup" (always ποτήριον) in a figurative sense occurs twelve times in the New Testament, as against thirteen occurrences when it means literally a cup, e.g. "cup of cold water" in Matt. 10.42. Owing to the use of the word ποτήριον in the LXX for the *kōs* of the Hebrew in the Old Testament in such places as Isa. 51.17f. many commentators have insisted that ποτήριον when used by our Lord in this figurative sense must have the meaning of "cup of wrath". The latest of these is Tasker.[2] He assumes that the cup of

[1] Op. cit. (ed. Luke), in loc.
[2] Op. cit., p. 34.

which our Lord speaks is the cup of wrath, but he explains: "We are not to suppose that... Jesus felt that God was angry with himself ... But he did experience the misery, the affliction, the punishment, and the death which are the lot of sinners... subject to the wrath of God." Now if Tasker were referring to the wrath simply as the *consequences of men's sins* this would be unexceptionable. We have seen that St Paul certainly believed our Lord suffered the consequences of sin, though in his case they were not wrath. But as a matter of fact, Tasker is saying something different here; he identifies an experience of the wrath with the feelings of one with whom God is angry. But, as we have seen, throughout the Bible, in the New Testament as well as the Old Testament, the wrath is not essentially a feeling at all, either God's or man's, but the effects of disaster, or a description of the effects of sin. Hence Tasker is astray in his very definition of the wrath. Also, though he refers to Isa. 51.17 he makes no reference to the inter-Testamental period. As we saw, there the cup which Jahveh gives has become dissociated from the wrath. It is given, for example, to Isaiah, with whom no one would suggest that God is wroth. It means in fact simply "the destiny of suffering" and nothing more. There is no necessary hint of divine displeasure in it. Even in the Old Testament, it is nowhere suggested that the innocent could drink of Jahveh's wrath. They could, and sometimes did as in the case of Jeremiah, experience misfortune from Jahveh's hand, but that is not wrath and is never described as such.

When we turn to the actual use of the word in the New Testament, the impression is confirmed that, unless ποτήριον is explicitly connected with wrath, it does not signify the wrath at all. It is used by all four evangelists in connection with Gethsemane (in the case of John in connection with his equivalent of Gethsemane). Mark has (10.38):

δύνασθε πιεῖν τὸ ποτήριον ὃ ἐγὼ πίνω; Are ye able to drink the cup that I drink?

and verse 39:

τὸ ποτήριον ὃ ἐγὼ πίνω πίεσθε. The cup that I drink ye shall drink.

Then in 14.36 our Lord's words in Gethsemane are:

παρένεγκε τὸ ποτήριον τοῦτο ἀπ' ἐμοῦ. Remove this cup from me.

JUDGEMENT IN THE SYNOPTIC GOSPELS AND ACTS

It is significant that immediately before Mark represents him as praying:

ἵνα... παρέλθῃ ἀπ' αὐτοῦ ἡ ὥρα. That the hour might pass away from him;

so that ποτήριον and ὥρα are practically identified. Luke has only one reference:

παρένεγκε τοῦτο τὸ ποτήριον ἀπ' ἐμοῦ. Remove this cup from me,

almost exactly copied from Mark (Luke 22.42). Matthew has the same references as Mark to the cup which James and John are to drink (Matt.20.22):

δύνασθε πιεῖν τὸ ποτήριον ὃ ἐγὼ μέλλω πίνειν... τὸ μὲν ποτήριόν μου πίεσθε. Are ye able to drink the cup that I am about to drink?... My cup indeed ye shall drink.

In his Gethsemane narrative he has a slight difference: 26.39 runs:

παρελθάτω ἀπ' ἐμοῦ τὸ ποτήριον τοῦτο. Let this cup pass away from me;

and verse 42:

εἰ οὐ δύναται τοῦτο παρελθεῖν ἐὰν μὴ αὐτὸ πίω, γενηθήτω τὸ θέλημά σου. If this cannot pass away except I drink it, thy will be done.

The Received Text reads in this verse: παρελθεῖν τοῦτο τὸ ποτήριον ἀπ' ἐμοῦ, no doubt as a gloss, correctly interpreting the sense. It is interesting to notice here the same tendency as in Mark to identify the ποτήριον with the ὥρα, thus making it even more unlikely that there is any wrath-reference here. In none of these places is wrath even hinted at. The cup is simply our Lord's destiny of suffering, sent indeed from God the Father, but not coming in the form of wrath. John's reference is precisely similar (18.11):

τὸ ποτήριον ὃ δέδωκέν μοι ὁ πατήρ, οὐ μὴ πίω αὐτό; The cup which the Father hath given me, shall I not drink it?

Here the connection with the Father is absolutely explicit. John does mention the ὀργή in another context, and it is a quite distinct conception from what one finds here. The suggestion that John thought this cup was the cup of wrath is grotesque. ποτήριον occurs four times in Revelation, where it is associated with the wrath; but a full investigation of its significance there is to be found in chapter 7.

The wrath of God is not mentioned in Acts—a sufficient refutation of those who would make "wrath to come" an essential part of the Christian evangel. But in several places the conception of judgement as something automatic and self-inflicted can be traced in the background. For example in Acts 3.23 Peter, preaching the Gospel message to the people, quotes first the well-known passage in Deut. 18.15f., about the prophet who was to come in the future, and then adds to it a quotation from Lev. 23.29:

> ἔσται δὲ πᾶσα ψυχὴ ἥτις ἐὰν μὴ ἀκούσῃ τοῦ προφήτου ἐκείνου ἐξολοθρεύσεται ἐκ τοῦ λαοῦ. And it shall be that every soul which shall not hearken to that prophet shall be utterly destroyed from among the people.

In what way does Peter imagine that this destruction will be brought about in the case of the New People, the Church? In Leviticus the destruction was certainly to be executed by the theocratic authorities, but Peter could hardly have had that in mind. In verses 19 and 26 of this chapter salvation seems to be primarily salvation from sin into the presence of the Messiah. Compare also 2.40 where σώθητε ἀπὸ τῆς γενεᾶς τῆς σκολιᾶς ταύτης, "Save yourselves from this crooked generation", seems to mean: "Save yourselves from this wicked world which is in a state of spiritual destruction." Indeed, there is good evidence that in the New Testament when γενεά is used in a bad sense it normally means, not all who happen to be alive at the time of the speaker, but "the class of those who reject the Messiah"; cf. especially Matt. 3.7: "generation of vipers" (Luke 3.7 also); Mark 8.12: "generation that seeks a sign" (Luke 11.29; Matt. 12.39); Mark 9.19: "O faithless generation" (Luke 9.41; Matt. 17.17). Compare also the passages in which future events are all to come to pass "on this generation" (Mark 13.30; Luke 11.50; 21.32; Matt. 23.36). This is confirmed by Büchsel, writing in the *Theologisches Wörterbuch zum Neuen Testament*,[1] who says that in the New Testament, when used in a figurative sense, it usually implies contemporaneity with the time of speaking, and therefore it can be used of any generation that rejects the Messiah. Hence in this Acts context, it seems likely that Peter is interpreting

[1] Ed. G. Kittel (Stuttgart 1935), art. γενεά.

ἐξολοθρεύσεται in purely spiritual terms. Luke seems to have added the Leviticus quotation deliberately, for in Deut. 18 a few verses separate the promise from the threat. Luke has left out the threat in Deuteronomy: "I will require it of him", and substituted the threat in Leviticus. It looks as though Luke was deliberately avoiding suggesting that God punishes directly; and substituting instead a suggestion of a state of spiritual destruction which is self-imposed.

A similar impression is conveyed by a quotation from Habakkuk cited in an address by Paul in Acts 13.41. The quotation, which is from the LXX of Hab. 1.5, runs:

ἴδετε οἱ καταφρονηταί, καὶ θαυμάσατε καὶ ἀφανίσθητε,
ὅτι ἔργον ἐργάζομαί ἐγω ἐν ταῖς ἡμέραις ὑμῶν,
ἔργον ὅ οὐ μὴ πιστεύσητε ἐάν τις διηγῆται ὑμῖν.
Behold, ye despisers, and wonder and perish.
For I work a work in your days,
A work which ye shall in no wise believe, if one declare it unto you.

In the context in which it is used in Habakkuk, the prophet is warning the Jews of a coming disaster. The M.T. here reads: *re'ū baggōyīm*, corresponding to the LXX ἴδετε οἱ καταφρονηταί. On the strength of this, Rackham[1] maintains that Paul is here addressing the nations, and that this was Habakkuk's intention also. But both Ward[2] and Wade's[3] interpretation of Habakkuk is that it is the Jews who are addressed here and the meaning of the M.T. is: "Look [you Jews] among the Gentiles."[4] But in either case it is the Jews, not the Gentiles, who are addressed. Hence what Paul is represented as saying here is that the Jews, who scorn the Gospel, must beware, because God *has done* a deed in their time which they will not believe. The fact that the LXX uses the present tense enables Paul to take the prophet's words as referring to a past act, even though he was really looking forward to a future one. In fact Paul is warning the Jews against their present state of unbelief which is itself the judgement. He is not threatening future judgement at all. Rackham insists on taking it as a threat of future punishment, for

---

[1] Ed. Acts (Westminster Commentary, 10th ed., London 1925), in loc.
[2] Ed. Habakkuk (I.C.C., Edinburgh 1912), in loc.
[3] Ed. Habakkuk (Westminster Commentary, London 1929), in loc.
[4] Ward actually maintains that the LXX has preserved the right reading here, and restores the meaning "ye wrongdoers" from בגדים בגוים.

he says: "St Paul knew a day of the Lord was being prepared for the unbelieving Jew", and then quotes 1 Thess. 2.16. One could hardly imagine a more unfortunate quotation for the purpose of supporting his contention! Foakes-Jackson is more to the point, for he comments[1]: "There is no hint in this address of eschatology, on which Paul subsequently lays so much stress." It is quite true that this passage is not eschatological, but, as we have seen, it can hardly be said that later on Paul's conception of judgement grew more eschatological—rather the reverse in fact. Of course it cannot possibly be maintained that the doctrine of eschatological judgement is not found in Acts: 17.31 alone would disprove that. But there are also several places where a much more realized conception of judgement can be traced. 18.6 is another one, where Paul says to the Jews: τὸ αἷμα ὑμῶν ἐπὶ τὴν κεφαλὴν ὑμῶν, "Your blood be upon your own heads." Rackham here well compares 13.46: οὐκ ἀξίους κρίνετε ἑαυτοὺς τῆς αἰωνίου ζωῆς, "Ye judge yourselves unworthy of eternal life." And indeed Paul's last words recorded in Acts are significant of this self-imposed judgement. He quotes Isa. 6.9,10. In this passage he carefully avoids any suggestion of God's having been responsible for the blindness of the Jews.[2] He only quotes ἐπαχύνθη in 28.27, not suggesting that it was God who made their heart dull. Rackham comments here that the force of the quotation is to show that the Truth itself brings judgement. We may add that the state of unbelief described in this quotation *is* the judgement.

It is, however, significant that all these traces of a conception of a self-operating judgement in Acts, definite though they are, are associated with utterances of apostles, Peter once, and all the rest Paul's. We cannot say for certain how much is due to Luke and how much to the source from which he draws, but we must attribute something to his sources, especially when he is reporting Paul. On the other hand, when he is simply describing events in his own words, we can find traces of a conception of divine punishment as direct and exemplary, such as meets us in 1 Cor. 10 and 11. It is also significant (and perhaps reassuring) that all these examples of direct punishment occur in the half of his work where on the whole his sources seem to be not first-

---

[1] Ed. Acts (Moffatt Commentary, London 1931), in loc.
[2] Contrast Luke 8.10; and see p. 114 f.

hand. For instance in Acts 1.18–20 we read of Judas' awful death. The quotation from Ps. 69.25 is used to emphasize the fact that this fate was God's punishment. The previous verse in this Psalm is:

Pour out thine indignation upon them,
And let the fierceness of thine anger overtake them.

So perhaps Luke saw Judas' death as an instance of God's wrath. Again in 5.1–11 the death of Ananias and Sapphira appears to be an instance of direct divine punishment, though this is not explicitly stated. The curse pronounced on Simon (Magus) in 8.20 affords another example; Peter uses the strong phrase: τὸ ἀργύριόν σου σύν σοι εἴη εἰς ἀπώλειαν, "Thy silver perish with thee", which might mean only spiritual destruction; but another sorcerer in 13.10,11 does not escape with merely spiritual punishment but is afflicted with blindness, apparently only temporary. A final example is Herod in 12.23, where Luke states explicitly that an angel of the Lord struck him. It is, however, only fair to point out that in all these four examples the persons punished or rebuked have committed sins very closely connected with God's revelation of himself in Christ and in the new dispensation. Ananias and Sapphira have tried to deceive that very Holy Spirit whose presence in the hearts of the believers was such a striking new feature in the Christian community. Simon Magus has committed the sin of idolatry; the two Old Testament quotations which Peter cites about him (Ps. 78.37 and Deut. 29.18) both refer to one whose mind is really given to an idol. Elymas was trying to turn the ruler of Cyprus away from the faith (13.8). Herod, as Luke says explicitly, was smitten "because he gave not God the glory" (12.23). There is an echo here of that contrast which is to be found in Maccabees, in Judith, and supremely in Revelation, between the true God and the human ruler setting up as a false god; cf. especially the people's slogan in 12.22: "The voice of a god, and not of a man."

6

JUDGEMENT IN HEBREWS, THE JOHANNINE WRITINGS, THE PASTORAL AND CATHOLIC EPISTLES

THE EPISTLE TO THE HEBREWS

In only one place does the author of the Epistle to the Hebrews explicitly mention the wrath,[1] but there is perhaps no work in the New Testament, with the exception of Revelation, where the wrath or judgement is implicitly referred to more often. He is constantly referring to divine punishment in reserved language, probably both because he does not wish to expatiate on so awful a subject and because he wishes to emphasize rather grace than wrath.

The first warning occurs in 2.2,3:

> εἰ γὰρ ὁ δι' ἀγγέλων λαληθεὶς λόγος ἐγένετο βέβαιος, καὶ πᾶσα παράβασις καὶ παρακοὴ ἔλαβεν ἔνδικον μισθαποδοσίαν, πῶς ἡμεῖς ἐκφευξόμεθα τηλικαύτης ἀμελήσαντες σωτηρίας; For if the word spoken through angels proved stedfast, and every transgression and disobedience received a just recompense of reward, how shall we escape if we neglect so great salvation?

Holmes[2] here well points out that ἔνδικον hints at the systematic nature of God's wrath. What is it that we cannot escape? Almost certainly spiritual, not physical punishment, or indeed destruction. We shall find that later on the author, when he compares the old dispensation with the new, characterizes the new as spiritual and the old as material.

In 3.7—4.13 we come upon a passage which bears a resemblance to 1 Corinthians 10, in that both passages cite examples of wrath in the Old Testament, and draw lessons for Christians therefrom. We may note to begin with that our author has no hesitation at all in accepting the fact of the wrath in the Old Testament. He quotes the words προσώχθισα, "I was displeased", and ὀργῇ μου, "in my wrath" without making any attempt to explain them away. This is in fact the

---

[1] Except in quotation from the Old Testament.
[2] Ed. Hebrews (Indian Church Commentaries, Calcutta 1917), in loc.

only place in the New Testament where a verb meaning "to be angry" is used of God; it is extremely important to note that it is in a quotation from the Old Testament (Ps. 95.10), and even then it is a translation of the Hebrew *qūṭ*, which is not really a wrath word at all, though it looks like one in the LXX. Similarly he uses παραπικραίνω, "provoke", in quotation; like Paul, and indeed all the New Testament writers and several Old Testament writers, he accepts traditional instances of the wrath without question. It is not, however, primarily with the wrath that our author is concerned here. He is not warning his readers against the fate of all Israel who provoked God, nor even of those whose corpses fell in the wilderness. He mentions these merely in order to show that there is a rest waiting for Christians which has not been preoccupied by those who might have been expected to take it, the Israelites in the wilderness. What he *is* warning them against is disbelief, the sin of that generation that had to live out their lives in the wilderness. These are not the people whose corpses fell in the wilderness, but merely those who disbelieved God's promises and therefore had to be kept out of the rest which God had prepared for them in Canaan. We can thus distinguish three categories of people here: (1) οἱ παραπικραίνοντες, "they who provoked", i.e. all Israel, (2) οἷς προσώχθισεν, "those with whom he was displeased", i.e. those who were slain at any time during the forty years; (3) οἷς ὤμοσεν ἐν τῇ ὀργῇ αὐτοῦ, "those to whom he swore in his wrath", i.e. those who survived to live forty years in the wilderness. Categories 2 and 3 are included in category 1, but are mutually exclusive. (The three categories are stated in 3.16-19.) It is only the people in category 3 whose bad example is held up to Christians to avoid. Notice also that in recapitulating category 3 in 3.18 he omits the words ἐν τῇ ὀργῇ αὐτοῦ. He does not want to stress the conception of the divine wrath, or indeed of "provoking God" here. He is therefore distinctly milder than Paul in his treatment of Old Testament wrath. He does not want to threaten his readers with destruction, as Paul does. His language is very reserved indeed when he speaks of Christians falling into the sin of disbelief; e.g. 4.1: δόκῃ τις ἐξ ὑμῶν ὑστερηκέναι, "any one of you should seem to have come short". Finally, notice his extremely lofty and spiritual conception of the judicial role of the word of God. It is (one should say "he is" by the end of the passage) an internal, not an external judge: κριτικὸς ἐνθυμήσεων καὶ ἐννοιῶν καρδίας, "quick to discern the thoughts and intents of the heart", and he judges by his own presence revealing the true nature of those with whom he comes in contact: καὶ οὐκ ἔστιν πᾶσα κτίσις ἀφανὴς ἐνώπιον αὐτοῦ, "and there is no creature that is not manifest in his sight" (4.12,13). The judgement of the Word, in fact, is not something that strikes from outside, but something that shows up from inside. He is not referring to eschatological judgement here.

In 6.4–8 we find a passage which echoes the same conception of judgement as we found in the passage just discussed. This passage is referring to the fate of those who have fallen away. It is most remarkable that judgement is here directly related to the Cross, for those who fall away are described as: ἀνασταυροῦντες ἑαυτοῖς τὸν Υἱὸν τοῦ Θεοῦ, "seeing they crucify to themselves the Son of God afresh". Just as the Cross is the judgement, so those who incur judgement in some sense reproduce the crucifixion. This is a feature of this Epistle that we shall have occasion to notice again, and it shows that in certain respects our author's conception of the judgement of the new dispensation was even more profound than that of St Paul, and is only equalled by the author of Revelation. Here also the process of judgement is compared to a natural process, the cycle of nature (verses 7–8), a significant indication of how God's judgement is conceived as working. The actual language he uses of those who are judged is extremely restrained. He merely says that they cannot be restored "*as long as* they crucify afresh, etc." Westcott[1] says that the participle here gives the moral cause of the impossibility. In drawing out his figure from the process of nature the author does use the phrase κατάρας ἐγγύς, "nigh unto a curse", a mild enough one, but it serves to identify the curse with the process of judgement as in Paul. Here we have both law and curse. Also he views the end of the judged as destruction (καῦσιν) not eternal punishment.

In 9.27,28 a difficult passage occurs, which when elucidated throws a valuable light on the author's conception of judgement:

καὶ καθ' ὅσον ἀπόκειται ἀνθρώποις ἅπαξ ἀποθανεῖν, καὶ μετὰ τοῦτο κρίσις, οὕτως καὶ ὁ Χριστός, ἅπαξ προσενεχθεὶς εἰς τὸ πολλῶν ἀνενεγκεῖν

[1] Ed. Hebrews (London 1903), in loc.

ἁμαρτίας, ἐκ δευτέρου χωρὶς ἁμαρτίας ὀφθήσεται τοῖς αὐτὸν ἀπεκδεχομένοις εἰς σωτηρίαν. And inasmuch as it is appointed unto men once to die, and after this cometh judgement; so Christ also, having been once offered to bear the sins of many, shall appear a second time apart from sin, to them that wait for him, unto salvation.

The final revelation of judgement on each man here is thought of as reserved till after death. Parallel to this is the contrast between Christ "having been once offered to bear the sins of many" and his appearing "a second time apart from sin, unto those that wait for him unto salvation". The reference to the Suffering Servant here: εἰς τὸ πολλῶν ἀνενεγκεῖν ἁμαρτίας, "to bear the sins of many", makes it likely that Christ is thought of not as in any sense having been involved in the guilt of sin, but as having accepted the consequences of sin, becomes voluntarily involved in the process of God's wrath; e.g. Isa. 53.4,5: "Surely he hath borne our griefs and carried our sorrows. . . . He was wounded for our transgressions, he was bruised for our iniquities; the chastisement of our peace was upon him; and with his stripes we are healed." The end of all things will be the consummation of this process, and then Christ will be χωρὶς ἁμαρτίας, "apart from sin", that is, the process will be finished, it will be no longer there for him to be involved in it. Those who are "in Christ" will be out of the sphere of sin, and those who have rejected him (if there be any; the author of Hebrews plainly believes that there will), will have destroyed themselves, having deliberately chosen to reject the way God offers of avoiding the destructive consequences of their sin, and that of others. But the author, with his characteristic reserve, though he speaks of Christ appearing to salvation for those who wait for him, does not explicitly speak about the destruction of those who do not wait for him. Holmes[1] thinks that κρίσις in verse 27 is the great judgement of the Last Day, but this interpretation deprives the comparison of one of its members. The analogy is surely this: as each individual dies once . . . and then his life is judged, so Christ died once . . . and then the great judgement day. The point lies surely in the final and unrepeatable quality of Christ's death; in verses 25–7 of this chapter the argument is that, whereas under the old law sacrifices had to be continually repeated, under the new dispensation one eternal sacrifice satisfies. In verses 27, 28

[1] Op. cit., in loc.

the argument is that as the death of a man is something unrepeatable and final, something that puts an end to, and reveals the full significance of, a concluded process, so the death of Christ is a perfecting and consummating event. Hence the κρίσις of verse 27 refers not specifically to the Last Judgement at the Second Coming, but to the natural fact that the death of a man is the signal for the final verdict on his life. The sense then is: just as you cannot see the final significance of a man's life until after his death, an irrevocable event, so the final meaning of all life is only to be understood in the light of the death of Christ. But whereas a man's life process is consummated by his death, the life of redeemed humanity in Christ is only consummated at the Parousia, i.e. when the process inaugurated by his death is worked out to its conclusion. This very Pauline conception of judgement as a showing up rather than an execution has already appeared in 4.12. It is only fair to point out, on the other side, that in 6.2: κρίματος αἰωνίου, "eternal judgement", follows ἀνάστασις νεκρῶν, "resurrection of the dead". But we may legitimately distinguish between κρίμα and κρίσις. κρίμα is the passing judgement, κρίσις is the process of judgement. Our author does not say of all men: ἅπαξ ἀποθανεῖν καὶ μετὰ τοῦτο κρίμα, "once to die, and after that, judging" but κρίσις "judgement". Westcott[1] supports this distinction; he says, commenting on 6.2: "κρίμα describes the sentence and not the process". So we legitimately take κρίσις in verse 27 of this chapter as "significance of the process of judgement".

Chapter 10.26–31 plunges us into one of the most difficult, interesting, and when carefully examined, illuminating passages on judgement in the whole Bible. We should observe first a number of outstanding characteristics of this passage: it is very eschatological in the sense that punishment (for which two words are used, τιμωρία and ἐκδίκησις) is reserved till after death, though it is not clear whether this is also associated with the Parousia or not. Also judgement is here associated with the Cross; those who deliberately sin after conversion are described as defiling the blood of the Covenant. Another important feature of the passage is that the only possible implication of his interpretation of the Old Testament usage points to his having a completely

---

[1] Op. cit.

JUDGEMENT IN HEBREWS, ETC.

spiritual conception of punishment under the new dispensation. Those who broke the law of Moses were punished with physical death; those who sin under the new order have a *worse* punishment; this can only mean spiritual death, annihilation, not everlasting torment. κρίσεως here seems to mean "passing of judgement" but (verse 27) there is no reason why we should not take φοβερὰ δέ τις ἐκδοχὴ κρίσεως as "a dreadful expectation of exposure". This is reinforced by the author's use of ἐμπίπτειν in verse 31. ἐμπίπτειν is used in six other places in the New Testament. In the three Synoptic references it is literal, e.g. Matt. 12.11 of a sheep falling into a pit. The other three places are 1 Tim. 3.6: εἰς κρίμα διαβόλου, "into the condemnation of the devil"; 3.7: εἰς ὀνειδισμὸν καὶ παγίδα τοῦ διαβόλου, "into reproach and the snare of the devil"; and 6.9: εἰς πειρασμόν "into a temptation". What is common to all these six references is the unintentional nature of the act and the fact that what is fallen into is something unpleasant. In only one of them can the thing into which one falls be described as active, Luke 10.30: "He fell among thieves." ἐμπίπτειν therefore does not normally mean "to be caught by". The more usual meaning is "to be entangled in", almost as in machinery. Even the thieves did not probably plan to catch that particular traveller. Hence to "fall into the hands of the living God" is not "to be caught by God". It is more like "to deliver oneself into his hands". For the discussion of the strange phrase πυρὸς ζῆλος, "a fierceness of fire", see Appendix 5.

Two references in chapters 10 and 11 show that same moderation and reserve in referring to judgement and ultimate destruction that we have learned to expect from the author. The first is 10.38. He quotes a passage from Hab. 2.3,4 about a coming judgement. The second line is rendered in the LXX which the author quotes as:

καὶ ἐὰν ὑποστείληται, οὐκ εὐδοκεῖ ἡ ψυχή μου ἐν αὐτῷ. And if he shrink back my soul hath no pleasure in him.

In 10.39, he adds:

ἡμεῖς δὲ οὐκ ἐσμὲν ὑποστολῆς εἰς ἀπώλειαν, ἀλλὰ πίστεως εἰς περιποίησιν ψυχῆς. But we are not of them that shrink back unto perdition; but of them that have faith unto the saving of the soul.

The reference here is uncompromisingly eschatological, and plainly destruction is seen as the fate of the disobedient, but the very mild word ὑποστολή, "drawing back", is used. Similarly in 11.7 Noah is described as having "condemned the world" by his belief in God and consequent building of the ark. Like Christians he "became an heir of the righteousness which is according to faith". It is not illegitimate to conclude that our author would apply this language to Christians also who became heirs of righteousness through faith; so we have here a reference to the contemporary, non-eschatological judgement which is passed by the existence in the world of Christ in his Church. This is a species of judgement which meets us again in the Apocalypse. A third instance of unemphatic judgement occurs in 12.15 where backsliders are referred to in the words: μή τις ὑστερῶν ἀπὸ τῆς χάριτος τοῦ Θεοῦ. Is this remarkable reserve due to the writer's sensitiveness to the awful nature of judgement, or is it because he thought of this sort of opposition to God as being primarily something one inflicts on oneself? "I miss my chance (ὑστερῶν) and therefore destroy myself" rather than "I offend God and he destroys me". Two verses later (17) the word ἀπεδοκιμάσθη is used of Esau; we have already seen Paul's fondness for this word (pp. 83f.) and no doubt the author uses it here in the same sense as Paul does: "stood self-condemned".

There follows the famous passage in which we read of the sort of company to which Christians have joined themselves (12.18–29). The whole point of this description is that the fire, the judgement, and the destruction which Christians are described as having come to are *not* material, but spiritual. Under a temporal dispensation the fate of the disobedient was temporal death; under a spiritual and eternal one, their fate is spiritual death, eternal annihilation. This should dispose once and for all of the crude notion that the New Testament speaks of material hell-fire, indeed the phrase "hell-fire" itself is utterly misleading unless it is clearly understood as symbolical of spiritual realities, not material.[1] The author of Hebrews believes that this sort of destruction is infinitely more terrible than material hell-fire, hence perhaps the reserve of his language. We may note also here the reference to the blood of Abel. It is strikingly like Rev. 19.13 (q.v. in chapter 7). The blood which is shed at the last great conflict described

---

[1] But see below the section concerning 2 Peter.

in that chapter is the blood of the Redeemer; and so here God is someone greater than the Avenger of blood; he is the Redeemer of the blood-guilty. But of course to reject such a love is indeed in itself death. Westcott remarks on κρίτης, "judge", in verse 23: "The action of the Judge is not to be limited to judgement only." Perhaps it would be better to say that the juxtaposition of God as Judge and Christ as Redeemer shows that the two functions are ultimately identical. He redeems and those who reject the redemption are thereby judged. The suggestion is confirmed by the very negative word παριτήσησθε, "refuse", in verse 25. *A propos* this verse, we may ask: Who is τὸν ἀπ' οὐρανῶν, "him that warneth from heaven"? It looks very much as if it was the same as τὸν λαλοῦντα, "him that speaketh", in verse 24, in which case it must refer to Christ (*sic* Westcott). But if so, οὗ in verse 26 will also refer to Christ, and consequently the writer is suggesting that the voice in Hag. 2.6 is that of the Son, not the Father, and we have an echo of the theory, hinted at in other parts of the New Testament and openly avowed by Justin Martyr and Tertullian, that wherever God is described as appearing or speaking in the Old Testament, it is God the Son, not God the Father.[1] The whole passage reinforces the point of verse 18f., that we are dealing with a heavenly, spiritual, and eternal dispensation, and not with an earthly, material, and temporary one, as in the Old Testament. The message of τὸν ἀπ' οὐρανῶν ἀποστεφόμενοι, "who turn away from him that warneth from heaven", then, is that formerly they had to deal with a God of earthly and temporal rewards and punishments, now we have to deal with a God who has revealed an eternal redemption, not an earthly theodicy. The significance of the two sets of references, one to the theophany in Ex. 19.12 and the other to the "shaking of the heaven and earth" in Haggai, is to show that the passage in Haggai was a prophecy of the Messianic dispensation. Let us note also that it has been fulfilled. The μετάθεσις τῶν σαλευομένων ὡς πεποιημένων, "a removing of things that are shaken" (verse 27), has already taken place. As Holmes well points out, in verses 18 and 23 it is προσεληλύθατε "ye are come", not προσέρχεσθε. The writer's eschatology is more fully realized here than

---

[1] This theory is discussed more fully in an article by me in *Hermathena* No. LIV, 1945 (Dublin and London), called "Theophanies in the Old Testament and the Second Person of the Trinity", p. 67.

perhaps anywhere else in the epistle. We cannot fail to note here also that profound characteristic of judgement which is not always evident in St Paul, its connection with the Cross.

The author ends this magnificent passage with the tremendous words: ὁ γὰρ Θεὸς ἡμῶν πῦρ κατανάλισκον, "for our God is a consuming fire", quoted from Deut. 4.24; Isa. 33.14. Westcott comments on this phrase: "He purifies by burning up all that is base in those who serve him, and all that is unfit to abide in his presence." This is no doubt legitimate comment, but it will hardly stand as an interpretation of the author's mind. An analysis of the use of πῦρ and cognates in the New Testament in a figurative sense shows that it is used in all 53 times.[1] Of these only five can be described as purgative, and of these five three occur in the same passage: 1 Cor. 3.13-15. The other two are 1 Pet. 4.12: πύρωσις "fiery trial", and Rev. 1.15: χαλκολιβάνῳ πεπυρωμένης, "refined in a furnace". Of the other 48 instances, in 45 the meaning of fire is either destruction, retribution, or judgement. Of the remaining three, two are doubtful (Jas. 3.6[2] and Acts 2.3), and the last is the passage in question, Heb. 10.29. In the only other passage in Hebrews where πῦρ is used in a figurative sense, πυρὸς ζῆλος (10.27), whatever the origin of the phrase, there can be no doubt that it is used in a retributive rather than a purgative sense (see Appendix 5). Hence we must conclude that destruction, and not purgation, is in our author's mind here.

One more passage in this Epistle should be mentioned. It is 13.13:

τοίνυν ἐξερχώμεθα πρὸς ⟨Χριστὸν⟩ ἔξω τῆς παρεμβολῆς, τὸν ὀνειδισμὸν αὐτοῦ φέροντες. Let us therefore go forth unto him [Christ] without the camp, bearing his reproach.

"The camp" here seems to stand for Judaism (*sic* Westcott), and hence for the Law. Christ transcended the Law (cf. 7.19) and was condemned by it; that is why he suffered "without the camp". Christians are to bear the ὀνειδισμός, "reproach", which he suffered, the reproach of the Law. Here is a link with Paul's conception of Christ having become a curse and sin *according to the law*; cf. also the discussion on Rev. 14.20: ἔξωθεν τῆς πόλεως, "without the city".

[1] Synoptics 16; John once; Acts twice; Paul 5; Hebrews twice; Catholic Epistles 7; Apocalypse 20. Mark 9.49 may refer to purgative fire, but the sense is doubtful.

[2] But this one cannot be purgative, whatever the real meaning is.

Hebrews, then, is an Epistle which in an oblique fashion is much concerned with the wrath. The author's conception of wrath shows a more eschatological emphasis than does St Paul's, though there are traces of realized judgement. On the other hand divine punishment is conceived as strictly spiritual, and we do not find the tendency to regard certain happenings as direct physical punishment, as we do sometimes in Paul's epistles and Acts. In the opinion of the writer the end of the obdurate is destruction, not eternal punishment. He shows the utmost reserve on the subject. Perhaps his greatest contribution to the New Testament conception of judgement is his connecting it with the Cross, a feature in which he is only surpassed by St John the Divine. Behind his references to judgement we can trace the conception common to all the main traditions in the New Testament that the sphere of judgement is the sphere of law, wrath, and curse. Apart from Old Testament quotations he only uses one word for the wrath, ζῆλος. It has been argued that this is in meaning more akin to *'aph* than to *qin'āh*.

THE FOURTH GOSPEL AND JOHANNINE EPISTLES

In the Johannine writings judgement and the wrath (as far as the latter is mentioned) are almost always conceived as already realized; judgement is something in which we already find ourselves, or something which we impose on ourselves, not something imposed from outside by God. In this respect the Fourth Gospel is the natural sequel to the later Pauline epistles.

John 3.16–21 might be described as the *locus classicus* for the Johannine conception of judgement. Judgement is not the direct act of God, it is a by-product of salvation. Moreover, judgement is already passed by our reaction to Christ (ἤδη κέκριται, "hath been judged already", verse 18). Westcott's comment on verse 16[1] is just: "Judgement is not an arbitrary sentence, but the working out of an absolute law." On ἀπόληται, "perish", in verse 16, Bernard[2] remarks that it is contrasted with "to have eternal life", and therefore refers to our final destiny, not to our present condition. He would also interpret ζωὴ αἰώνιος "eternal life", as referring primarily to a future state in this passage. But

[1] Ed. Gospel of St John (London 1889), in loc., p. 56.
[2] Ed. Gospel of St John (I.C.C., Edinburgh 1928), in loc.

in view of verse 18 ἤδη κέκριται this seems unlikely; compare the use of οἱ ἀπολλύμενοι and οἱ σωζόμενοι in Paul to describe a present condition. ἀπόληται then must be taken as describing a present state, just as ἔχῃ ζωὴν αἰώνιον is present. He came to a world which was under judgement. His coming finally pronounced that condemnation. οὐ κρίνεται, "is not judged", in verse 18 means that we are taken out of the realm of automatic judgement. Verse 19 then refers to Christ's whole life, culminating in the crucifixion. With verse 20 compare Luke 23.30 and Rev. 6.16; 9.6. This is a rejection of the love of God because it involves penitence. What the author of the Fourth Gospel here describes in terms of turning from the light, the author of Revelation describes in terms of God or the Lamb slaying his enemies.

In 3.36 we find the only explicit use of the phrase ὀργὴ τοῦ Θεοῦ, "the wrath of God", in the Johannine writings: ἡ ὀργὴ τοῦ Θεοῦ μένει ἐπ' αὐτόν, "the wrath of God abideth on him". Notice the use of μένει here. It is a pre-existing condition. Westcott[1] here comments: [the wrath of God] "is the general revelation in which man as a sinner stands towards the justice of God". But he fails to see that the Cross makes any difference to this, for he adds: "St John goes back from the revelation of God as Father to the original idea of God as God." He also adds: "Only faith can remove the consequences of sin which must otherwise bring God's wrath upon the sinner." The Wrath of God is revealed by the Incarnation and Cross; the revelation of God as Father is itself indirectly a revelation of the wrath. Also the consequences of sin should not be described as *bringing* the wrath of God: they *are* the wrath of God. In the same verse Hoskyns and Davey[2] commenting on οὐκ ὄψεται ζωήν, "shall not see life", say: "The eschatological future tense ... remains in the context of the wrath of God ... in spite of the preceding present tense [ἔχει ζώην]", and they compare Rom. 2.5; Eph. 5.5. We have already discussed Rom. 2.5 (see pp. 85f.). It is certainly the most eschatological wrath passage in Paul; others of a much more realized character could be cited (e.g. 1 Thess. 2.16). Even in Rom. 2.5 the δικαιοκρισις, "the righteous judgement", is *revealed*. Eph. 5.5 is a very doubtful example of eschatological wrath. There the unclean, οὐκ ἔχει κληρονομίαν ἐν τῇ βασιλείᾳ, "no forni-

---

[1] Op. cit., p. 63.   [2] Ed. John, London 1940.

cator... hath any inheritance in the kingdom"; the ὀργὴ τοῦ Θεοῦ ἔρχεται, "the wrath of God cometh", which might just as well mean "is now coming". Moreover, it is very difficult to see how ἡ ὀργὴ τοῦ Θεοῦ μένει can possibly be interpreted in a purely eschatological sense. οὐκ ὄψεται ζωήν should rather be taken as "shall not see life as long as he disobeys". Had the author written οὐχ ὁρᾷ it would have been a truism. Just the same conception of judgement as a by-product of salvation appears in 5.22-4; the Father has given all judgement to the Son, and yet the Son judgeth no man. These two statements are compatible because in the New Testament judgement is normally not something which God applies, but something which applies itself, or which one applies to oneself. Just because Jesus is the Son, he judges; that is the meaning of all judgement being given to the Son. This note reappears in 5.45, where the Jews are already judged by their failure to recognized the Messiah of the Scriptures. There is no room here for a future judgement.

This language might seem to conflict with verses 28, 29 of chapter 5, where we have the apparently un-Johannine conception of a bodily resurrection at the last day. Those who have done good are to come out to an ἀνάστασις ζωῆς, "resurrection of life", and those who have done evil to an ἀνάστασις κρίσεως, "a resurrection of judgement". Bernard says that the two resurrections, to life and to judgement, are mentioned in Dan. 12.2. As a matter of fact, the phrase ἀνάστασις κρίσεως does not occur either in the LXX of Dan. 12.2, or in Theodotion's version.[1] The LXX translates ἀναστήσονται εἰς ὀνειδισμόν, "they shall arise to shame", and Theodotion has ἐγερθήσονται εἰς ὀνειδισμόν, "they shall be raised... to shame". The LXX adds after ὀνειδισμόν the words οἱ δὲ εἰς διασπορὰν καὶ αἰσχύνην αἰώνιον, "but some to dispersion and eternal dishonour". (Theodotion adds only καὶ αἰσχύνην αἰώνιον.) In both translations the language is very moderate. There is a significant difference between Daniel and John. Daniel describes the punishment, αἰσχύνη or ὀνειδισμός. John describes the condition of being under condemnation. Just as those who will wake to life will wake to enjoy what they already possess, so those who rise in the ἀνάστασις κρίσεως will find themselves already

[1] Not that John could have read Theodotion's version! But his version may have been based on an older version known in the first century A.D.

judged. But even with these qualifying considerations, the passage still seems something of an anomaly.

In 6.48 we seem to have a passage in which John reads into the Old Testament that indirect connection of judgement with salvation which he finds in the new dispensation. The reference seems to be to Ex. 32.6, also quoted by Paul in 1 Cor. 10.7: "The people sat down to eat and drink and rose up to play." Hence the meaning in the context in which John uses it is not "Though your fathers ate the manna, they were mortal men after all", but "Your fathers ate and drank judgement to themselves in the wilderness". They received the supranatural food and scorned it; you may accept it and avoid judgement. This view is confirmed by verses 31 and 32 of this chapter, where John emphasizes the God-given and heavenly character of the manna. John's view of the incidents in the wilderness is the same as Paul's here. It is not that of the Epistle to the Hebrews, where the Old Testament is contrasted with the New Order, as the material and temporal with the spiritual and eternal. Just as Paul speaks of a πνευματικὸν πόμα, "spiritual drink," in the wilderness, so here John is arguing that Israel has always had the choice of life or death in the presence of God's living grace. He is not concerned to contrast the physical food in the Old Testament with the spiritual in the New Testament. But he does say: "The issue is supremely before you now." We can point to several other examples of this sort of treatment of the Old Testament in John; another is 12.37–41, where John quotes Isa. 6.9 to show that in Isaiah's time also the revelation of salvation brought automatic judgement to those who refused it. Indeed here he is even more like Paul's "and that Rock was Christ" (1 Cor. 10.4), for he seems to claim that Isaiah saw the glory of Christ in the Temple; τὴν δόξαν αὐτοῦ, "his glory", in verse 41 can hardly refer to anyone else. διὰ τοῦτο therefore in verse 39 will mean something like "because of this principle", i.e. the principle that salvation also brings judgement. See also 15.25, where John seems to be tracing the same principle in Psalm 69.4[1]: ἐμίσησάν με δωρεάν "They hated me without a cause." His argument is that, just as in the Psalmist's day the man who loved God incurred unjustifiable hostility, so also when Love himself comes down. A final example occurs in

---

[1] Bernard thinks this more likely than Ps. 35.19, as Ps. 69 was generally considered Messianic.

13.8: "Yea, mine own familiar friend, etc." The betrayal by the familiar friend was fulfilled in the betrayal by Judas, who has destined himself for eternal ἀπώλεια, "perdition". In so far as the Old Testament was a revelation of God's character, it must be also a revelation of men's reaction to that character. According to John, the reaction which involves judgement can be traced also in the Old Testament. It is an approach to the Old Testament which might, if developed by later Church Fathers, have led to something much more compatible with the post-critical conception of the Scriptures than what we actually find in their writings.

In 8.21–8, judgement is related, not to the Parousia, but to the Cross. The disbelieving Jews are to die in their sins. But it is only when the Son of Man is lifted up on the Cross that this judgement is made plain. The same thought occurs in 12.31, John's version of Gethsemane. Christ is speaking if he was already in his passion, and he says: νῦν κρίσις ἐστὶν τοῦ κόσμου τούτου, "Now is the judgement of this world." His reference in the same verse to the prince of this world being cast down recalls Rev. 12.9; 20.10, the casting down of Satan from heaven and his being cast into the lake of fire. Final judgement has been pronounced in principle on the Cross. The Apocalypse seems to take it even further back. There is another interesting parallel with Rev. in 8.44. Jesus is the Truth, and he is the Son of the Father. The Devil is the Father of Untruth.[1] The parallel with the rival dispensation of Satan, more fully described in Revelation, is implicit here.

Finally in 12.47,48 a most interesting distinction is made between Jesus and ὁ λόγος ὃν ἐλάλησα, "the word that I spake". Jesus does not judge the man who fails to keep his ῥήματα; but there is one who judges him: ὁ λόγος ὃν ἐλάλησα. This prompts an investigation into John's use of λόγος, λόγοι, ῥήματα, in his Gospel. He uses these words in a whole gamut of meanings, from the Incarnate Λόγος of the Prologue to the mere spoken or written word in Scripture or elsewhere. Moreover, the farther the meaning is from the

---

[1] αὐτοῦ must refer to ψεῦδος, understood in 8.44. Westcott would understand τις between λάλῃ and τὸ ψεῦδος, and translates: "Whenever anyone tells a lie he speaks out of the devil's store, because the devil is a liar and father to such a man." But this is gnomic and unlike John's style.

Incarnate Λόγος the more likely is it to be described as judging. In fact, judgement is conceived of as an impersonal process: the Incarnate Λόγος is a person, so he does not judge. The λόγος or λόγοι, which are just teaching or principles, can be said to judge because they are impersonal. We might express this another way by saying that the Λόγος is the Person of God in Christ; the λόγος or λόγοι, ῥῆμα or ῥήματα, are the significance of God's saving action, and part of that significance consists in its aspect as judgement. The distinction between Λόγος and λόγος etc. is not absolute. It is rather a gradual declension from the Word, meaning the personal self-disclosure of God in Christ, to *verba Christi*, the actual words or sounds he uttered. We can trace the declension as follows:

1. Λόγος in the prologue: the Incarnate Lord.

2. John 5.38: τὸν λόγον αὐτοῦ ⟨sc. Θεοῦ⟩ οὐκ ἔχετε ἐν ὑμῖν, μένοντα "Ye have not his [God's] word abiding in you". This might almost be pointed τὸν Λόγον αὐτοῦ, and is the nearest parallel in the rest of the Gospel to the Prologue.

3. 10.35: πρὸς οὓς ὁ λόγος τοῦ Θεοῦ ἐγένετο, "unto whom the word of God came". Both Westcott and also Hoskyns and Davey agree that, though the reference is primarily to the oracles of God having come to men under the old covenant, it also suggests that it was the pre-existent Word that spoke in the Old Testament. It is significant that the quotation referred to here is from the Psalms (82.6), where so often New Testament writers interpret the Son as speaking. These two examples suggest that there is not such a big gap between the Λόγος conception of the Prologue and the rest of the Gospel as some scholars have imagined.

4. 17.6,14,17: ὁ λόγος is here God's revelation of himself but with a certain emphasis on its intellectual aspect; it is, however, very personal; see especially verse 17.

5. Three passages: 8.51: ἐάν τις τόν ἐμον λόγον τηρήσῃ, "if a man keep my word"; 14.23: τὸν λόγον μου τηρήσῃ, "he will keep my word"; 15.3: ὑμεῖς καθαροί ἐστε διὰ τὸν λόγον ὃν λάληκα ὑμῖν, "ye are clean because of the word which I have spoken unto you". In all these the λόγος has a very inward spiritual reference. It

is only less personal because it is ὁ ἐμὸς λόγος, "my word", and not ἐγώ, "I".

6. In the next group ὁ ἐμὸς λόγος, "my word", is the beginning of faith, something which must grow into full personal relationship, e.g. 8.31: ἐὰν ὑμεῖς μείνητε ἐν τῷ λόγῳ τῷ ἐμῷ, ἀληθῶς μαθηταί μού ἐστε, "if ye abide in my word, then are ye truly my disciples". Westcott comments: "The sentence is a gracious recognition of the first rude beginning of faith." To this group also belong a number of passages where ἀκούειν, "hear", is used of the λόγος: 5.24; 8.43. Here also belongs 14.24, with its τοὺς λόγους μου οὐ τηρεῖ, "keepeth not my words", and ὁ λόγος ὃν ἀκούετε, "the word which ye hear". This looks very like 8.51; but in the first sentence it is λόγοι not λόγος, which is more intellectual and external; and in the second sentence ἀκούειν is used, which makes it nearer the spoken word and farther removed from the Λόγος who is to be personally appropriated. In this group also must go 8.37: ὁ λόγος ὁ ἐμὸς οὐ χωρεῖ ἐν ὑμῖν, "my word hath not free course in you", where Westcott's comment is: "The idea required is not that of 'abiding' but of growth and movement." The λόγος here is the more external and intellectual apprehension that may lead on to personal faith in the Word.

7. The ῥήματα passages: e.g. 3.34: τὰ ῥήματα τοῦ Θεοῦ "the words of God"; 5.47: γράμμασιν ... ῥήμασιν[1]; 8.47: τὰ ῥήματα τοῦ Θεοῦ ἀκούει, "heareth the words of God"; 15.7: τὰ ῥήματά μου ἐν ὑμῖν μένει, "my words abide in you", 17.8: τὰ ῥήματα ἃ ἔδωκάς μοι, "the words which thou gavest me". In these instances the use of the plural indicates that what is described is something short of full personal confrontation, and the emphasis is rather on the intellectual significance of the Incarnation. To these we may add 6.63,68: τὰ ῥήματα ἃ λάληκα ὑμῖν πνεῦμά ἐστιν, "the words that I have spoken unto you are spirit", and ῥήματα ζωῆς αἰωνίου ἔχεις, "thou hast the words of eternal life". In these two places ῥήματα is not used so much to emphasize the intellectual side, as to show that it is a beginning: "they lead to the enjoyment of the Spirit"; "thou hast the words which lead to eternal life".

---

[1] ῥήμασιν instead of λόγοις no doubt partly for the sake of the play on words. One might paraphrase: "If ye believe not this teaching, how shall ye believe my preaching?"

8. The last group consists of passages where λόγος or λόγοι means literally a spoken or written word: e.g. 10.19; 15.20,25.¹ The very fact that the distinctions between the various usages of these words are so subtle and that they lie below the surface is an indication that they represent a deep, perhaps semiconscious, conviction in the writer's mind, the conviction that the divine judgement cannot be described as a direct act of God, but as an impersonal process.

In the Johannine epistles we meet with very much the same conception of judgement as being something revealed by the reaction which men show to Christ. Thus in 1 John 2.19, the departure of the heretics from the Church is interpreted as a sign that they never really belonged to Christ. It is like: "I never knew you" of Matt. 7.23. The use of θάνατος, "death", in this Epistle is exactly the same as the use of ὀργή in John 3.36,² cf. especially 1 John 3.14: ὁ μὴ ἀγαπῶν μένει

---

² With this whole discussion cf. Heb. 4.12,13; 1 Pet. 1.23. C. H. Dodd in *The Interpretation of the Fourth Gospel* (Cambridge 1953) has an interesting classification of John's use of λόγος, though he is primarily thinking of its metaphysical significance. His categories are roughly parallel to those given here, and his note on p. 342 comes to very much the same conclusion about the author's variation in significance from λόγος to λόγος. He would not, however, admit any significant difference between λόγος and λόγοι in such places as 8.51 and 14.24 (see op. cit., p. 265 (iii)). I still believe that the plural has some significance. The phrase "keep my words" is very reminiscent of Ps. 119 (118), where it occurs several times. There the LXX does not use τηρεῖν but φυλάσσεσθαι. (τηρεῖν λόγους does not occur in any undisputed passage in the LXX: τοὺς λόγους μου οὐκ ἐτήρησεν in 1 Kingdoms 15.11 represents הֵקִים in the Hebrew, and A's ἔστησεν may well be right. But see Prov. 3.1, where τὰ ῥήματά μου τηρείτω σὴ καρδία represents וּמִצְוֹתַי יִצֹּר לִבֶּךָ). φυλάσσεσθαι λόγους or λόγια occurs in verses 9, 17, 67, 101, 158. It represents שָׁמַר דְּבָרִים or אִמְרָה. Compare also Luke 11.28: μακάριοι οἱ ἀκούοντες τὸν λόγον τοῦ Θεοῦ καὶ φυλάσσοντες. In all the occurrences in Ps. 119 what is kept is in fact the detailed commandments of the Law. Hence the associations of the phrase τηρεῖν λόγους in the Fourth Gospel are with keeping a set of precepts rather than with apprehending a personal revelation. Dodd does comment (op. cit., p. 209) on the contrast between the Son, who does not judge, and his word, which does; but his explanation of the contrast is not really convincing. He believes that it implies a condemnation of "a crude misrepresentation of the idea of Christ as Judge", and he thinks that this misinterpretation is to be found in the Apocalypse. This great scholar's antipathy to the Book of Revelation is well known (see also op. cit., p. 213, note 3) and it may have coloured his judgement here. It is the contention of Chapter 7 of this present work that the conception of the Judgement of Christ to be found in the Christian apocalypse is anything but a crude misinterpretation.

² The use of the word implies destruction, not eternal punishment, and is thus in line with Hebrews.

ἐν τῷ θανάτῳ, "he that loveth not abideth in death". It is a spiritual condition here, not an act of condemnation. In 3.20,21, we have a passage which seems to outline the same conception that we have found in Paul concerning the duty of Christians to judge themselves so that they may not come under divine judgement: "God is greater that our heart, and knoweth all things." It is not suggested here that God knows we are mistaken in condemning ourselves, but rather that if we condemn ourselves honestly he will not condemn us.

1 John 4.17,18 presents us with a problem of interpretation:

As he is, even so are we in the world. There is no fear in love, but perfect love casteth out fear, because fear hath punishment (κόλασιν ἔχει).

Westcott[1] interprets "as he is" as referring to "his character as it is at present and eternally, and not to the particular form in which it was historically manifested". But this is perhaps to read nineteenth-century philosophical conceptions into the text. It is more consonant with the rest of the New Testament, especially the Apocalypse, to take "as he is, even so are we in the world" to refer to Christ's life in the Church. Our sufferings as Christians are his sufferings, and thus the sense will be that as Christ by pure love saved and judged the world, but was not judged by it, so we through love can transcend all judgement. With this interpretation Dodd[2] agrees: "Hence, to remain in love, living in this world as Christ lives, means for us that we keep our place in God's family." If this interpretation is correct, then κόλασις must mean "punishment" not "torment", and the phrase will really signify: "fear is its own punishment". With this Westcott agrees, but Bennett[3] argues that it means that fear springs from an anticipation of future retribution. It does not, however, seem necessary to limit fear to this alone. The fear to which John refers is the λύπη τοῦ κόσμου "the sorrow of the world", which works death, of 2 Cor. 7.10. Pakenham-Walsh[4] argues that κόλασις is the "kind of punishment that corrects and improves". But κόλασις and cognates are never used in this sense in the New Testament. It only occurs in three other places: Matt. 25.46: κόλασις αἰώνιος, "eternal punishment"; Acts 4.21: of

[1] Ed. Johannine Epistles (London 1886), in loc.
[2] Ed. Moffatt Commentary (London 1946) in loc.
[3] Ed. Johannine Epistles (Century Bible, London 1900) in loc.
[4] Ed. Johannine Epistles (Indian Church Commentaries, Madras 1910), in loc.

the punishment received by the apostles at the hands of the Sanhedrin; and 2 Pet. 2.9: ἀδίκους εἰς ἡμέραν κρίσεως κολαζομένους τηρεῖν, "to keep the unrighteous under punishment unto the day of judgement". Here the notion of corrective punishment is entirely absent. Dodd's comment is just: "Perhaps his meaning is that fear carries punishment with it."

We must also give some attention to a remarkable phrase in 1 John 5.16: the ἁμαρτία πρὸς θάνατον, "a sin unto death". This passage is like Rom. 9.22 in that editors have done their best to soften the apparent rigour of the writer here. Westcott quotes many Fathers, some of whom interpret the sin as deliberate persistence in evil (e.g. Augustine, *De Serm. Dom.* 1.22,73). Westcott himself describes it as a characteristic of sin rather than a specific sin. Pakenham Walsh speaks in the same strain. Dodd takes a more realistic view, and argues that it must mean an actual sin, apostasy perhaps, or a denial of the Incarnation. There is, however, one mitigating argument brought forward by commentators which certainly will not stand the strain of examination. Bennett, who thinks that it refers to deliberate and continued apostasy, emphasizes that ἁμαρτία πρὸς θάνατον means "a sin tending towards death", but not "a sin necessarily involving death". Westcott appears to support this, quoting John 11.4: ἀσθένεια πρὸς θάνατον "a sickness unto death". But this quotation is fatal to the argument. Even though Lazarus's sickness resulted in temporary death, it is described as *not* being an ἀσθένεια πρὸς θάνατον, "sickness unto death". Surely then, *a fortiori*, a sickness that could be described as πρὸς θάνατον must result in some sort of (more than temporary) death. By the same analogy ἁμαρτία πρὸς θάνατον, "sin unto death", must mean "a sin that results in death". This conclusion is confirmed by the fact that the phrase "a sin unto death" occurs in Jubilees 21.22 (only the Ethiopic is preserved), where the sense is undoubtedly "a sin that results in death". Editors have however apparently forgotten that for John θάνατος=ὀργή, and is a spiritual condition, not necessarily, in this life at any rate, an irrevocable sentence. Hence the ἁμαρτία πρὸς θάνατον brings the sinner into death now, in this life. But there is nothing in this epistle positively forbidding us to believe that he who has been brought into death by his sin may yet be brought out again before the final consummation.

THE PASTORAL AND CATHOLIC EPISTLES

The word "wrath" does not occur in any of the Pastoral or Catholic Epistles, but the conception of judgement as being to a greater or a lesser degree realized does, and the contrast between the legal character of the sphere of judgement and the grace character of the sphere of salvation also occurs.

In 1 Pet. 4.17,18 we find a conception which has already appeared prominently in Hebrews, the connection of judgement with the Cross. Selwyn's comment is: "The divine judgement is already operative in the trials suffered by the Christian community." The writer interprets the sufferings of Christians in the terms of a judgement, and in verse 13 of this chapter those sufferings are identified with Christ's. The quotation, as Beare points out, is from Prov. 11.31 (LXX; the Hebrew is quite different):

εἰ ὁ μὲν δίκαιος μόλις σώζεται, ὁ ἀσεβὴς καὶ ὁ ἁμαρτωλὸς ποῦ φανεῖται;
And if the righteous is scarcely saved, where shall the ungodly and sinner appear?

It is very likely that the author understood this as a prophecy of the final judgement, for the previous verse in the LXX is

ἐκ καρποῦ δικαιοσύνης φύεται δένδρον ζωῆς,
ἀφαιροῦνται δὲ ἄωροι ψυχαὶ παρανόμων.
From the fruit of righteousness grows a tree of life,
But the souls of the lawless are carried away and vanish (my trans.),

which an early Christian exegete would naturally interpret as referring to eternal life. The judgement in this passage *begins* with the Christians (the house of God). Hence it is not a case of two separate judgements, one of the house of God, and one for sinners, as Beare, for example, understands it. It is all one process of judgement. It is true that the writer envisaged the end of all things as close at hand, but he was only foreshortening what is true of all Christian history. Christ in the Cross accepts the judgement of the Law, and emerges triumphant—and by the same act all other men are judged too. It is very closely related to the conception in Revelation of the Lamb triumphing through the deaths of the martyrs. In the quotation, ποῦ φανεῖται does not mean "What will happen to the ungodly?" as Beare assumes. It means rather

"Will he survive? Is it the second death for him or not?" The writer is not interested in the nature of the punishment, but rather suggests that the ungodly will not survive the trial. Probably, like the author to the Hebrews, he believed in the ultimate destruction of the obdurate.

James in two places uses θάνατος, "death", in the sense which we have met in 1 John, as the equivalent of ὀργή in the Fourth Gospel: James 1.15; 5.20. In 2.12,13 we find a passage which shows considerable insight into the nature of the Christian's relation to the law. He speaks of Christians ὡς διὰ νόμου ἐλευθερίας μέλλοντες κρίνεσθαι "as men that are to be judged by a law of liberty", and goes on to say that "judgement is without mercy to him that hath showed no mercy; mercy glorieth against judgement." Here is the true Pauline apprehension of Christians having been taken altogether from the sphere of judgement (κρίσις), and the conviction that if you will not accept grace (here called ἔλεος) all that is left is the merciless sphere of legal judgement. What does the νόμος ἐλευθερίας, "law of liberty", mean? Mayor[1] takes it as the importance of having the right motive, the love of God, in our hearts. If we have this, there will be no question of legalism. Plumptre[2] agrees. It does seem that the author of this epistle has understood Christianity as something that transcends law, even though he uses the word νόμος. He does not, however, give any hint that the law of liberty is only for those who are justified by faith in Christ.

There is one small point in 2 Timothy. In 2.15 and 3.8 δόκιμος and ἀδόκιμος seem to be used in a Pauline sense. In 2.15 the sense is plain; the merit of Timothy is to be proved by his own life. In 3.8 editors on the whole seem to accept "reprobate" as the right sense rather than "useless" (*contra* Scott).[3] Falconer compares Rom. 1.28. The word seems to imply a condition of obduracy achieved by deliberate turning from God.

In Titus 1.16 and 3.11 the author of the epistle seems to be anxious to prove that the adversaries against whom he writes are so outrageously perverted that they condemn themselves. He uses both ἀδόκιμος,

---

[1] Ed. James (London 1897), in loc.
[2] Ed. James (Cambridge Bible, 1909), in loc.
[3] Ed. Pastoral Epistles (Moffatt Commentary, London 1936), in loc.

"reprobate", and αὐτοκατάκριτος, "self-condemned". It is curious how much in the post-Pauline epistles adversaries are described as deliberately sinning against the light. Is it because the Church leaders wanted to be justified in condemning them outright, committing them to Satan, which they felt would be too severe a punishment for those who were merely mistaken? Perhaps we can see here the germ of the later habit of accusing heretics of every other error, both intellectual and moral, as well as their particular heresy.[1]

1 Tim. 1.16 introduces us by its use of the word μακροθυμία, "longsuffering", to a study of that word's use in the New Testament. In the Old Testament μακροθυμία and cognates are invariably used to translate *'erek 'appayim*. It is therefore really a wrath word. This is much less so in the New Testament. Paul uses μακροθυμία of God twice in Romans. The first place is Rom. 2.4 where it does certainly mean "restraining his wrath up to a point" and since he speaks of the ἡμέρα ὀργῆς, "day of wrath", in the next verse, it is plain that when that point is reached the wrath will not be restrained any longer. As we noted in chapter 4, Rom. 2.4f. is probably the most eschatological wrath passage which Paul wrote. The other reference is Rom. 9.22:

⟨Θεὸς⟩ ἤνεγκεν ἐν πολλῇ μακροθυμίᾳ σκεύη ὀργῆς. [God] ... endured with much longsuffering vessels of wrath.

Here the meaning of μακροθυμία is not quite the same as in 2.4. We have argued that the σκεύη ὀργῆς must be understood to be quite as much instruments of the wrath as recipients of it, so Paul must be thinking of the contemporary wrath process and of God's μακροθυμία as permitting that process to go on without his signal intervention in one direction or another. In so far as the μακροθυμία has an end here, it will be in the Incarnation–Cross–Resurrection series of events, and not in the Parousia as in Rom. 2.4. This passage then is like Luke 18.1–8 (see p. 123), where God's μακροθυμία ends not with the Parousia, but with the Cross and Resurrection. This is a specifically Christian use of μακροθυμία. In the five other places where Paul uses μακροθυμία it is a Christian virtue (2 Cor. 6.6; Gal. 5.22; Eph. 4.2; Col. 1.11; 3.12), and of course there is no suggestion that the θυμός should ever be shown by Christians at all, a significant usage and one

---

[1] See also p. 157 on Jude's similar tendency.

which must throw light on Paul's conception of the μακροθυμία of God. Besides Luke's use of the word in connection with God, it is used in Matt. 18.26f. in the Parable of the Unmerciful Servant. Both the Unmerciful Servant and his debtor say:

> μακροθύμησον ἐπ' ἐμοί, καὶ πάντα ἀποδώσω σοί. Have patience with me, and I will pay thee all.

This means only: "Defer your wrath until a time when it will not be necessary." But of course it is not used directly of God, and we cannot infer from this that Christians should say μακροθύμησον, "have patience with me" to God. 1 Tim.1.16 shows an interesting use of the word:

> ἵνα ἐν ἐμοὶ πρώτῳ ἐνδείξηται Ἰησοῦς Χριστὸς τὴν ἅπασαν μακροθυμίαν. That in me as chief might Jesus Christ show forth all his longsuffering.

It is possible that there is an echo of Rom. 9.22 here, ἐνδείξασθαι τὴν ὀργήν, "to show his wrath", but if so the contrast is very remarkable. Another link with that passage and this one is that in both cases the μακροθυμία is shown in order eventually to win over a bitter opponent. But in the 1 Timothy passage there is no end at all to the μακροθυμία envisaged, no suggestion at all that θυμός could ever be associated with Christ. Falconer here well translates it: "Jesus Christ might prove that there are no limits to his longsuffering." In fact it is a very Christian use of the word. A somewhat similar use occurs in 1 Pet. 3.20:

> ὅτε ἀπεξεδέχετο ἡ τοῦ Θεοῦ μακροθυμία ἐν ἡμέραις Νῶε κατασκευαζομένης κιβωτοῦ ... κτλ. When the longsuffering of God waited in the days of Noah, while the ark was a-preparing.

The primary reference of this passage is to the temporary μακροθυμία of God, which lasted as long as it took to build the ark and was exclusively shown to those eight persons who entered the ark. But the whole passage refers to Christ's having preached after his Crucifixion to the spirits of those who failed to take advantage of that period of μακροθυμία, and therefore it has also a reference to the far greater μακροθυμία of God in allowing even these an opportunity of hearing the Gospel. Moreover, the reason why the writer refers at all to Christ's Passion is in order to exhort Christians to show similar patience and longsuffering, though he does not use the word μακροθυμία of Christians. So in fact this passage also shows a very Christian connotation in its use of μακροθυμία. The Epistle to the Hebrews uses the word twice (verb once, noun once) in Heb. 6.12,15, where it means simply "be patient" and "patience", without any thought of ultimate wrath. This is of human patience. Indeed there cannot be any thought of θυμός, for it was towards God's promises that this patience was shown. Finally the word occurs in 2 Pet. 3.9–15 where it means simply: "God's holding off his wrath for a season", with a view, be it said, to the ultimate salvation of all except the false teachers. But the author has no doubt about ultimate wrath.

Μακροθυμία and cognates thus afford us in a certain respect a vignette of the wrath conception of the writers of the New Testament. It is not really, taken literally, a very suitable word in a New Testament context; the main message of the New Testament is not: "God has given you one more chance." So we find that on the one hand the word tends to lose all wrath connotation at all, and means merely patience, and on the other that when a term to the μακροθυμία is thought of it is sometimes seen, not as the Parousia and Last Judgement, but as the Cross and Resurrection. In a few places, one in Paul, and one, as we might expect, in 2 Peter, it seems to have its full Old Testament connotation. Incidentally, it is interesting to notice that in several places in the inter-Testamental literature the word is apparently devoid of wrath-connotation and means simply "patience"; cf. Ecclus. 5.4; Baruch 4.25; Test. XII Patriarchs, Gad 4.7.

When we turn to Jude and 2 Peter we seem to have entered a new and coarser atmosphere. All the restraint and sensitiveness about judgement and final punishment which meet us in the rest of the New Testament is gone, and instead we have crude pictures of judgement after death used as horrible warnings against false teachers. The comprehension of the true meaning of judgement not only falls far short of the rest of the New Testament, but also of the highest insights of the Old Testament writers.

In Jude 4 we seem to have an unreflecting adoption of reprobation. The author speaks of certain ungodly persons as:

οἱ πάλαι προγεγραμμένοι εἰς τοῦτο τὸ κρίμα. They who were of old set forth unto this condemnation.

Plumptre[1] would take this simply as "marked out [by their behaviour] for some time past as condemned", but this seems an attempt to render the writer's thought theologically respectable, rather than anything else. Wand[2] probably rightly sees a reference to Enoch 67.10, and suggests that τοῦτο τὸ κρίμα, "this condemnation", is the last great judgement. He also attempts to palliate the reprobation by saying that they were pre-ordained to being condemned for their impiety, rather than to impiety itself, a distinction which is hardly likely to have occurred to the writer of the Epistle.

We find both in Jude and in his imitator, the author of 2 Peter,[3] what we find in no other part of the New Testament, a literal and explicit description of the sort of punishment sinners are to meet at the last day. Paul, it is true, warns his Christians against the destruction in which the Israelites were involved in the desert, but when he speaks definitely of future judgement himself he restricts himself to the word ἀπώλεια, "perdition". Our Lord speaks (or is represented as speaking) of fire and brimstone, and the worm that dieth not, but we can be quite certain that this language is symbolic; the same can certainly be said of the Lake of Fire in Revelation. But there is no symbolism in these two epistles. Jude mentions the δεσμοῖς ἀϊδίοις, "everlasting bonds", of the fallen angels (verse 6), the πυρὸς αἰωνίου, "eternal fire", of Sodom and Gomorrah (verse 7) and the ζόφος τοῦ σκότους, "blackness of darkness" prepared for the false teachers (verse 13). In 2 Peter at first it looks as if the writer is going to be more restrained; in 2.1 he contents himself with claiming that the false prophets bring on themselves ταχινὴν ἀπώλειαν, "swift destruction", but we are not long left in doubt as to the nature of that destruction. In 2.4 he describes God punishing the fallen angels: σείροις ζόφου ταρταρώσας, "committed them to chains of darkness" (R.V. adopts another reading, *vide infra*); then come the Flood and the fall of Sodom and Gomorrah. In 2.9 he tells us of the unrighteous (un-Pauline word in this context!) εἰς ἡμέραν κρίσεως κολαζομένους, "under punishment unto the day of judgement". After that comes in verses 15 and 16 what appears to be a still more awful punishment, that of being rebuked by an ass! The

---

[1] Ed. Jude (Cambridge 1897), in loc.
[2] Ed. 2 Peter (Westminster Commentary, London 1934), in loc.
[3] Unless, as some hold, the relationship is the other way.

final threat occurs in 2.17 where he says of the false teachers: οἷς ὁ ζόφος τοῦ σκότους τετήρηται, "for whom the blackness of darkness hath been reserved". It cannot unfortunately be maintained that these descriptions are symbolical. They seem to be taken from the Apocalyptic literature, largely the Book of Enoch. Wand points out that ὑπὸ ζόφον in Jude 6, "under darkness", probably refers to Enoch 67.4–7, where the fire prepared for the wicked is described as located under the Dead Sea. Similarly it would be difficult to take δεσμοῖς ἀϊδίοις, "everlasting bonds" (Jude 6), or σείροις ζόφου, "chains of darkness" (2 Pet. 2.4), in anything but a literal sense. The variant reading for σείροις ζόφου(= "chains of darkness", a strange phrase) is σείραις ζόφου "pits of darkness" (S R m). This would be even more unmistakably literalistic. The language in both these epistles is violent and ill-considered. Jude actually compares those against whom he is writing to the Israelites who disobeyed in the wilderness, the fallen angels, the cities of the plain, Satan, Cain, Balaam, and Korah. One cannot resist the impression that he is simply piling up every example of divine punishment, scriptural and unscriptural, of which he can think, and hurling them against these adversaries. The pity is that so many subsequent ecclesiastical councils imitated his example and not the reserve of the Author to the Hebrews. The author of 2 Peter shows a certain resemblance to the Book of Revelation, which, of course, he may well have read. Like St John the Divine, he describes the destruction of the world by fire, the annihilation of the wicked, and the creation of a new heaven and a new earth. But there are also certain marked differences; in 2 Peter there is no reference to the centre of John's scheme of things, the Lamb as it had been slain; there is no eschatological climax, no analysis of the forces of anti-God, and the whole is not placed against the background of world history, as is John's picture. Perhaps the only redeeming feature in 2 Peter (like the saving last two verses of Jude) is the gracious reference to God's μακροθυμία, "long-suffering", in 3.9,15, where it is emphasized that God wishes *all* (except presumably the false teachers) to be saved. But Jude and 2 Peter together show us the low-water mark of the New Testament conception of judgement. In both we meet a crude and materialistic conception of both judgement and divine punishment, used in a violent and intemperate manner to bludgeon adversaries. The restraint and insight of the rest of the New Testament stand out all the more clearly by contrast. This fact alone should surely prove the non-apostolical origin of these two Epistles.

7

THE WRATH IN THE APOCALYPSE

The concept of the wrath of God is more prominent in the Book of Revelation than in any other part of the New Testament. Nearly all scholars have assumed that St John the Divine's conception of the wrath is not different from that of the Apocalyptists in the Old Testament and inter-Testamental period, and it does not seem to have occurred to anyone to try to trace any connection between Paul's conception of the ὀργή and John's. Modern editors vary between on the one hand apologizing for the un-Christian emphasis on the divine wrath which they believe they find in Revelation and, on the other, assuming that St John's conception of the wrath is essentially that of the Apocalyptists and must be somehow reconciled with the Christian revelation.[1] But closer investigation of how St John the Divine uses his wrath vocabularly, and especially of the antecedents in the Old Testament of the phrases he uses, reveals that John, far from being a sort of throw-back to the Old Testament in his treatment of the wrath, presents us in fact with a more carefully thought out conception of the divine wrath even than Paul, one which is more closely related to the central message of Christianity, and which forms a completion and crown of all that is said about the wrath in the rest of the Bible. We must begin therefore by studying his vocabulary.

John uses ὀργή six times of the divine wrath; twice it is in connection with θυμός: ἡ ὀργὴ τοῦ θυμοῦ, "the fierceness of the wrath" (16.19 and 19.15). He uses θυμός of the divine wrath eight times. In this, with the exception of one occurrence in Paul, he is unique in the New Testament. His use of θυμός, however, is by no means haphazard. Of the eight occasions on which he uses it, in seven it is in more or less direct connection with the word οἶνος, "wine" or ληνός, "winepress"; 15.7: ἑπτὰ φιάλας χρυσᾶς γεμούσας τοῦ θυμοῦ τοῦ Θεοῦ, "seven golden bowls full of the wrath of God", is not an exception, for here φιάλη represents the Hebrew *kōṣ*. Charles points out that φιάλη was actually adopted into Hebrew and Aramaic about the beginning of

---

[1] For an example of the latter category cf. Tasker, op. cit., p. 47: "The fact that the Lamb is also the Lion adds to the terribleness of his Wrath."

the Christian era, and he quotes the Targum on Isa. 51.17, here the Hebrew *kōs* is explained as *pyly*. Therefore in this passage the reference is to the wine of the wrath. The eighth passage is 15.1: ἐν αὐταῖς ἐτελέσθη ὁ θυμὸς τοῦ Θεοῦ, "in them is finished the wrath of God". Charles[1] regards this as an interpolation, and it is perhaps significant that this is the only passage in which θυμός is used not in an explicitly "wine" passage. But there is an indirect reference to the wine, for αὐταῖς refers to the ἑπτὰ πληγαῖς, "seven plagues", and in chapter 16 these take the form of φίαλαι poured out. Thus we may fairly claim that θυμός of God is always used with more or less direct reference to the wine or cup figure. John also uses ὀργίζειν and θυμός of the Dragon in 12.12,17, and ὀργίζειν of the nations in 11.18, in an Old Testament reference. As we study John's use of the five words, ὀργή, θυμός, οἶνος, ποτήριον, ληνός, we are struck by one remarkable feature; they invariably refer, not to purely eschatological wrath, but to wrath worked out in the events of history. This is as a matter of fact what we should have expected in view of the past history of the "cup of wrath" figure. We have seen that the cup of Jahveh's wrath in the Old Testament is never used of what is to happen at the end of history. It always refers to certain specific events in history, either in the past or in the near future. This is almost as true of the "pouring out of the wrath" figure (see p. 35f.). All editors of Revelation seem to have assumed that, because the author was dealing with the Last Things, his reference to the divine wrath must be purely eschatological also. But this does not follow at all; most of his references to the wrath, especially those in which the wine-figure occurs, refer to the fall of Babylon, by which he meant the fall of the Roman Empire. This, he believed, was to be an event in future history, and not the last event, either; nor was it to be an event brought about by direct divine action, but rather by the action of men in history, the kings from the East, in fact. To this event or rather series of events, he applies the language of divine wrath. In so doing he is entirely in line with the Old Testament conception of the divine wrath, but he is *not* treating the wrath as purely eschatological. On the contrary, it is fundamentally just as Paul describes it, the working out in history of the consequences of men's sins;

---

[1] Ed. Revelation (I.C.C., Edinburgh 1920), in loc.

the fact that St John the Divine uses the vivid personal phrases of divine wrath taken from the Old Testament has misled many commentators into imagining that he conceived of the wrath as personal and direct. But this is not so. An examination of some of the places where he uses wrath language should make this clear.

In 14.8, Babylon is described in the words:

ἡ ἐκ τοῦ οἴνου τοῦ θυμοῦ τῆς πορνείας αὐτῆς πεπότικεν πάντα τὰ ἔθνη.
Which hath made all the nations to drink of the wine of the wrath of her fornication.

This is the first occurrence of the phrase ὁ οἶνος τοῦ θυμοῦ, "the wine of the wrath". It is interesting to note that the phrase ὁ οἶνος τοῦ θυμοῦ τοῦ Θεοῦ in 14.10 is peculiar to Revelation; it is never found in the LXX of any of the "cup of wrath" passages in the Old Testament. Charles would excise τοῦ θυμοῦ in 14.8 as a gloss, on the grounds that in the Old Testament "the wine of the wrath" always applies to God and never to man. As a matter of fact, if we follow the M.T. this is not accurate. The M.T. of Hab. 2.16 does represent the wine of the wrath as referring to man, though we have argued that the M.T. cannot be accepted and the passage must be altered.[1] Also, even to excise τοῦ θυμοῦ in 14.8 does not exclude the reference to wrath: ἡ ἐκ τοῦ οἴνου τῆς πορνείας αὐτῆς πεπότικεν, "who hath made them drink of the wine of her fornication", would still have a wrath reference in view of John's use of οἶνος throughout his work. It would also mean excising the phrase in 18.3, as Charles admits. The phrase here certainly is used in a new sense, but St John the Divine never has any hesitation in using Old Testament language in a different *sense* if it suits his purpose. It means primarily here: "the evil influence or destiny of Rome". By her evil influence she had involved all the nations in her destiny. But there is also a reference to the divine wrath, for the wine of her fornication means the wrath process, whereby not only individuals but also whole nations are involved in the complex of sin and suffering which is the history of the Roman Empire. The thought of the wrath as a process in history is here very clear. Similarly in 14.10, it is said of him that worships the Beast:

αὐτὸς πίεται ἐκ τοῦ οἴνου τοῦ θυμοῦ τοῦ Θεοῦ τοῦ κεκερασμένου ἀκράτου ἐν

---

[1] See Appendix I.

τῷ ποτηρίῳ τῆς ὀργῆς αὐτοῦ. He also shall drink of the wine of the wrath of God, which is prepared unmixed in the cup of his anger.

Now this verse occurs in a context which refers to the downfall of Babylon, and worshipping the Beast means taking part in the idolatrous worship of the Emperor,[1] so the meaning here is that the Emperor-worshippers will share in the downfall of Rome. As invariably in the Old Testament, so here also the ποτήριον τῆς ὀργῆς "the cup of the wrath", is an historical destiny of disaster and suffering. This wrath is not eschatological, it is worked out in history. Charles explains ἄκρατον as "unmixed with water" and κεκερασμένον as "mingled with spices". The whole phrase emphasizes the terrible nature of the historical disaster which is to befall Rome. In 14.19 occurs the phrase: τὴν ληνὸν τοῦ θυμοῦ τοῦ Θεοῦ τὸν μέγαν, "the winepress, the great winepress, of the wrath of God". It occurs also in 19.15. Later on in this chapter we shall be dealing with the meaning of these two passages more fully. Here it will be sufficient to note that the phrase is unprecedented in the Bible. There are two references to the winepress of God in the Old Testament, one in Lamentations, and one in Joel,[2] but neither has a specific reference to the wrath. The phrase in both these places in Revelation must be connected with the wine of the wrath, and it must refer to the culmination of the process elsewhere described as the drinking or the pouring out of the wine of the wrath. *A propos* 16.19: δοῦναι αὐτῇ ⟨Βαβυλῶνι⟩ τὸ ποτήριον τοῦ οἴνου τοῦ θυμοῦ τῆς ὀργῆς αὐτοῦ, "to give unto her [Babylon] the cup of the wine of the fierceness of his wrath", Charles remarks that the order θυμὸς ὀργῆς is less frequent in the Old Testament than ὀργὴ θυμοῦ. In fact, the two words are used absolutely interchangeably in the LXX and there cannot be the slightest significance in the order in which they occur in the LXX (see Appendix I). For some examples of ὀργή followed by θυμός see the LXX of Num. 12.9; 32.10; Deut. 7.4; 31.17; for θυμός followed by ὀργή see LXX of Num. 14.34; 32.14; Deut. 13.17.

---

[1] I am assuming that Charles' main contentions about Revelation are correct; viz. that Babylon refers to the Roman Empire, and the worship of the Beast to the cult of the Emperor. Farrer's recent book does not seem to have established his alternative. For a more detailed working out of Charles' interpretation, see Preston and Hanson ed. Revelation (Torch Commentary, London 1949).

[2] Lam. 1.15; Joel 3.13.

These examples are taken from the Pentateuch alone. It would, however, be a mistake to assume therefore that John uses ὀργή and θυμός interchageably.[1] On the contrary, he uses θυμός very carefully only in a context of the wine of the wrath. In this actual passage the reference is certainly to the historical fall of Rome. There does not seem to be any great significance in John's adding ὀργή to θυμός as he does twice (here and 19.15); he has this much in common with the LXX that he uses the two words together to give added emphasis, not to distinguish two kinds of wrath. But we can claim that θυμός is always a sign of the wrath process worked out in history.

In chapters 17 and 18 the phrases οἶνος, θυμός, and ποτήριον occur very frequently in connection with Babylon (= the Roman Empire). In 17.2, it is said:

ἐμεθύσθησαν οἱ κατοικοῦντες τὴν γῆν ἐκ τοῦ οἴνου τῆς πορνείας αὐτῆς. They that dwell on earth were made drunken with the wine of her fornication.

This will have the same meaning as 14.8: all nations are involved in Rome's fatal destiny. In verse 4, she is described as having a golden cup in her hand (ποτήριον χρυσοῦν) with which she intoxicates all the nations. This is an echo of Jer. 51.7, where Babylon is described as "a golden cup in the Lord's hand". The meaning here is very much the same; the cup is the destiny of sin and suffering which Rome has brought upon the nations. It is very much the Lord's cup, even though Babylon wields it, but it is possible that the thought of the wrath is in the background here. This is not a parallel with the cup of Gethsemane; there, there was no reference at all to the wrath. Here the fact that the cup intoxicates shows that in the background is the conception of Rome's corrupting influence as part of the wrath process. She herself is described in verse 6 as "drunk with the blood of the saints". Drunkenness here means disaster, and it is a profound indication that by her persecution of the Church the Roman Empire was already incurring that process called the wrath of God which is to lead to her fall.[2]

---

[1] Büchsel in Kittel's *Theologisches Wörterbuch zum Neuen Testament*, article θυμός (Stuttgart 1933) makes this mistake.
[2] Notice that there the wrath is connected with the Cross; for a fuller exposition of this central conception of the Apocalypse, see below in this chapter.

In 17.3 we read:

> ἐκ τοῦ οἴνου τοῦ θυμοῦ τῆς πορνείας αὐτῆς πέπωκαν πάντα τὰ ἔθνη. For all the nations have drunk the wine of the wrath of her fornication.

(The R.V. follows one of the alternative readings given below in a footnote and translates differently.)[1] The reference is once again plainly to Rome's historical destiny in which all the nations are involved, the wrath process. In 18.6 we have an indication of the nature of the wrath process:

> ἐν τῷ ποτηρίῳ ᾧ ἐκέρασεν κεράσατε αὐτῇ διπλοῦν. In the cup which she mingled, mingle unto her double.

The wrath-sin process brings its own dreadful interest; it is akin to the uttermost farthing of the parable. Once we realize that the reference here is to the impersonal process of the wrath in history, which does as a matter of fact bring compound interest, we are relieved from the necessity of imagining that John represents God as deliberately giving Babylon twice as much punishment as she deserved. The use of ποτήριον first for Babylon's cup and then for God's cup here is not as unprecedented as it looks. There is really only one cup, God's, but he allows Babylon to use it for a period. The conception is as old as Isaiah (10.5): "Ho Assyrian, the rod of mine anger." In the historical process Rome plays the part of mistress for a while, but sooner or later that same process brings about her downfall. In 18.10 John writes: μιᾷ ὥρᾳ ἦλθεν ἡ κρίσις σου, "in one hour is thy judgement come". The word κρίσις is here used in the sense of "culmination of the process". The climax came very suddenly. It cannot mean that there was no judgement before, for the wrath-cup has been much in evidence throughout Rome's history. Note that in this book so much concerned with the Last Things, κρίσις is something that takes place entirely within history. We may therefore sum up John's use of θυμός, οἶνος, and ποτήριον by claiming that when he uses these words, he is *always* referring to the wrath process as worked out in history; he never uses

---

[1] Charles would follow a group of cursives in reading here πεπότικεν for πέπωκαν. Between these two readings there is not much to choose as far as the meaning of the passage is concerned. πεπότικεν is more powerful. ℵ and AC are plainly wrong in reading πεπτώκασι and πέπτωκαν respectively.

these words in a purely eschatological sense.¹ He does not use θυμός interchangeably with ὀργή, but he uses it chiefly to point out a reference to the historical process, and it is therefore always used in the context of the wine of the wrath, a figure which is indissolubly bound up with the manifestation of the wrath in history, and not solely at the Last Day.

So far, then, we have established that John's conception of the wrath is closely allied to Paul's. For both, the wrath is something that is worked out in history. We must now go on to show that John the Divine had an even deeper conception of the wrath than Paul, and one that reminds us of the Epistle to the Hebrews: he connected the wrath with the Cross. We must begin by examining John's use of the concept of victory. He uses νικᾶν and cognates fifteen times in all. In eleven instances it means conquest by sacrificial death (seven times in the Letters to the Churches and also 5.5; 12.11; 15.2; 21.7). Amongst these eleven instances we should notice especially 3.21:

> He that overcometh, I will give to him to sit down with me in my throne, as I also overcame, and sat down with my Father in his throne.

This is a key-passage for the understanding of the meaning of victory and war in the Apocalypse. Christians share in Christ's victory, which has been attained by His voluntary death. This is the victory obtained by the blood of the Lamb, and both "blood" and "Lamb" retain this significance throughout the book. In three passages (6.2; 11.7; 13.7) victory means conquest by violence. In all "victory" passages, Christ and the saints conquer by dying; Satan and the powers of evil by physical force. 6.2, where death is represented as coming forth "conquering and to conquer" (νικῶν καὶ ἵνα νικήσῃ),² does not fall in either category, as death is not a power of evil. This instance therefore does not affect the argument either way.³ This leaves only 17.14:

> οὗτοι μετὰ τοῦ 'Αρνίου πολεμήσουσιν καὶ τὸ 'Αρνίον νικήσει αὐτούς.
> These shall war against the Lamb, and the Lamb shall overcome them.

---

¹ This is not to say that the wrath has no reference to the end of history; but it never refers purely to that end. It is always a process; sometimes a process viewed as culminating in the End.

² I have counted these two words as once instance.

³ It should also be pointed out that Westcott and Hort bracket the phrase νικῆσαι αὐτούς in 13.7.

There seems therefore to be a strong presumption at least that this passage also must be interpreted in terms of conquest by sacrificial death; in fact it bears a reference to the victory of the Cross. On the whole this is borne out by the use of νικᾶν and cognates in the rest of the New Testament: it occurs ten times in the sense of spiritually overcoming the world or sin; once in a moral sense (Rom. 12.21, two instances counted as one); once in a juridical sense (Rom. 3.4); once of death's conquest (1 Cor. 15.55); and once of physical violence (Luke 11.22).[1] There is an interesting contrast between Revelation's use of the concept of victory and that which appears in the Book of Enoch. In Enoch 46—50 there is a passage which is in many ways reminiscent of the Christian Apocalypse. There is a picture of the Son of Man, who will destroy sinners; the cry of the righteous and their blood comes up before him. In 50.2 occurs the phrase:

And the righteous shall be victorious in the name of the Lord of Spirits.

But there is in Enoch no hint of the victory of the Cross; there victory must be understood in a literal sense. This in itself should make us hesitate about calling Revelation a purely Jewish book in spirit, as some have done.

We have then established that there is a close resemblance between Paul's conception of the wrath and that which appears in Revelation; and we have also seen that throughout the book the victory of Christ and the saints is the victory of the Cross, which is won not by killing others but by undergoing voluntary death. We must now go on to enquire how John connects the Cross with the wrath. For this purpose it is more convenient to comment on a series of passages throughout the book, taking them in the order in which they occur.

In 1.16 we have the first occurrence of the word "sword" in the book:

ἐκ τοῦ στόματος αὐτοῦ ῥομφαία δίστομος ὀξεῖα ἐκπορευομένη. And out of his mouth proceeded a sharp two-edged sword.

John uses ῥομφαία when it refers to Christ's power of judgement. He

---

[1] Oscar Cullman has noticed the peculiar use of νικᾶν in Revelation: "Dans l'Apocalypse, le verbe 'vaincre' n'a pas le sens secondaire et pejoratif de 'vaincre par la violence'; il designe, au contraire, un acte divin" (*Christ et le Temps*, Neuchâtel—Paris 1947); but see Rev. 11.7 and 13.7.

uses ῥομφαία six times[1] and μάχαιρα three times.[2] With one exception, ῥομφαία is always used of the divine sword. That exception occurs in 6.8, where it is said of death that he is given power ἀποκτεῖναι ἐν ῥομφαίᾳ, "to kill with the sword". This however seems to be an echo of Ezek. 5.12: τὸ τέταρτόν σου ἐν ῥομφαίᾳ πεσοῦνται, "and a fourth part of thee shall fall by the sword" (R.V. follows Heb. with a slightly different text). The three uses of μάχαιρα all refer to the sword of men, counting 6.4, where the man on the red horse signifies human wars. In the five instances in which ῥομφαία refers to the divine sword, it is called "the sword of his mouth" in four instances, and in the other (2.12) the reference must imply that it is "the sword of his mouth" as it plainly echoes 1.16. In two instances it is also called δίστομος, "two-edged", and in three ὀξεῖα, "sharp". All these five instances are based on Isa. 11.4, where the Messiah is described in the LXX in the words: καὶ πατάξει τὴν γῆν ἐν λόγῳ τοῦ στόματος αὐτοῦ, "and he shall smite the earth with the word of his mouth". We cannot help comparing Heb. 4.12,13. We are forbidden therefore to take ῥομφαία in a literal sense. It refers to the judgement of the Messiah; as we shall see, this is the judgement of the Cross. John uses ῥομφαία not μάχαιρα by way of indicating that the Messiah's judgement is something different from the judgement of men.[3] The rest of the New Testament on the whole tends to use μάχαιρα in a figurative sense rather than ῥομφαία. Excluding all places where "sword" occurs in its literal sense, we find five references to a figurative sword: Matt. 10.34; Luke 2.35; Rom. 13.4; Eph. 6.13; Heb. 4.12. In all these, μάχαιρα is used, except the Luke passage, where ῥομφαία occurs.

In 2.22 we read:

> Behold, I do cast her [the false prophetess] into a bed. . . . I will kill her children with death [R.V. margin, "pestilence"; Greek is θανάτῳ].

This is not symbolical language, and John seems to envisage the possibility of direct punishment by Christ. It is very similar to Paul's

---

[1] 1.16; 2.12; 2.16; 6.8; 19.15; 19.21.

[2] 6.4; 13.10 (2 counted as one); 13.14.

[3] Precisely the same conclusion holds for John's use of πόλεμος and cognates; with the exception of 16.14, divine war in Revelation always refers to the Lamb's war (2.16; 17.14; 19.11; 19.19; 20.8). And 16.14 seems to be fulfilled in 19.19. The method of the Lamb's war is the same as the method of the Lamb's victory, Cross and death.

suggestion in 1 Cor. 11.30, that some have died and some are sick as a punishment for misbehaviour at the Eucharist. It is not at all incompatible with a much deeper conception of the mode of the divine judgement. We have already commented on the great significance of 3.21 where the victory of the martyrs is directly associated with the victory of Christ, and both are shown to be nothing else but the death of the Messiah on the Cross, a death reproduced and continued in the death of Christians under persecution. The same thought is expressed less clearly in 2.26,27. There, "he that overcometh" is to rule as Christ rules over the Gentiles: ὡς κἀγὼ εἴληφα παρὰ τοῦ Πατρός μου, "as I also have received of my Father".[1] All this language is descriptive of the victory of the Cross, and that victory is itself a judgement, hence the reference to Ps. 2.8,9, where the Messiah is represented as judging the Gentiles. Christ had received this position of judge from the Father through the Cross and Resurrection and that is the way in which the martyrs also are to receive it. John's meaning is not exhausted by the simple scheme: first death, then victorious judgement. That is the order in which he represents it at the end of his book, where Christ reigns a thousand years with the saints. But that reign is only a symbol expressed in temporal terms of the deeper significance, which is that victory *is* judgement; the Cross *is* the treading of the vintage of divine judgement. We shall find traces of this profound conception as we go through the book.

5.5–6 presents us with one such instance: here in verse 5 we read:

ἰδοὺ ἐνίκησεν ὁ Λέων ὁ ἐκ τῆς φυλῆς Ἰουδά . . . ἀνοῖξαι τὸ βιβλίον. Behold, the Lion that is of the tribe of Judah . . . hath overcome to open the book.

The reference is to Hos. 5.14: "For I will be unto Ephraim as a lion, and as a young lion to the house of Judah: I even I, will tear and go away; I will carry off and there shall be none to deliver." This is a threat of dreadful judgement, and the phrase ἀνοῖξαι τὸ βιβλίον, "to open the book", also refers to judgement in Rev. 5.5. The book contains the judgements that are to come. Then in verse 6 we find that he who was described as this devouring lion is Ἀρνίον ὡς ἐσφαγμένον "a Lamb . . . as though it had been slain". It is he who judges. The contrast with Hosea could not be more acute. In the Old Testament

---

[1] Cf. also 12.11.

THE WRATH IN THE APOCALYPSE

God judges by inflicting suffering; in the Apocalypse he judges by accepting suffering. So the judgements that follow in chapter 6 are judgements of the Cross, judgements precipitated by the fact that the Lamb is still being slain in the world in the persons of his persecuted followers.[1] This "realized" interpretation of John's conception of judgement is borne out by the fact that, as we have seen, when John proceeds to give us examples of the wrath and the judgement of God, they occur in history; they are the actual events of the fall of Rome and consequent collapse of the Emperor cult. These events of the fall of Rome and the rest John interprets as the judgements of the Cross. It is because the Empire has rejected and persecuted the Messiah in the persons of his saints that this judgement comes upon it, in history. In 6.11 we find a hint that what is happening is a process of judgement; for the martyrs are encouraged to wait a short time: ἕως πληρωθῶσιν καὶ οἱ σύνδουλοι αὐτῶν, "until their fellow-servants also ... should be fulfilled", cf. Matt. 23.32.

Then in 6.15,17 comes what is perhaps the deepest insight concerning the doctrine of the wrath of God which we find anywhere in the Bible. It is also the passage which has perhaps given most offence to modern editors. The kings of the earth and all the rich and mighty hide themselves in the caves and the rocks, exclaiming:

> πέσετε ἐφ' ἡμᾶς καὶ κρύψατε ἡμᾶς ἀπὸ προσώπου τοῦ καθημένου ἐπὶ τοῦ θρόνου καὶ ἀπὸ τῆς ὀργῆς τοῦ Ἀρνίου, ὅτι ἦλθεν ἡ ἡμέρα ἡ μεγάλη τῆς ὀργῆς αὐτῶν, καὶ τίς δύναται σταθῆναι; Fall on us, and hide us from the face of him that sitteth upon the throne, and from the wrath of the Lamb: for the great day of their wrath is come; and who is able to stand?

Charles comments that several editors have excised the words "and from the wrath of the Lamb" on the ground that they are out of keeping with the character of the Lamb in the rest of the book. Charles defends them because in Judaism the Messiah was expected to judge the world, and he compares the Book of Enoch. Now it would

---

[1] C. H. Dodd in *The Interpretation of the Fourth Gospel*, pp. 230 ff., has an interesting discussion of the significance of the name "Lamb" for the Messiah. Its general tenor is to suggest that it was not so unprecedented and startling a title as might at first appear, and that the Messiah might well be thought of as both a Lamb and a Lion together. But the significance of St John the Divine's use of the symbol of the slaughtered Lamb still remains, whatever the precise significance of "Lamb" in the Fourth Gospel.

certainly be a mistake to excise the phrase. For one thing, it is very difficult to imagine who would have inserted it. If a reference to the Lamb were needed, ἀπὸ προσώπου τοῦ καθημένου ἐπὶ τοῦ θρόνου καὶ τοῦ ᾽Αρνίου, "from the face of him that sitteth upon the throne and from the Lamb", would have been quite sufficient. Also, if the phrase is omitted αὐτῶν in verse 17 must be changed to αὐτοῦ, as is indeed read by some MSS. But Charles is not on such sure grounds in comparing the Book of Enoch. In several apocalyptic works we read of the judgement of the Messiah, but nowhere in any of them is anything said about the wrath of the Messiah. Still less do we meet so astonishing a phrase as "the wrath of the Lamb". Its very incongruity should make us look at it more carefully. Wrath in the rest of the book always means "the working out in history of the consequences of sin", and this is undoubtedly the meaning it has here. But it is the wrath of the *Lamb*, the Lamb who is to us the living representative of the sacrificial love of God. "The Lamb" is no *epitheton ornans* in a writer like John. So the "wrath of the Lamb" is here the working out in history of the consequences of the rejection and crucifixion of the Messiah. It is extremely significant that Luke represents our Lord as using this same quotation from Hos. 10.8 to describe precisely the long-term consequences to the Jews of their rejection of the Messiah (Luke 23.30). The rest of chapter 6 in Revelation gives a description of various judgements which, as we have seen, are precipitated by the Cross, not only the historical crucifixion on Golgotha, but its continuance in the sufferings of the martyr Church. So we have here no throw-back to a more primitive conception of God, but the expression in the language of myth and symbol of the profound truth that the power and judgement of Christ are manifested in the disastrous consequences working out in history of his rejection by the Jews and the persecution of his followers by the authorities of the Roman Empire. The wrath here is not purely eschatological; it is a process, stretching from the Cross to the Parousia.

We have already noticed a link between the third Gospel and the Apocalypse. Another link between Luke and John occurs in 11.16–19, which affords a striking parallel to Acts 4.23–31. In the Acts passage we have a prayer made by the Church when it was being persecuted by the Jews; in Revelation it is a prayer made by the heavenly host after the persecution, death, and resurrection of the two witnesses.[1] The two passages have in common a quotation from the Psalms which describes the commotion or anger of the Gentiles. The two passages are too long to quote in full, but if we analyse their contents in parallel columns we find the following resemblances:

Acts 4.23–31	*Rev.* 11.17–19
The faithful are in prayer.	The heavenly host prays.
Invocation of God as Creator.	Invocation of God as omnipotent.
Quotation from Psalms.	Quotation from Psalms.
Reference to the Crucifixion (verses 26, 27).	Reference to God's wrath and judgement.
It was according to God's will (verse 28).	
Prayer for power and healing.	

In each of the two columns, except for the prayer for pardon and healing in Acts 4.29, 30, there is always something corresponding. Swete[2] has noticed the resemblances, but does not drive the point home. He says: "With a wider outlook the Seer of the Apocalypse sees in it [the quotation from the Psalms] the hostility of the world against the Church... the futile violence of men is answered by the effective judgement of God." The point here is that the crucifixion in the Acts passage is represented by the ὀργή and judgement of God in the

---

[1] Something must be said about the Old Testament text quoted. Acts 4.25 quotes: ἵνα τί ἐφρύαξαν ἔθνη; Revelation 11.18 has καὶ τὰ ἔθνη ὠργίσθησαν. Acts is certainly quoting the LXX of Ps. 2.2, which is ἐφρύαξαν ἔθνη. On the other hand the Hebrew of Ps. 2.1 is רָגְשׁוּ. It is possible that the author of Revelation is echoing Ps. 99 (98).1; where the LXX runs κύριος ἐβασίλευσεν, ὀργιζέσθωσαν λαοί. In that Psalm ὀργιζέσθωσαν is a possible, though not an accurate translation of the Hebrew יִרְגְּזוּ; some such word as ταρασσέσθωσαν would be a more accurate rendering. Charles thinks that here John is echoing Ps. 99.1, but also has Ps. 2.1 in mind. Swete thinks that here John is referring primarily to Ps. 2.1. It is quite possible of course that John was translating from the Hebrew direct, in which case we must admit that ὠργίσθησαν is probably a translation of יִרְגְּזוּ in Ps. 99 rather than of רָגְשׁוּ in Ps. 2. There is also the possibility that he had a different version of the Septuagint.

[2] H. B. Swete, ed. the Apocalypse of St John (London 1909), in loc.

Revelation passage. What Swete seems to ignore is that the two passages are referring to the *same* process of events, but Acts looks at it from the point of view of those who live immediately after the crucifixion, and John looks at it from the view point of the end of history. John is not referring, as Swete seems to imagine, to a separate act of God's wrath. The crucifixion and its consequences in history are the means by which that wrath is manifested. The shaking of the place where the disciples prayed in Acts and the earthquake in Revelation both signify the fulfilment of the prayer. 13.10 and 14.12, with their repeated ὧδέ ἐστιν ἡ ὑπομονὴ καὶ ἡ πίστις τῶν ἁγίων, "Here is the patience and the faith of the saints," give us an insight into the nature of the wrath process. This is especially emphasized in 13.10:

> If any man is for captivity, into captivity he goeth; if any man shall kill with the sword, with the sword must he be killed.

This is the legal retributive process of the wrath to which those who reject Christ are abandoned. The patience of the saints, and also their faith, consists in understanding the nature of this process. Here is another link with Paul, who suggests in several places that faith is needed to understand the wrath as well as the love of God. τὴν πίστιν Ἰησοῦ, "the faith of Jesus", in 14.12, therefore, means not just "faith concerning Jesus" but "the same faith that Jesus manifested in his life and death"; cf. Gal. 3.22. The word ὑπομονή, "patience", is frequently in the Apocalypse connected with suffering as Christ suffered; cf. 2.3,10,13,19; 3.10. So both πίστις, "faith", and ὑπομονή, "patience", are connected with the process of the wrath, a process manifested in the sufferings of the saints.

Chapter 13 also introduces us to the Rival Dispensation of Satan, a theme which we have observed in other parts of the New Testament; but this rival dispensation is worked out in greater detail here than anywhere else. The theme of the rival dispensation of Satan has its origin no doubt in the Old Testament, especially in the Book of Daniel, where the king who made himself a god, Antiochus IV Epiphanes, is portrayed as the arch-enemy of the true God and his people. We find the themes taken up to some extent in the Apocrypha, especially in the Books of Maccabees. It also occurs in Judith, where Holophernes no

THE WRATH IN THE APOCALYPSE

doubt represents the Greek power and even Epiphanes in particular; cf. Judith 3.8:

And it had been given unto him to destroy all the gods of the land.

Compare with this Rev. 6.2; cf. also Judith 6.2 with Rev. 13.4, and see the Greek Add. to Esther 13.14. The Dragon, the First Beast, and the Second Beast offer a sort of Satanic Trinity, Satan becomes incarnate in the figure of Nero Redivivus, the first great persecutor of the Church whom John believed to be in some way about to return soon. Nero Redivivus even has a death and resurrection (cf. 13.3 with 5.6). Satan produces a world-church, with a distinguishing mark akin to baptism (13.16). There is not only the divine μυστήριον, "mystery", referred to in 10.7, but there is also a Satanic μυστήριον belonging to Babylon in 17.5. Finally the Dragon (who is Satan) is actually described as ἔχων θυμὸν μέγαν, "having great wrath", in 12.12 and in 12.17 as ὠργίσθη, "waxed wroth". But here is a significant difference: the Dragon is described as having θυμός without any reference to the historical process which a connection with the "wine of the wrath" would imply, and the verb "to be angry" is used of him, which John, in common with all the writers of the New Testament, scrupulously avoids using of God. The Rival Dispensation of Satan is worked out in such detail in order that we may be able to see for ourselves the essential difference between the methods of Satan, who operates by inflicting suffering, and of God, who operates by accepting suffering. It is not for nothing that John calls them the Beast and the Lamb respectively.[1]

We next approach two related passages, which on the surface would seem among the most difficult for the modern Christian to accept because of their apparently ruthless description of God's wrath and judgement. But closer examination reveals them as in fact very closely related to the Cross. The first is 14.14–20. In these verses there seems to be some confusion; there are too many angels, and the phrase καὶ ἄλλος ἄγγελος ἐξῆλθεν, "and another angel came out", is repeated three times. Charles suggests that verses 15–17 are an editorial insertion after John's death intended to make the passage conform more closely to Joel 3.13; certainly this conjecture removes the confusion.

---

[1] The significance of the Rival Dispensation has been worked out in greater detail by Preston and Hanson, op. cit., pp. 96–7.

But even if those verses are retained, the main significance of the passage is not altered. Farrer[1] would explain 15–17 as giving us two harvests, the wheat-harvest being the harvest of the faithful, and the vintage being the harvest of the unfaithful. But in the New Testament harvest of any sort is a symbol of judgement, and judgement implies a separation between the good and the bad. To have two harvests ruins the symbolism. There is an interesting parallel here with Mark 4.29:

ὅταν παραδοῖ ὁ καρπός, εὐθὺς ἀποστέλλει τὸ δρέπανον, ὅτι παρέστηκεν ὁ θερισμός. But when the fruit is ripe, straightway he putteth forth the sickle, because the harvest is come.

Here there is no thought of two harvests. The rest of the New Testament always uses the figure of the wheat harvest. John deliberately changes it to the vintage in order no doubt to emphasize the conection with the wine of the wrath. Then in verses 19, 20 the strange words:

καὶ ἐτρύγησεν ⟨sc. ὁ ἄγγελος⟩ τὴν ἄμπελον τῆς γῆς καὶ ἔβαλεν εἰς τὴν ληνὸν τοῦ θυμοῦ τοῦ Θεοῦ τὸν μέγαν· καὶ ἐπατήθη ἡ ληνὸς ἔξωθεν τῆς πόλεως καὶ ἐξῆλθεν αἷμα ἐκ τῆς ληνοῦ ... And [the angel] gathered the vintage of the earth, and cast it into the winepress, the great winepress of the wrath of God, and the winepress was trodden without the city and there came out blood from the winepress ...

The angel seems undoubtedly to be the Son of Man of verse 14; so important a task would hardly be given to anyone else.[2] The omission of verses 15–17 makes this reference clearer. The passage is founded on Joel 3.13 with its reference to the wine-press as the symbol of judgement; and also Isa. 63.1–6. This latter passage, as we have seen, is a terrible picture of God coming, possibly from Edom, with his garments sprinkled with the blood of his enemies. What does John mean by using these two figures? It is Christ who tramples the wine-press of the wrath. That wine-press means nothing else than the effects of the rejection of the Messiah working themselves out in history. The image of vintage emphasizes the conception of a process. Again, the wine-press is trodden ἔξωθεν τῆς πόλεως, "without the city". Charles takes this as a proleptic reference to the heavenly Jerusalem that is

---

[1] Farrer, *A Rebirth of Images*, p. 152–3 (London 1949).
[2] Farrer, op. cit., in loc., agrees.

later described as descending. But he adds that it may refer to the historical Jerusalem, pointing out that in Jewish tradition the last judgement was to take place just outside Jerusalem (cf. Joel 3.2,12). But is it not more likely that "without the city" refers to the Crucifixion? Compare with this Heb. 13.10–16, where Jesus is described as suffering "without the gate" and Christians are urged to "go forth unto him without the camp, bearing his reproach". Swete gives this cross-reference, but does not draw out its significance. On this interpretation then, the treading of the wine-press of the wrath of God refers primarily to the judgement of the Cross perpetuated no doubt in the martyrdom of the Church. Further light is thrown on this interpretation by the second passage, Rev. 19.11–16. Here Christ is described as:

περιβεβλημένος ἱμάτιον βεβαμμένον αἵματι . . . καὶ αὐτὸς πατεῖ τὴν ληνὸν τοῦ οἴνου τοῦ θυμοῦ τῆς ὀργῆς τοῦ Θεοῦ τοῦ παντοκράτορος. Arrayed in a garment dipped in blood . . . and he treadeth the winepress of the fierceness of the wrath of Almighty God.

(R.V. follows a different reading and translates "sprinkled with blood".) This passage is founded on the same two passages and we find the same implicit reference to the judgement of the Cross. As in the first passage, we must ask: "What city?" so here we must ask: "In whose blood is Christ's robe dipped?" Charles claims it cannot be his own, since he is here Slayer and not slain, Judge and not victim. The blood cannot be that of the nations, since their death is recounted later. It must therefore be that of the Parthian hosts, a reference to whose overthrow has been lost. This is a desperate expedient. In order to answer the question satisfactorily we must go back to those principles which we have seen to be implicit in John's conception of the wrath throughout the book. Christ here treads the winepress of the wrath; this is a reference to events of history. It is Christ who treads it, therefore it is the consequences of the Cross that are working themselves out. More than that, this is a picture of the victory of Christ *and his Saints*. In 19.14 we read:

And the armies which are in heaven followed him.

Swete would refer this to the angelic hosts, but he seems to have overlooked 17.14, which refers to the victory of the saints and uses the very phrase we find in 19.16: Κύριος κυρίων καὶ Βασιλεὺς βασιλέων, "King of kings and Lord of lords." They must be the martyr hosts (notice also they are clad in pure linen, a mark of the triumphant martyr). Now we have seen how Christ and the martyrs triumph in the rest of the book: they triumph through the blood of the Lamb, through the all-prevailing death of Christ. But here is a reference to blood. Christ's robe is βεβαμμένον αἵματι, "dipped in blood". Surely it must be his own blood? The word βεβαμμένον is not without significance. The point is that it is not suitable to the passage Isa. 63.3.[1] On the strength of this, Swete would read in Rev. 19.13 instead of βεβαμμένον the word ῥεραμμένον, which has some MSS. support here. But this is quite unnecessary. John never quotes the Old Testament slavishly; he always adapts it for his own purposes, and here may he not be thinking of the Messiah's baptism of blood? Compare Mark 10.38:

> δύνασθε πιεῖν τὸ ποτήριον ὃ ἐγὼ πίνω, ἢ τὸ βάπτισμα ὃ ἐγὼ βαπτίζομαι βαπτισθῆναι; Are ye able to drink the cup that I drink? Or to be baptized with the baptism that I am baptized with?

In the difference between Jahveh's garments being sprinkled with blood and Christ's robe being dipped in blood lies all the difference between the Old Testament and the New Testament, the difference between the conception of God judging his enemies by shedding their blood and the conception of his judging them by shedding his blood for them. Just as in the Marcan passage there is a reference to the ποτήριον, "the cup", so here there is an echo of the wine of the wrath figure. But whereas in the Gospel the Cross is thought of in its aspect of salvation attained through suffering, here it is thought of as an act of judgement upon those who rejected that salvation. Swete comes near to this interpretation: "He [the author] could hardly have failed to think also of the 'blood of the Lamb' which was shed in the act of treading the enemy underfoot", and he quotes Hippolytus and Origen as interpreting the ἱμάτιον, "the garment", as Christ's flesh. He adds, however: "But this view, if admitted, must be kept subordinate to the other. In this vision Christ is not presented as the Redeemer, but as the

---

[1] There the Hebrew is: וְיֵז נִצְחָם עַל־בְּגָדַי. The LXX as we have it does not offer an exact translation, but some MSS. render נִצְחָם by ἐρραντίσθη or ἐρράνθη.

Judge and Warrior." Here is the unfortunate "either-or" which commentators seem to have derived from Hosea and the author of Psalm 85. They will present God as either loving or angry, Christ as either the Redeemer or the Judge. They do not seem to be able to attain the height of John's thought, which sees him as both the Redeemer and Judge. Not one after the other, but one because of the other. In these two passages we do have indeed a picture of judgement, but it is the judgement of the Cross. It is not intended to tell us that Christ and the saints will some time in the future conquer and judge their enemies, but to tell us that by virtue of the victory won once for all on the Cross, he and his faithful followers "are more than conquerors", and that this applies to all post-incarnational history, that is, to the time from the Cross to the Parousia. Once accept the full implications of John's symbolism, and he proves far more of a Christian than most of his editors permit him to be.[1]

In 16.9 men are described as "blaspheming the name of God". Blasphemy in Revelation refers always to a denial of the sovereignty of God. Thus in 13.1 and 17.3 the "names of blasphemy" are the imperial titles, such as "*dominus et deus noster*", which attribute divinity to the emperor. So here in 16.9 men blaspheme God by not acknowledging that the plagues from which they are suffering have their origin in the divine call. Similarly in 9.20 where it is said that men have not repented, it is added that they go on worshipping idols. Hence "giving God glory" in 16.9 must mean recognizing the working of the divine wrath in the processes of history. This is important, for it shows that for John, as for Paul, faith was necessary for an understanding of the wrath, and that what John describes as plagues and the visitation of wrath might seem to one who had not faith to be the ordinary course of human history. In 19.9 John refers to the marriage feast of the Lamb: compare with this Luke 14.15,17,[2] where the king makes a feast, and contrast with it the grim feast of Rev. 19.17. In the Synoptic parable, the feast means no doubt the rejection of the Jews and the accession of the Gentiles. In Revelation, the overthrow of Rome is closely associated with

---

[1] Most of this paragraph has already appeared in *Theology*, Vol. XLIX, No. 311, May 1946; cf. also Preston and Hanson, op. cit., pp 37–8, 104–5 (2nd ed. 1951).

[2] The Synoptic parallel is Matt. 22.2–10; Matthew does not use δεῖπνον but he does call it a marriage-feast (γάμοι) which Luke does not.

the marriage-feast of the Lamb. The two uses of "feast" in Rev. 19 show the juxtaposition of love and judgement. Similarly in 21.9 it is one of the Angels of the Seven Vials of the Wrath who shows John the New Jerusalem. The last words of the book, 22.18,19, seem utterly incongruous with the extremely profound conception of wrath and judgement which we have traced throughout the book, and very much incline one to accept Charles' suggestion that they are the addition of an editor or later copyist. Assuming that these verses are not from John's pen, we may sum up the concept of the wrath of God in the Apocalypse by saying that in this book the wrath always refers to the process of history wherein those who reject the saving love of God are involved. It is never purely eschatological, though it often looks towards the end of the process. Similarly the divine victory is always achieved through death and suffering, as contrasted with the satanic victory, which is achieved through physical violence and trickery. Moreover, wrath and judgement are essentially connected with the Cross; the Messiah judges by dying. Paul's conception of the process of law and wrath can be clearly traced in Revelation, and in this book also faith is needed in order to discern the wrath. In short, the concept of the wrath in the Book of Revelation is more profoundly Christian than that which is found in any other part of the New Testament.

A SUMMARY OF THE NEW TESTAMENT EVIDENCE CONCERNING THE WRATH OF GOD

After reviewing all the evidence about the wrath of God in the New Testament, we should be in a position to see the doctrine in perspective. It seems to resolve itself into five main assertions:

1. The concept of the wrath of God is found in the Pauline Epistles, the Epistle to the Hebrews, the Fourth Gospel, and in Revelation. In all these there is a consistent conception of the wrath to be found, which views it as primarily the consequences of men's sins worked out in history and consummated in the Parousia, and that Parousia is conceived of as a showing up of the real state of affairs and not merely a passing of a sentence. The sphere of law, sin, curse, and wrath is that in which all who do not believe Christ live.

2. The Wrath is connected with the Cross—only occasionally in

Paul, more clearly in Hebrews, by implication in the Johannine writings, and most essentially in Revelation. The wrath is both revealed on the Cross as the most terrible consequences of the most terrible sin, and also the rejection and crucifixion of the Messiah (and subsequent persecution of the Church) effect in themselves judgement on those who brought them about; to such people the Cross is that which concludes them under the wrath.

3. In the rest of the New Testament (Synoptics, Acts, Pastorals, James, and 1 Peter) it is constantly implied that unbelievers are in the sphere of sin, law, and curse. It is also implied that this is the sphere of impersonal judgement. In view of this, Dodd's statement that the concept of wrath does not appear in the teaching of Jesus[1] seems questionable. The essential idea of judgement as an impersonal process can be traced in much of his teaching.

4. There are a few exceptions to this common New Testament conception of the wrath as an impersonal process in history; e.g. 1 Cor. 10.22; where the possibility that Christ may be provoked is allowed; also 1 Cor. 11.30 and Rev. 2.22,23, where "direct action" judgement is envisaged. Also in Jude and 2 Peter the apocalyptic tradition of external, eschatological judgement appears, and the main New Testament tradition is ignored.

5. Negatively, we may say that in the New Testament the wrath is never appeased or propitiated; neither is God or Christ ever described as angry or as being angry, nor is there any place in which a tension appears between the love and the wrath of God.[2] (But see p. 92.)

[1] C. H. Dodd, ed. Romans (London 1932), pp. 20–4.
[2] The one passage in the New Testament that seems to be an exception to this is Rom. 11.22–3, where, it is to be noted, there is no explicit word for the divine wrath. But Paul does contrast the χρηστότης and the ἀποτομία of God. The former is shown in his forgiving the Gentiles, the latter in the fact that most of the Jews have "fallen away". Paul speaks of "breaking off" the boughs that represent the Jews, but what he means is that they hardened themselves. It was not something that God did, it was something that God suffered them to do (see Rom 9.22). But his goodness was shown in accepting the Gentiles in Christ. Hence the ἀποτομία is shown in the impersonal process of moral retribution and the χρηστότης in active personal love. Moreover the very purpose of the ἀποτομία is to show great mercy to the Jews in the end (Rom. 11.31). Hence there is not really in this passage a contrast between the personal wrath and the personal love of God such as we find in Hosea. We might almost borrow the language of modern prophylactic medicine and say that according to Paul God is the same God to all men, but his character "takes" differently on men, to those who accept his mercy he appears as loving; to those who refuse it he appears as stern, because they have chosen the path of wrath.

THE WRATH OF THE LAMB

With the exception of one faint indication in 1 Cor. 10.13, the wrath is never disciplinary. The wrath is not an attitude of God, but a condition of men.[1]

[1] Vocabulary: ὀργή for the wrath of God is used 29 times in the New Testament. (Paul 18; Synoptics 3: Hebrews 1 (in Old Testament quotation); Revelation 6; John 1). ζῆλος is used once in Hebrews; παραζηλῶ once in Paul. προσοχθίζω and παραπικρασμός (not counting repetitions, including cognates) are used once each in Hebrews in quotation from the Old Testament, ἀγανακτεῖν once of our Lord in Mark. θυμός is used for the wrath 9 times (Paul 1, Revelation 8).

8

THE WRATH OF THE LAMB AS AN ELEMENT IN CHRISTIAN DOCTRINE

THE rise of higher criticism of the Bible in the nineteenth century caused most theologians to revise fundamentally their approach to many aspects of Christian doctrine. The concept of the wrath of God is certainly one about which the higher criticism has caused a great deal of doubt and confusion. Even to-day, a hundred years after the first impact of the new approach in England at least, there are many well-educated Christians who would find it very difficult to say what place they would give to the concept of the wrath of God in their system of thought and belief. So we may take the middle of the nineteenth century as a convenient point from which to begin a survey of what scholars have said about the wrath of God. To go back earlier is to step back into the same atmosphere, as far as the approach to the Bible is concerned, as the Fathers and the Reformers breathe; it would be a valuable investigation, but is outside the scope of this work.

In the year 1859, Albert Ritschl published a Latin treatise *De Ira Dei*.[1] In it he reviews briefly the Biblical evidence about the wrath of God, an enterprise which does not seem to have been repeated till this present work. It is a valuable attempt to tackle what must at the time have been a thorny question, but it suffers from being on the whole pre-critical, though not literalistic. He is perhaps the first to put forward the theory, maintained as we have seen by later scholars without further examination, that the cause of the divine wrath against Israel is always a falling away from the Covenant (p. 19), but he had at least the excuse that in his day the distinction between JE, of which this theory is not true, and D, of which it is, had not yet been made. He interprets almost all references to the wrath in the New Testament as eschatological, another tendency which appears in later scholars; this involves some explaining away of passages where it seems to be realized (pp. 16f.); e.g. 1 Thess. 2.16, about which he uses a phrase that has more than a hint of realized eschatology in it: "*Ira finali, quae iam tunc efficax esse coeperit*"—"Eschatological wrath, which even then

[1] Bonn 1859.

began to be effective". So also Eph. 2.3: φύσει τέκνα ὀργῆς "by nature children of wrath", is explained as "*destinatos ad iram*", "destined to wrath", and in John 3.36: ἡ ὀργὴ τοῦ Θεοῦ μένει ἐπ' αὐτόν, "the wrath of God abideth on him", μένει is interpreted as "impends". All this explaining away is occasioned by a well-intentioned desire to avoid the notion (orthodox in his day) of God having already condemned the great mass of mankind to feel forever the effects of his wrath. He very rightly objects to the thought of Christ propitiating the wrath of God (p. 20). In a later work[1] he definitely stigmatizes the concept of God's wrath as one that ought not to be included in a scheme of Christian theology, and he points out that Paul "clothes the idea of God's wrath against those who are lost in the guise of a perpetual determination of his will, all the characteristics of a passing emotion being stripped away". He has here come near to the notion of the impersonal wrath which does form the centre of Paul's thought about the wrath. On the other hand, both here and in his early work Ritschl insists that the wrath of God must be thought of as being primarily disciplinary. In his Latin treatise he describes it as "*castigatio a patre immissa*", "chastening sent from the Father" (p. 23), and in the later work[2] he says: "Every evil they [mankind] experience even in consequence of sin should be reckoned, never as a destructive penalty, but as a means of education." As we have been, the overwhelming testimony of both Old and New Testaments is against this view of the wrath.

McLeod Campbell, writing a few years later than Ritschl's first work, makes a fine protest against the suggestion that Christ's sufferings are penal.[3] But he is not free from the mistaken idea that the wrath of God represents an attitude of God. Christ, he says on p. 117, interposed "himself between sinners and the consequences of that righteous wrath". He seems here to distinguish between the wrath (which he thinks of as an attitude of God) and the consequences of wrath, which are some sort of suffering. The New Testament knows nothing of such a distinction. The wrath in the case of sinners *is* the consequences of

---

[1] A. Ritschl, *The Christian Doctrine of Justification and Reconciliation*, Vol. III (E. 71, Edinburgh 1900), p. 323.

[2] Op. cit., p. 323.

[3] John McLeod Campbell, *The Nature of the Atonement* (London 1872), p. 222.

sin; Christ bore the consequences of sin, but in him they were not wrath. He goes on to say: "That is accorded to divine justice which is its due, and could alone satisfy it." Here we have the suggestion, much more prominent in Dale, that God's justice had somehow to be propitiated or vindicated, though McLeod Campbell, unlike Dale, does not speak of satisfying or propitiating the wrath of God, only the justice of God.

Dale[1] has much to say about the wrath, since his work was written in order to vindicate a substitutionary doctrine of the Atonement. He does deal to some extent with the wrath in the Old Testament. For example, he says (p. 167): "The Jews never attribute to Jehovah the unreasoning and unreasonable passion which was ascribed to heathen deities." This can hardly be maintained if the implications of passages such as 1 Sam. 6.19 and 2 Sam. 6.6,7 are faced honestly. What is significant is the efforts of later writers to modify them. When he treats of the New Testament, Dale uses phrases which, no matter how natural in the context, are not actually found in the New Testament, and therefore do insensibly give a misleading twist to his account of the wrath. Thus à propos Rom. 1.18 he writes (p. 232): "St Paul's intention was to demonstrate that the whole world is exposed to the divine wrath and that if men are to be saved, that wrath must be somehow averted." Now there is nothing in the Greek of the New Testament which corresponds exactly to either of the two English phrases, "exposed to the wrath" and "the wrath must be averted". This phrase "exposed to the wrath" occurs again on p. 242 and on p. 257 it is in this sense that he interprets Eph. 2.3: τέκνα φύσει ὀργῆς, "by nature children of wrath". In this respect he joins hands with T. K. Abbott, who, as we have seen (p. 103, *supra*), interprets the phrase as meaning a possible contingency later to be averted by love. Another phrase not found in the New Testament[2] but used by Dale is "provoked the Divine anger" (e.g. p. 255), and on p. 242 he does not hesitate to describe God as hostile to us, a step which Paul scrupulously avoids.[3] It is in accord with this treatment of the wrath that Dale should insist (p. 327f.) that the wrath in the New Testament is exclusively eschatological; he proves this by

---

[1] R. W. Dale, *The Atonement* (London 1884).
[2] With the exception of a hint in 1 Cor. 10.13.
[3] But not auct. Ep. James; see James 4.4.

quoting the more eschatological passages in the New Testament and ignoring the others. In fact, Dale's conception of the wrath is much more like the Old Testament conception than the New Testament one, except that he leaves no room for the impersonal element in the wrath which is found in the Old Testament.

In his conclusions (p. 432) Dale uses language about the death of Christ which has been echoed by many later theologians[1]; he says that the death of Christ was the revelation or the vindication of the righteousness of God. Now it is quite true that Paul does view Christ's death (and resurrection) as a revelation of God's righteousness, but does that revelation necessarily mean a vindication in the sense that "justice had to be done"? The point really turns on the translation of the phrase (Rom. 3:25): ἔνδειξις τῆς δικαιοσύνης τοῦ Θεοῦ, "to show his righteousness" (R.V.). Dale and his school would translate it "a vindication of the justice of God". But an alternative translation is "a revelation of the righteousness of God", and an examination of the passages in which this sort of language occurs strengthens the case for the alternative translation. What Dale has overlooked is the intimate connection in Paul's mind between God's righteousness and the way of faith. We have already had occasion to notice again and again in the New Testament that the sphere of law is the sphere of wrath; therefore the sphere of love is the sphere of faith, and God's righteousness is not a legal righteousness. In the background of Paul's mind is always this contrast between Law and faith, wrath and love. Thus in Romans 1.17 he says: δικαιοσύνη γὰρ Θεοῦ ἐν αὐτῷ ⟨εὐαγγελίῳ⟩ ἀποκαλύπτεται, "for therein is revealed a righteousness of faith", which must mean the "strange, non-legal righteousness of God" not "the abstract justice of God". It is a faith context. Again Rom. 3.5 at first sight seems to support Dale's view: our unrighteousness commends God's righteousness. God who is not unrighteous, "brings wrath to bear". But Paul goes on to argue that God has as a matter of fact forgiven us all. Hence his first concluding us under sin and then forgiving us does not really "vindicate his justice", rather the reverse; but it can be said to reveal his peculiar righteousness, a righteousness that is not by works, but of faith. He could have vindicated his justice by leaving us in sin; he

[1] Cf. Tasker, op. cit., p. 20

chose to reveal his righteousness by sending his Son to live the life and die the death of faith. Rom. 3.21 with its emphasis on the unlegal character of God's righteousness supports this. The most crucial passage is Rom. 3.25:

ὃν ⟨Χριστὸν⟩ προέθετο ὁ Θεὸς ἱλαστήριον διὰ πίστεως ἐν τῷ αὐτοῦ αἵματι εἰς ἔνδειξιν τῆς δικαιοσύνης αὐτοῦ διὰ τὴν πάρεσιν τῶν προγεγονότων ἁμαρτημάτων ἐν τῇ ἀνοχῇ τοῦ Θεοῦ πρὸς τὴν ἔνδειξιν τῆς δικαιοσύνης αὐτοῦ ἐν τῷ νῦν καιρῷ, εἰς τὸ εἶναι αὐτὸν δίκαιον καὶ δικαιοῦντα τὸν ἐκ πίστεως Ἰησοῦ. Whom [i.e. Christ] God set forth to be a propitiation through faith, by his blood, to show his righteousness, because of the passing over of the sins done aforetime, in the forebearance of God; for the showing, I say, of his righteousness at this present season; that he might himself be just, and the justifier of him that hath faith in Jesus.

It may be best to tabulate our comments on this:

1. The meaning of ἱλαστήριον, "propitiation", is a very much vexed question into which we have not space to enter here. But it may be said that there is no necessity in this passage to take it in any other sense than "means of removing sin", and this translation has excellent authority behind it.[1]

2. Wherever the phrase ἔνδειξις τῆς δικαιοσύνης, "to show his righteousness", is used in this passage, it is closely connected with forgiveness or faith. God's justice was certainly not vindicated by the πάρεσις τῶν ἁμαρτημάτων, "the passing over of the sins", nor by Gods ἀνοχή. Besides if God's justice was vindicated in the death of Christ, whatever that transaction may be described as, it cannot be called the ἀνοχὴ τοῦ Θεοῦ, "the forebearance of God".

3. There is no word in the Greek that can be honestly translated as "vindicated"; the Greek for that would be ἐκδικεῖν (cf. Luke 18.6–8).[2]

Other passages which support the translation "righteousness" rather than "justice", and "revelation" rather than "vindication", are 1 Cor. 1.30; 2 Cor. 5.21, where we can hardly be described as being "the justice of God"; Phil. 3.9. The only place where δικαιοσύνη

---

[1] Cf. Rashdall's discussion in *The Idea of the Atonement in Christian Theology*, pp. 131–2 (London 1919).
[2] Cf. also Rom. 9.22: ἐνδείξασθαι τὴν ὀργήν, where there would be no point at all in translating "vindicate his wrath".

means something different from the "righteousness of God" is James 1.20, where the sense seems to be "the righteous will of God". But in Paul the sense of δικαιοσύνη τοῦ Θεοῦ is invariably "the strange supra-legal righteousness of God" which operates, and is apprehended, by faith. Such a righteousness needs no vindication. It is revealed in Christ, in his life, his death, his resurrection.

Orr, in his article in Hastings' *Dictionary of the Bible*[1] "Anger (Wrath of God)", has a very inaccurate section on the wrath in the Old Testament. "Anger in God has thus always an ethical connotation" (p. 98) is a statement which it would be difficult to defend; even David's conscience revolted at the death of Uzzah. Again he says: "No real distinction can be predicated between the earlier and later descriptions of the Divine Wrath in the Old Testament, except, as Ritschl points out . . . they tend in the prophets to become more eschatological." Both the statement and the qualification are highly inaccurate, as we can see from chapters 1 and 2. T. B. Kilpatrick, writing in Hasting's *Encyclopaedia of Religion and Ethics* (art. "Anger of God"),[2] well points out that "the New Testament never does, in words, connect the death of Christ with the Divine anger". But he does describe God as angry and, like Orr, obviously thinks of the wrath as an attitude or affection of God. In fact, like so many scholars, he has not really passed beyond Hosea's insight. Love and wrath are two opposite affections that must be allowed for in the divine nature: "Our anger is certainly not a part or aspect of our love", he says, and concludes that therefore the divine wrath is not just the complement of his love. And he goes on to bring in again the appeasement of the wrath, which he seemed at first sight to repudiate. "In the sufferings of Christ, the love of God reaches its consummation, and by them the wrath of God is stilled for evermore." The contradictions which these two scholars experience in reconciling the wrath and the love of God are a clear indication that to treat the wrath as an affection or attitude of God is to encounter insuperable difficulties.

Moberly in *Atonement and Personality*[3] makes a valiant effort to shake off the traditional substitutionary doctrine of the Atonement.

[1] Edinburgh 1898.
[2] P. 477 (Edinburgh 1908).
[3] London 1901.

Like McLeod Campbell, he will not (p. 23) accept the word "penal" for Christ's sufferings. On the other hand, his alternative of penitence for punishment does not seem ultimately to mean anything very different, as far as the wrath is concerned at any rate. He says[1] that Christ "took the whole responsibility and burthen of its [sin's] penance". Is this really what Paul meant in the two crucial passages, Gal. 3.13 and 2 Cor. 5.21? A little later on (p. 333) he says *à propos* 2 Cor. 5.21 that "the phrase must be interpreted along the line of sacrificial phraseology". This seems to be inclining towards Augustine's interpretation of ἁμαρτία here as "a sin-offering"; but, as we have seen, such a translation is impossible. Moberly's only direct reference to the wrath seems to be on p. 304: "The wrath of Jesus of Nazareth was—and is— uncompromising and very terrible." This is the same point that Tasker has recently stressed: if Jesus in the days of his flesh is described as showing anger, then we can ascribe anger to God. We have already discussed this question on pp. 113f., and concluded that such a simple transference of Jesus's human attributes to God is not possible.

P. T. Forsyth in *The Work of Christ*[2] devotes a special addendum to the wrath of God. He represents a more sensitive return to the tradition of Dale. He begins by allowing that the wrath is the working out of God's judgement in the moral order, but he cannot accept that it is in any sense impersonal. God, he maintains, cannot be personal in his love and impersonal in his wrath. Wrath is not, he says, "the automatic recoil of his moral order upon the transgressor" nor "exposure to the action of the vast moral machine". He says of Christ: "Was he just caught in the works?" And he accuses those who accept the impersonal nature of the wrath of being deists. Now we may well be thankful for a theologian who has devoted something more than a passing mention to the subject of the wrath of God; but it is difficult to deny that Forsyth has ignored the strong evidence in the New Testament for the impersonal character of the wrath. The fact that all the New Testament writers, without exception, refrain from using ὀργίζεσθαι, "to be angry", or any other similar verb, of God has immense significance. Forsyth writes also of the wrath under certain conditions being appropriate to God's nature, and, pressing the parable

---

[1] Op. cit., p. 110.   [2] Pp. 236 f. (London and New York 1910).

of the Prodigal Son beyond what the text allows, he says: "Does not the best of sons suffer from the angry gloom that spreads from the father over the whole house at the prodigal's shameless shame?" He seems, in effect, to want to attribute θυμός to God. We have seen already that this is only done in the New Testament within certain very carefully observed limits. As for the "angry gloom" of the prodigal's father, if we read the parable, the only place where we encounter angry gloom is in the person of the elder brother. Again, the fact remains that Paul pre-eminently, but also the other writers of the New Testament in their own ways, saw the sphere of wrath as the sphere of law. It was in fact its very impersonal character that made the Law to be law; that is the difference between law and faith. The Law, according to Paul, was good because of its very impersonal nature; but, just because of its moral demand, divorced from the personal faith-relationship, it shut us all up unto sin. Christ's very breaking of the Law by incurring its curse made it fulfil its function and thereby cease. If there could have been a personal element in the Law, by it salvation might have come. Wrath is part of the natural moral order, and it is no more deistic to conceive of God as allowing the process of the wrath to work impersonally, than it is to conceive of his allowing the process of the laws of nature to work impersonally. Just as moral life is erected on a foundation of natural order, so life in the Spirit is erected on a foundation of impersonal moral laws. We are freed from the bondage to natural law, to which the animals are subject, by the fact of our moral nature; and we are taken out of the impersonal process of the wrath by faith in Christ, by the faith of Christ. "Was Christ just caught in the works?" No, but we were, and he voluntarily became involved in the mechanism like an ordinary worker, in order to free us.[1]

Rashdall, writing nine years later than Forsyth,[2] is in the full Liberal tradition which reacted, not without some justification, against the implications of the substitutionary or penal theory of the atonement. In commenting on Gal. 3.13 (p. 93) he assumes that Paul really thought

---

[1] Compare L. Hodgson, *Towards a Christian Philosophy* (London 1943), p. 110: "But as true freedom is only to be won through moral progress, man has the choice either by co-operation with God to become a rational being capable of the eternal mode of reality, or to sink back into the impersonal mechanistic order from which he has come."

[2] Op. cit.

of Christ as cursed of God, and comments: "It illustrates the complete dependence of St Paul's argument upon the authoritative letter of prophecy." A closer study of what Paul is saying, however, gives a contrary impression, if the interpretation on p. 74 *supra* is correct, Paul's contention is that the "curse of the Law" is *not* the "curse of God". On pp. 131-2 of his work, in discussing the meaning of ἱλαστήριον in the New Testament, Rashdall admits a tension in the Godhead between wrath and love. He quotes with approval Weinel's interpretation of Paul's meaning: "His [God's] love wished to help them [men] and reconcile them to himself. Simple forgiveness of sins was not, however, possible for God. He was bound to show his justice, which mankind might begin to doubt." All this interpretation depends on the assumption that Paul meant by δικαιοσύνη, "justice", and by ἐνδείξασθαι, "vindicate". But, as we have argued throughout, God has not any need to vindicate his justice. God's peculiar righteousness was (not "must be") demonstrated in Christ's career of faith. Rashdall also suggests in the same passage that the reference in 4 Macc. 17.22 noted on p. 43 of this work to the deaths of the martyrs being an expiation of the wrath "was the source of Paul's thought and expression". Seeing that neither Paul, nor anyone else in the New Testament, ever suggests that the divine wrath needs any expiation at all, this suggestion seems ill-founded.

Kirk, writing in 1926,[1] criticizes Paul for his whole conception of justification by faith, and for his conception of the wrath which is bound up with it. He says that Paul introduces the Jewish conception of the wrath of God, from which man needs forensic justification. But he does note Paul's impersonal notion of the wrath, and agrees that this tendency eliminates to a large extent the difficulties we find in the conception. It is perhaps doubtful whether Dr Kirk would still have maintained so extreme a view about the Pauline doctrine of justification by faith to-day. At any rate, his suggestion that Paul's doctrine of the wrath is an unfortunate survival from Judaism cannot be left unchallenged, as also his statement that the wrath is something from which man needs forensic justification. Paul did of course receive the conception of the wrath of God from the Jewish tradition in which he was brought up,

---

[1] In *Essays Catholic and Critical*, ed. Selwyn (London 1926), pp. 265-71.

but, as we have seen, he modified it considerably in order to fit it in with his essentially Christian scheme of thought, and even then did not accept all the various strands of thought about the wrath which the Old Testament contains. Moreover, there is no suggestion whatever, in the Old Testament or anywhere else, that man can be justified from the wrath. On the contrary, wrath, both in Old Testament and inter-Testamental literature, is always something that must be worked out. The Old Testament does sometimes speak of averting the wrath, but this, as we have seen, is not a thought which finds expression anywhere in the New Testament. Kirk's contention that Paul's doctrine of justification imposes on us "the bonds of Rabbinic legalism" is not borne out by Paul's language. Grace, accepted by faith, takes us out of the realm of law altogether. Perhaps Kirk has been misled by the fact that in a few places Paul uses νόμος in referring to the new dispensation; but this is only for the sake of symmetry,[1] and much more often he contrasts the impersonal law with the personal rule of Christ. Anyway, if Kirk wished to remove the conception of the law-wrath process from the New Testament, he would have had to deal not only with Paul, but with nearly every other New Testament writer, for, it is implicit in a great many places where the word ὀργή or even νόμος is not used.

Barth[2] is on the whole a little disappointing on the subject of the wrath. He does acknowledge in one place (pp. 204–5) that it needs faith to apprehend the wrath as well as the love of God. What he says is: "God's wrath and judgement is only the hard shell, the '*opus alienum*' of God's grace, but it is the man who knows about grace, about the '*opus Dei proprium*', who, and who alone, knows what God's wrath and judgement are." But later on (pp. 268–9) he speaks of "God's wrath with man", and of the "mercy of God triumphant in wrath over wrath" and of the seriousness of God's wrath against sin. All this language seems to imply that he thinks of the wrath as an affection of God beside his love. Even the phrase "the wrath of God against sin" is not really in accordance with New Testament usage, unless it is made quite clear that the phrase means nothing more than the consequences of sin itself visible in human history.

---

[1] See Appendix 4, p. 210.
[2] *The Doctrine of the Word of God* (tr. Thompson, Edinburgh 1936).

THE WRATH AS AN ELEMENT IN CHRISTIAN DOCTRINE

Edwyn Bevan in his Gifford lectures[1] has a most useful and illuminating discussion of the wrath, only marred by the fact that it is not founded on an examination of the Biblical evidence, and therefore seems like a series of brilliant guesses rather than a number of firmly established conclusions. He argues (pp. 214f.) that righteous indignation is justified against bad desert, and that retributive punishment means simply giving a man what he deserves. From this he concludes that the conception of divine wrath is morally justifiable. But in fact in the Bible the remarkable characteristic of the divine wrath is that in it wrath and punishment are identified. Once we try to separate wrath from the effects of wrath we go astray, and find ourselves attributing wrath to God as an affection, which the New Testament never does. Bevan also (p. 231) uses the same argument as we have found in Moberly, that if Jesus showed wrath, then we can predicate wrath of God. It is remarkable, as a matter of fact, that wrath and punishment are only explicitly mentioned together in the New Testament three times: Rom. 12.19; 13.4; Heb. 10.27, and in all these places the wrath is plainly something that God does, not something that he feels. In all other places it is assumed that the wrath is the punishment. In his conclusion about the wrath, however, Bevan is most penetrating. He says (p. 241) that punitive pains rightly endured become vicarious suffering. This is in fact the nexus between the wrath and the Cross. Wrath is only wrath so long as the attitude of him who endures the wrath is unchanged. There is never any question of appeasing wrath or reconciling God, but of recognizing and accepting the wrath as "the law of consequences arranged and willed by God", which is exactly the New Testament conception.

With the reaction towards biblical theology in the thirties came, perhaps inevitably, a reconsideration of the substitutionary theory of the atonement. A. B. Macaulay's book *The Death of Jesus*[2] is an attempt to rehabilitate this theory, and very naturally he has something to say about the wrath of God. His argument is, however, vitiated throughout by the assumption that the wrath means an attitude of God. This is made clear by his words on pp. 157-8: "Christ's experience was to be subject to a perfect consciousness of the divine reaction

---

[1] *Symbolism and Belief* (London 1938).   [2] London 1938.

to sin." The wrath of God is exhibited on the Cross, as the author of Revelation shows, because the wrath is the consequences of men's sins working themselves out in history, and the Crucifixion was the supreme sin in history. But he who hung on the Cross did not experience the wrath. In this sense, Macaulay is right when he speaks (p. 169) of "the dual impression which the death of Christ immediately produces of divine condemnation and divine love". But in a later passage (pp. 171-2) he commits himself definitely to an expiatory view of the atonement: "The idea of the inexorable repulsion of God to sin expressed by the term 'wrath' (ὀργή) . . . if taken in its plain sense . . . describes just that divine attitude which demands propitiation." Nothing could show more clearly that if you think of the wrath as an attitude of God you cannot avoid some theory of propitiation. But the wrath in the New Testament is never spoken of as being propitiated, because it is not conceived of as being an attitude of God.

Finally we should consider an article by Archdeacon Harrison in the issue of *The Churchman* of September 1951.[1] In certain ways his paper comes to conclusions about the wrath which are nearer to those above in this work than any which we have so far considered. Discussing our Lord's use of "cup" as reported in the Synoptic Gospels he points out that "with one possible exception all the Old Testament references [to the cup of wrath] . . . are concerned with suffering which is penal". He does not indicate which he considers is to be the exception, and he has apparently overlooked the references in Nahum 3.11; Obad. 16; Job 21.20; Zech. 12.2, also two out of the four in the Psalms. But his contention is certainly right, that all the Old Testament references to the wrath-cup signify penal suffering. From this he draws the conclusion that when our Lord speaks of his cup, he too must mean a destiny of penal suffering. He has not however considered the three references to the wine or cup of Jahveh which occur in the interTestamental period, in all of which the cup or the wine means disaster indeed, but not necessarily penal disaster. The nature of the disaster must be indicated before we can assume that it is penal.[2] This is in fact what we find in the New Testament. In Revelation, where the cup is

---

[1] D. E. W. Harrison: "The Apostolic Testimony to Christ Crucified", in *The Churchman*, Vol. LXV, No. 3 (*London* 1951).
[2] Pss. Solomon 8.15; Martyrdom of Isaiah 5.13; 2 Baruch 13.8.

penal it is explicitly associated with the wrath. In the Synoptics the wrath is not mentioned with it, and we are at liberty to understand it as meaning "destiny of suffering" without any suggestion of punishment. Archdeacon Harrison shows a fine understanding of Paul's use of ὀργή. He emphasizes its connection with law—and is perhaps the first to do so. On the other hand, he is hardly accurate when he says: "Elsewhere in the New Testament, the phrase [ὀργή] is either an Old Testament quotation or is used eschatologically." (He has excepted John 3.36.) Quite apart from the Apocalypse, where, as we have seen, the ὀργή is *not* purely eschatological, the phrase ὀργὴ τῷ λαῷ τουτῷ, "wrath unto this people", in Luke 21.23 is not strictly speaking eschatological, since it refers to the fall of Jerusalem, an event in history that had already taken place when Luke wrote his Gospel. Harrison does give one hint that he is not entirely free from the misapprehension of conceiving of the wrath as an attitude of God, and thus thinking of it as personal rather than impersonal, for he says: "The responsibility is man's but the divine reaction is conceived personally: God gave them up." But surely this is evidence not of a personal, but an impersonal reaction. If the wrath were conceived personally, surely Paul would have said: "God was angry with them." Instead of that God allows them to incur the impersonal process of the wrath. Following his own line of exegesis Harrison is compelled to interpret πρὸς τὴν ἔνδειξιν τῆς δικαιοσύνης, "to show his righteousness", in Rom. 3.26, as meaning not only to "reveal his righteousness" but also in some sense "to vindicate his justice". "God's action in Christ is to vindicate his character." Though Harrison does full justice to the first translation, it is doubtful if it is possible to read both meanings into the phrase—and ἔνδειξις does not mean "vindication"; that would be ἐκδίκησις.

If any clear conclusion emerges from this discussion it is surely this: we must follow St Paul's clue, and take the impersonal nature of the wrath seriously. If we once allow ourselves to be led into thinking that a reference to the wrath of God in the New Testament means that God is conceived of as angry, we cannot avoid some sort of theory of expiation. We cannot avoid maintaining that in some sense the Son endured the wrath of the Father, we cannot avoid thinking in forensic terms, with all the strain and violence to our God-given sense of moral justice that such a theory involves. But once accept the profound conclusion of Paul, echoed in the rest of the Bible and most magnificently in Revelation, that the wrath is simply the impersonal process of the consequences of men's sins working itself out in history, and these appalling difficulties do not present themselves. Christ endured the consequences of men's sins, but himself was sinless. What was wrath to all others, was in him the process of redemption, and can now be so to all who are united to him by faith.

Two questions finally suggest themselves: Why did the concept of the wrath of God develop in the scriptures in the way outlined above? And what is the relevance of the concept of the wrath of God to Christain theology to-day?

Why did the concept of the wrath develop as it did? As we have seen, by the end of the Old Testament period, two main tendencies had shown themselves in the way in which the biblical writers viewed the wrath of God. The first was the conception of an impersonal, majestic, remote wrath; it is found in the Chronicler and Daniel and certain of the Psalms. The other tendency was towards an apocalyptic conception, in which the wrath was extremely personal and on the whole nationalistic rather than universalist. This conception is found in most Old Testament apocalyptic, with the exception of Daniel, and also in the prophetic tradition. The danger of the first tendency was that it might develop into a sort of deism, or else assimilate the ideas of Greek philosophy, as happend to a large extent in Philo. The end of this process would be a god of the philosophers rather than the personal God revealed in the Old Testament. The dangers of the second tendency were anthropomorphism and an unhealthy other-worldliness.

The New Testament writers viewed the concept of the wrath from the farther side of the life, death, and resurrection of the Messiah. Consequently, their experience of God as personal was infinitely deepened. Indeed it formed one of the main characteristics of the revelation they had apprehended. On the other hand, their apocalyptic expectations had been partly realized; whatever was to come with the Messiah had come, in embryo at least. One might therefore expect them to lean heavily to the side of the apocalyptic conception of the wrath. The reason that they did not do so was that the revelation of God which they had experienced in the Messiah was of God as personal *love*. This impression was so strong and so definite that they could not think of him at the same time as personal wrath. On the other hand, outside the circle of those who were aware of God's love they saw an impersonal kingdom of sin. It was no invention of the theologians; it was something from which they felt themselves delivered through Christ. Its existence is implied in the existence of the salvation they enjoyed. Paul did not invent this sphere, but he brought it into conscious relation with the sphere of salvation by his doctrine of the law-state from which we are delivered by grace. Now to this sphere of law the wrath conception of Chronicles applied very adequately, and it was no doubt Paul who first applied it. The author of Revelation built on Paul's conception, using the mythical and symbolical language of apocalyptic without the unchristian pre-suppositions of the older apocalytpic; and he worked out with greater profundity than Paul the relation between the two spheres. This was no doubt because he was less concerned with the many other important practical and theoretical problems that occupied Pauls' mind, and was provoked by the circumstances of the Church in his day to concentrate on the great problems of the relation of wrath and grace. But, impersonal though the wrath certainly is in the New Testament, the God of the New Testament writers is no "Barthian" God entirely unconcerned with anything outside the area of revelation. That sin should bring its own retribution to infinite consequence is a law of the universe created by God; so the wrath is the wrath of God.

The danger of speaking about the wrath of God is obvious; it gives the impression of undue anthropomorphism, or else it seems to present an Old Testament Jehovah, rather than the God revealed in Jesus Christ. This danger is most marvellously avoided in the New Testament; but it certainly has not been avoided in the history of Christian thought and preaching. A study of the wrath of God in the Fathers would certainly show that they were not so scrupulous as were the writers of the New Testament in avoiding speaking of God as angry. Indeed, the beginning of this declension can be traced in the New Testament itself; we have noticed how great a contrast Jude and 2 Peter present in this respect. A misapprehension of the meaning of the wrath of God in the New Testament has given rise or has prepared the ground for the appearance of several highly distorted theories of the atonement. Calvin could say of Christ: "He bore in his soul the tortures of a condemned and lost man."[1] Even as late as Dale, we have traced in his concept of the wrath an Old Testament rather than a New Testament vision of God. Why then use the concept "wrath of God" at all? Why not speak, for example, of "moral retribution" instead?

In the first place, before we jettison the phrase "wrath of God" it is important to realize that the fundamental New Testament conception of the law–sin–wrath sphere is a true one. The sphere of sin is the sphere of legal, impersonal retribution. Sin is a depersonalizing agency. To-day we should have no difficulty in recognizing this; there is a renewed emphasis on the personal nature of God and of real living. We are existing in a society which is largely depersonalized; we constantly hear denunciations of the mechanical, impersonal nature of modern industrial civilization. Moreover, the impersonal, legal nature of sin is not a concept peculiar to Christianity. It is found in the Hindu doctrine of *karma* (see Appendix 6); it is the great theme of Aeschylus' *Oresteia*. Indeed it is interesting to observe Aeschylus' solution to the problem of δράσαντι παθεῖν. The last scene in the *Eumenides* is a trial scene, but he does not really solve his problem on legal grounds. The Eumenides are infuriated at the decision to acquit Orestes, and have to be propitiated. Aeschylus' propitiatory solution was a dramatic *tour de force*, and is inadequate morally; but it is significant that his solution, such as it was, is more in terms of grace than of law. Indeed, the impersonal character of the operations of sin is capable of great development as a philosophical principle. It is no Rabbinic quirk inherited from Paul's university days. In a sense, Paul plays a sort of theological Hegel to the Kant of the author of Deuteronomy. Kant gloried in the autonomy of the moral ideal, but it was the very autonomy of the Law that proved its ineffectiveness to Paul. It was because the Law said: "He that doeth me shall live by me" (and Paul read into it "and by me alone") that Christ had to transcend the Law by his life of faith. So the wrath principle as it is understood in the

---

[1] Nor did Cranmer avoid this mistaken view of the wrath of God. If the main thesis of this book is correct, "Be not angry with us for ever" in the Litany, and "provoking most justly thy wrath and indignation against us" in the Communion Service in the Book of Common Prayer are not phrases that should be used in Christian worship.

New Testament is not something that we can afford to ignore to-day or at any time.

And we must also call it the wrath of God. If we do not say that it is in some sense the creation or arrangement of God, we must accept either some form of dualism or the Hindu doctrine of *karma*. According to orthodox Hindu teaching, even Brahma cannot alter *karma*; it is the very principle of the universe (see Appendix 6). But if we call this law of retribution the wrath of God, we are reminding ourselves that ultimately it is within God's dispensation and serves God's ends. In this sense, perhaps, and only in this very teleological sense, the wrath can be looked on as disciplinary. We can at least hope—there is nothing in the New Testament that forbids it—that ultimately all who are under the wrath will accept the love of God. The alternative in the New Testament, when an alternative is spoken of, is destruction, not eternal punishment. And the very name wrath surely has its value as bringing into full prominence the awfulness of sin. So both terms of the concept are still needed to-day.

But while we keep the phrase, we must stress the New Testament conception of the wrath, not the Old Testament one, not even the Old Testament at its best and highest. The wrath of God is not an attitude which God adopts towards sinners, still less is it an emotion which can be attributed to God. To adopt either of these conceptions is to involve ourselves in endless difficulties. The attempt to delineate a God who is both loving and angry is made in the Old Testament, and the difficulty was never resolved there. If one attempts to do it, one must either ultimately leave it as an unresolved paradox, but an agonizing one, or else adopt some shift like the "*communicatio idiomatum*". Just as Leo said that our Lord showed his divinity in his miracles and his humanity in Gethsemane, so one has to say that God shows his love to the faithful and his wrath to the unfaithful. He loves the redeemed but is angry with the unredeemed. Or perhaps one tries to attribute both love and wrath to him at the same time, and draws a picture of God embarrassed by the conflict of his own attributes. The worst development of this idea is the conception of an angry Father and a loving Son. Perhaps it is only a matter of terms. We may say, if we like, that God is angry with the unfaithful (*pace* the New Testament), as long as by his being angry we do not mean anything but the fact that the unfaithful are entangled in their own sins. But is this really best described as God being angry? The wrath of God is the punishment of God, and the punishment of God is what he permits us to inflict on ourselves. God loves the most obdurate infidel as much as he loves the most devoted saint. He permits wrath, but he is love.

The biblical concept of the wrath of God, therefore, has its place in Christian thought to-day. Indeed, when properly understood, it is peculiarly relevant. What the doctrine of the wrath of God really does is to supply us with a Christian theology of power, and the problem of power is obviously one of the most acute in the atomic era. It is in the Book of Revelation that this theology of power is most completely worked out, so it will be convenient to consider it in the context of that Book.

If we read beneath the symbolical and mythological language used by St John the Divine, we shall find that, according to St John, God's power is manifest in two ways in the world. The first way is in the wrath of God. By this John meant the working out in history of the consequences of men's sins. It could be called judgement, but John also calls it "wrath" because God's power is really displayed in it, and it is, so to speak, by God's arrangement that the universe is a moral one and that sin has its consequences. We first find this power in Revelation working itself out in the comparatively milder visions of judgement in chapter 6: plague, war, famine. We should understand these visions as typical pictures of judgement. It is as if John were saying: "This is what happens when men fall out; and this when they ignore the living conditions of their fellow men; and this when human selfishness gets control."

This is not to claim that John ignores the possibility of "particular judgements". Though he emphasizes the judgement which comes through the automatic, impersonal operation of the wrath far more, he does, as we have seen, allow a place for particular judgements on individuals (see Rev. 2.22,23 and cf. 1 Cor. 11.30 and the earlier chapters of Acts). But these particular judgements are not integrated into his Christian theology as is the doctrine of the wrath. We find very much the same belief among the prophets of the Old Testament. See Ezekiel 11, where the fact that the men of Judah who worship idols in Jerusalem are to be punished by the sack of the city by the Babylonians

THE WRATH AS AN ELEMENT IN CHRISTIAN DOCTRINE

does not prevent Ezekiel from interpreting the sudden death of Pelatiah as a particular judgement on him.

Later on in Revelation the operation of God's power through the wrath is seen on a larger scale and is apprehended even more clearly through the fall of Rome. Again and again the overthrow of "Babylon" is described as an instance of the wrath, and indeed the complicated historical situation which produced the evils of Roman rule denounced by John is also described as Babylon having intoxicated the nations with the wine of her wrath. Yet all this operation of the wrath which John depicts was taking place or was to take place in history. In Rev. 17.16,17 it is the kings of the East, led by the figure of Nero returned from hell, who overthrow the empire at last, and not some eschatological judgement that destroys it. Hence we can trace in John's work another profound truth about the operation of the wrath of God: the wrath is the working out of the consequences of sin, but sin is self-destructive. Babylon in Revelation is constantly portrayed as an empire founded on the pursuit of power for its own sake. Indeed the great difference between the two symbolical animals which dominate in Revelation, the Lamb and the Beast, is that the Lamb conquers through suffering, the Beast conquers through coercion. This is another way of saying that an empire that abandons itself to the pursuit of power for its own sake is bound to destroy itself in the end. This self-destructive tendency must have been unmistakably obvious to those who lived through the year of the Three Emperors, from the suicide of Nero in A.D. 68 to the accession of Vespasian in A.D. 70. All this is implied in the great picture of the winepress of the wrath of God in Rev. 14 and 19, that winepress which runs over not with wine but with blood. John uses the symbol of the wrath, not to vent his personal hatred against his persecutors, but to express the undoubted truth that power, pursued for its own sake, brings about its own destruction. This truth is one which needs to be emphasized to-day, when one of the two great world empires is dominated by men who seem to have no other ultimate aim but the pursuit and retention of power.

But, according to St John the Divine, God's power is also manifest in a second way in the world. Inside the Roman Empire the Church suffers persecution; and here also are the power and the victory of God to be seen. The second manifestation of the power of God is through suffering voluntarily accepted, and it finds its focus in the crucifixion of the Messiah. In Revelation also we find it demonstrated that:

The foolishness of God is wiser than men;
and the weakness of God is stronger than men.

This suffering of the Cross is perfected in history by the suffering of the Christian Church, in John's day persecuted nearly to extinction (John probably thought it *would* be to extinction) by the authorities of the Roman Empire. Of this second manifestation of the power of God, the Lamb is the symbol. But it is important to bear in mind that this sort of power also brought judgement. It was not just that men were handed over into the power of their sins, enduring the consequences of their own and others' misdeeds to the end; the act of salvation itself brought in a special way judgement as well as redemption. The Cross was a manifestation not only of the love, but also of the wrath of God. Not that God was angry with men for crucifying his Son, but that those who rejected the love of God manifested in the life, death, and resurrection of Jesus Christ abandoned themselves utterly to self-destruction, to the process of the wrath. God had spoken finally in Christ, so those who rejected God rejected Christ also. The wrath is closely related to the Cross, and will be to the end of history. When God's last word is spoken it is inevitable that at the same time there must be left to man the supreme opportunity of destroying himself. Hence the powerful symbolism of Revelation is always valid for human experience. Looked at in its deepest significance, the symbolism of the Apocalypse is not exhausted in either a description of what has happened, or in a description of what is going to happen at some particular time in the future. It is a parable of the relation of God to man, and we are particularly concerned with that relation as it influences man's exercise of his God-given power in history. The relation described in Revelation includes the end of history, but the end is only a culmination of a process already in operation.

So the New Testament concept of the wrath of God enables us to apprehend in some degree the operation of the divine power in history. That concept is adumbrated in Paul's writings, is implicit in most of the rest of the New Testament, and becomes explicit (although only through symbol and myth) in the Christian Apocalypse. It supplies us with a Christian doctrine of power, and relates the action of God in Christ essentially to what we men try to do with the world in which we live. The concept of the wrath of God is therefore one of the great foundation principles of Christian thought. We may call it by other names if we choose, but we attempt to remove it from the New Testament at our peril.

APPENDIX 1

THE CORRECT RENDERING OF HABAKKUK 2.15, 16

Hab. 2.15 runs as follows in the M.T.:

הוֹי מַשְׁקֵה רֵעֵיהוּ מְסַפֵּחַ חֲמָתְךָ וְאַף שַׁכֵּר
לְמַעַן הַבִּיט עַל־מְעוֹרֵיהֶם:

The first line can only be translated:

> Woe to him who gives his neighbour to drink, adding to it [or "outpouring"] thy fury and wrath that makes drunk.

This is hardly sense; some sort of emendation is necessary. Fortunately such emendation is now supplied by the text of Habakkuk found in the Dead Sea Scrolls (see M. Burrows: *The Dead Sea Scrolls of St Mark's Monastery*, Vol. I, New Haven 1950). The reading of Hab. 2.15 there is as follows:

הוי משקה רעיהו מספח
חמתו אף שכר למען הבט אל מועדיהם

This is translated by Brownlee as follows (see *Bulletin of the American Schools of Oriental Research*, No. 112, pp. 8–18, Jerusalem–Baghdad, Dec. 1948):

> Woe to him that gives drink to his neighbour,
> Venting his wrath to make him drink too,
> So as to gaze upon their festivals.

This is presumably to derive מספח from the root ספח, a variant of סחף "to pour down" (see Koehler-Baumgartner, *Lexicon in Veteris Testamenti Libros*, Leiden 1953, p. 664). Perhaps a better translation of חמתו would be "his venom". In the last line the M.T. reading of מעוריהם seems preferable to מועדיהם, as there seems no point in a reference to festivals, while shame is often associated with drunkenness, and actually appears thus in verse 16.

By this reading therefore the notion of the cup of wrath being given into the hand of an individual to administer disappears. The passage is simply a protest against the excessive drinker who corrupts his neighbour, bringing shame on both. We may translate:

APPENDIX I

Woe unto him that gives drink to his neighbour,
Pouring out his venom to make him drink also,
So that one may gaze upon their nakedness.

It is interesting to notice that in verse 16 the Dead Sea Scrolls text reads instead of the M.T. וְהֵעָרֵל ("and be uncircumcised"), the word והרעל ("and reel"). This would make excellent sense, but the M.T. reading is just as appropriate and fits in well with the "foul shame" of the end of the verse. The commentator on Habakkuk whose work is included in the Dead Sea Scrolls assumes the M.T. reading even though his text has והרעל.

APPENDIX 2

THE DATE OF JEREMIAH 25.15–31 AND 51.1–58

Peake (op. cit., in loc.) considers that Jer. 25.15–31 was uttered by Jeremiah. Duhm (op. cit., in loc.) treats it as a much later prophecy, but he holds a theory that all Jeremiah's prophecies against the Gentiles are later compositions. He points out however that the phrase in verse 18: "Jerusalem, and the cities thereof, and the kings thereof", would not be appropriate in Jeremiah's day. Cornill (quoted by Elliott-Binns, West. Comm., London 1919, in loc.) thinks that the passage as a whole is taken from Jeremiah, but has received later additions. It is treated here as later than Jeremiah's day for the following reasons:

1. The wine is specifically mentioned. In all previous passages it is wrath, not wine, that is drunk. A later writer, modelling himself upon Deutero-Isaiah, would be more likely to incorporate the wine as part of the symbolism.

2. The phrases "this fury" in verse 15 and "as it is this day" in verse 18 seem to refer to an event which has already taken place. This would point to an exilic date.

3. Peake relegates verses 27–9 to a later period, nearer Deutero-Isaiah; but it is difficult to separate them from verses 18–26, and equally difficult to separate verses 18–26 from verses 15–17. In verses 27–9 occurs the thought of nations attempting to refuse the cup. But this sounds like a later elaboration of the figure, and is surely later than Isa. 51.17f., where there is no question of a nation refusing its destiny.

4. This passage in Jeremiah is prose. In the history of the development of a mythological theme such as the wrath-cup figure, poetry would naturally come first. Prose is likely to be a commentary on, or elaboration of, poetry. But if this passage is written by Jeremiah, it will be the first, or among the first, where this figure occurs. Hence we conclude that this passage was written after Isa. 51.17–23, possibly at the end of the Exile or in the early post-exilic period. It may well have been founded on a prophecy of Jeremiah's (cf. Jer. 13.13), but we cannot claim that the cup of wrath figure originates with him.

APPENDIX 2

Nearly all modern editors are agreed that Jeremiah 51 is not by Jeremiah. Most would put it at the very end of the Exile, e.g. Elliott-Binns (op. cit., in loc.). It must be later than Isa. 51.17–23. If therefore a later period than the end of the Exile is indicated, it will hardly be found before the overthrow, or imminent overthrow, of the Persian Empire (in this prophecy Babylon equals Persia on this supposition) in the fourth century B.C. Only the very conservative Rabbi Freedman insists on Jeremiah's authorship (ed. Jeremiah, Soncino ed., London 1949, in loc.).

APPENDIX 3

THE TRANSLATION IN THE SEPTUAGINT OF WORDS FOR THE DIVINE WRATH

THE way in which the Septuagint version renders the various phrases for the wrath is specially interesting, both because in some respects it forms a second century B.C. commentary on the text, and also because the writers of the New Testament were more influenced by the Greek translation than by the original Hebrew. (Throughout this book H. B. Swete's edition of the Old Testament in Greek (Camb. 1930–4 ed.) has been used. It must also be borne in mind that the LXX text available to the writers of the New Testament must have differed from what we have in some respects and is not always recoverable by us.) The characteristics of the Greek translation do not seem to vary very much throughout the Old Testament in its treatment of the language of the wrath. The Greek has two words with which to render almost every variation of the Hebrew words for the wrath; these are θυμός and ὀργή. They are used absolutely interchangeably, and are combined in order to render a strong expression of wrath in the Hebrew. In combination they are used equally interchangeably. Thus חָרָה־אַף is normally translated θυμωθεὶς ὀργῇ (e.g. Ex. 4.14), but ἐθυμώθη alone is also used (e.g. Num. 11.33); so is ὀργὴ θυμοῦ (e.g. Num. 12.9), and ὠργίσθη θυμῷ (e.g. Num. 32.10). The other wrath words are rendered by the same pair, severally or in conjunction; e.g. Ex. 15.7, חָרֹן is rendered by ὀργή, and אַף in the second half of the verse by θυμός. יִקְצֹף in Lev. 10.6 is translated θυμός ἔσται, and חֵמָה in Lev. 26.28 by θυμός. In Num. 16.26 קֶצֶף is rendered by ὀργή. If further proof is still needed that the two words are used interchangeably, compare the following six passages, where precisely the same phrase in Hebrew is translated in the first instance by ὀργή or ὀργίζω followed by θυμός or θυμῷ, and in the second by θυμός or θυμῷ followed by ὀργή or ὀργίζω.

Cf.: Exodus 22.24 with Exodus 4.14;
Numbers 12.9 with Numbers 32.14;
Deuteronomy 7.4 with Deuteronomy 11.17.

APPENDIX 3

When the Greek met a word for wrath which it did not know or was doubtful about it seems that it fell back on the well-tried combination: e.g. תְּנוּאָה in Num. 14.34 is translated by θυμὸς τῆς ὀργῆς, and הִתְאַנָּף in Deut. 1.37 by ἐθυμώθη.

The Greek, however, does contrive to muster a set of new words to translate the meaning of "provoke", "move to anger", in the Hebrew usually כעס or קצף both in Hiph'il. These are: παροξῦναι (e.g. Deut. 9.18, for Hebrew לְהַכְעִיסוֹ(?)); παροργίσαι (e.g. Deut. 31.29 for Hebrew לְהַכְעִיסוֹ(?)); and παραπικράναι (e.g. Deut. 32.16 for the same Hebrew word). In fact, though the Greek shows such lack of originality in translating the Hebrew words for the divine wrath, it shows more inventiveness than the Hebrew in translating words for "move to wrath". In the following places words other than ὀργή or θυμός are used to translate words for the wrath: Jer. 3.12 μηνίω (cf. also LXX of Isa. 13.3); Lam. 2.6 ἐμβριμάματι ὀργῆς for זַעַם־אַף (but cf. Codex Marchalianus marg. in LXX of Ezek. 21.31); Isa. 59.18 ὀνείδος for חֵמָה; Isa. 66.14 ἀπείλησις and Hab. 3.8 ὅρμημα, both for עֶבְרָה.

In a number of places there are more or less clear traces of a desire on the part of the Greek translators to tone down the Hebrew, usually through fear of anthropomorphism. Examples are Gen. 6.6 ἐνθυμώθη and διενοήθη for נחם and עצב respectively. The Greek does not like the idea of God repenting. Compare also Deut. 32.36, where יִתְנֶחָם is translated παρακληθήσεται. Again, in Gen. 18.30 the Hebrew has אַל־נָא יִחַר (of Abraham to God); the Greek offers κύριε, ἐὰν λαλήσω, which looks like a modification. The same phrase occurs in Gen. 31.35 of human wrath (Rachel to Laban) and the Greek translator has μὴ βαρέως φέρε. But contrast Jud. 6.39, where Gideon speaking to God says אַל־יִחַר אַפְּךָ בִּי, and the LXX translates μὴ δὴ ὀργισθήτω ὁ θυμός σου ἐν ἐμοί. Does this perhaps suggest a different translator of this passage? A clearer instance of deliberate modification of the translation is Deut. 32.27, where Jahveh is said to fear the provocation of Israel's enemies, a very anthropomorphic conception indeed. The M.T. is:

לוּלֵי כַּעַס אוֹיֵב אָגוּר
פֶּן יְנַכְּרוּ צָרֵימוֹ

For this the Greek has:

εἰ μὴ δι' ὀργὴν ἐχθρῶν, ἵνα μὴ μακροχρονίσωσιν,
ἵνα μὴ συνεπιθῶνται.

Codex Ambrosianus offers: μακροχρόνιοι ὦσιν as an alternative to μακροχρονίσωσιν. The Greek therefore gives a much less primitive conception: Jahveh was anxious lest the Israelites should have to suffer too long at the hands of their enemies. The sense of the Hebrew is that Jahveh was afraid lest the enemies of Israel should provoke him to anger, or else mock at Israel because of his apparent impotence. συνεπιθῶνται seems to mean "put on still more" or "seize to one's own advantage" (the latter sense is quoted from Polybius by Liddell and Scott). It looks like an alternative to μακροχρονίσωσιν. It is quite possible that the LXX translators did not know what נכר meant, but in any case it is hard to acquit them here of deliberate modification.

There are two interesting examples of Septuagintal modification in 1 Sam. 15.11 and 2 Sam. 6.8. In both these places devout men (Samuel in the first and David in the second) are described in the Hebrew as wroth with Jahveh because of his severity with individuals (Saul and Uzzah respectively). In each place the LXX translates the Hebrew וַיִּחַר as ἠθύμησεν, a distinct modification. Similarly in 2 Kings 3.27, where we have the shocking instance of the effective wrath of an alien god, the LXX translates καὶ ἐγένετο μετάμελος μέγας ἐπὶ Ἰσραήλ.

Finally, it is interesting to note that the evidence of the wrath vocabulary in the LXX of Jeremiah confirms the suggestion made by Thackeray (quoted in Elliott-Binns, op. cit., p. lxxviii) that Jer. 1–38 (LXX) was translated by a different hand to Jer. 39–51 (LXX). A sentence occurs twice in the Hebrew, once in 23.19,20 and once in 30.23,24 (LXX 37.23,24). It is as follows:

> Behold the tempest of the Lord, even his fury (חֵמָה) is gone forth, yea a whirling tempest... The anger of the Lord shall not return...

In the first occurrence of the passage the Greek offers:

ἰδοὺ σεῖσμος παρὰ Κυρίου καὶ ὀργὴ ἐκπορεύεται εἰς σύνσεισμον...
καὶ οὐκέτι ἀποστρέψει ὁ θυμὸς Κυρίου.

APPENDIX 3

This merely rings the changes on ὀργή and θυμός. But in 30.23,24 (LXX 37.23,24) we find:

ὀργὴ Κυρίου ἐξῆλθεν θυμώδης, ἐξῆλθεν ὀργὴ στρεφομένη.
οὐ μὴ ἀποστρέψει ὀργὴ θυμοῦ Κυρίου.

This is a better attempt at varying the vocabulary. Similarly in 18.8 the text runs:

I [Jahveh] will repent of the evil that I thought to do.

Here the LXX has μετανοήσω without any sign of embarrassment at the thought of God repenting. But in 42.10 (LXX 49.10), where the Hebrew has:

I repent me of the evil that I have done unto you,

the LXX translates:

ἀναπέπαυμαι ἐπὶ τοῖς κακοῖς οἷς ἐποίησα.

But undoubtedly the main significance of the LXX translation for the purpose of our study is the huge preponderance of ὀργή and θυμός to translate every variety of Hebrew words expressing the divine wrath. This has great importance for our study of the New Testament.

APPENDIX 4

W. D. DAVIES' SUGGESTION THAT PAUL THOUGHT OF CHRIST AS THE NEW TORAH

In Rom. 10.6 Paul quotes Deut. 30.12,13 in connection with his exegesis of the relation of the Law to faith: μὴ εἴπῃς ἐν τῇ καρδίᾳ σου, τίς ἀναβήσεται εἰς τὸν οὐρανόν; κτλ. W. D. Davies in *Paul and Rabbinic Judaism* (London 1948), commenting on this passage, argues that for Paul Christ was the New Torah. If this were true, it would much alter our understanding of Paul's conception of the wrath of God, so his arguments must be examined. But first it is necessary to establish the fact that Paul really does look on Deut. 30.12,13 as a prophecy of Christ. This is challenged by Sanday and Headlam. They maintain that because Paul does not introduce the quotation as specifically from Scripture, but merely says: ἡ δὲ ἐκ πίστεως δικαιοσύνη οὕτως λέγει, he is not here suggesting that Moses wrote this passage with the righteousness of faith in mind, but that he is merely using the quotation as an illustration of what he means; as if he were to say: "The following words could well be applied to what I mean by the righteousness of faith." The editors of the I.C.C. commentary on Romans emphasize that Paul was not really suggesting that Christ is to be found in this passage. But in fact, if Paul did not consider Deut. 30.12,13 to be a prophecy of the righteousness of faith in Christ, it was a most extraordinary illustration for him to have chosen, for it must have been plain to him that on the surface the words refer to the Law. One can hardly imagine Paul as saying: "These words from Scripture are the sort of language one might use to express what I mean by the righteousness of faith, though as a matter of fact Scripture uses them to describe the righteousness of the Law." He had in fact to claim Deut. 30.12,13 as a prophecy of the righteousness in which he believed, or else admit that it was a most damning piece of evidence on the other side.

We may accept, then, the conclusion that Paul, by quoting Deut. 30.12,13 in Rom. 10.6 is in fact claiming that this passage from Deuteronomy refers not to the Law, but is a prophecy of the righteousness of faith which was later to be revealed in Christ. This is somewhat

APPENDIX 4

confirmed by Rom. 10.16, where a quotation from Isa. 53.1 is described as ῥῆμα Χριστοῦ. Paul would no doubt have described this Deuteronomy quotation also as ῥῆμα Χριστοῦ. All this Davies accepts, and on the basis of this makes his assertion that Paul thought of Christ as the New Torah. On p. 154 of his work he maintains that because Paul applies here to Christ words which in Deuteronomy were applied to the Torah, Paul must have thought of Christ as the New Torah. He sums up his argument on pp. 172–3: "For St Paul the person and teaching of Jesus had replaced the Torah as the centre of his religious life, and had assumed for him therefore that character of a New Torah. Once this step had been taken, however, that of substituting Jesus for the Torah of Judaism, Paul's mind would inevitably move forward to transfer to Jesus those attributes with which Judaism had honoured the Torah . . . if, as we have maintained, Paul's thoughts were centred on the New Torah, he would have no need to employ the term Logos, and if even in Colossians it was of the Torah that Paul was thinking, this would help to explain his neglect of the explicit term Wisdom." Now the statement that Christ was for Paul the New Torah is one which is surely not borne out by the evidence. As we have already seen, the Law was for Paul the sphere of the wrath. It was not a new Law that Christ brought, but something which transcended the Law altogether. After all, if the mere fact that in Rom. 10.6 Paul applies to Christ a quotation that in its context in Deuteronomy describes the Law is to be so significant, one could point to the fact that in the previous verse he refrains from applying a similar quotation (Lev. 18.5) to Christ, as being equally significant on the other side. It is true that in some places Paul uses the word νόμος for the dispensation of grace and faith (cf. Rom. 3.27 νόμος πίστεως; and also Rom. 8.2f.), but this is only for the sake of symmetry, and he does not develop the characteristics of the νόμος πίστεως in the same way as he shows the wrath–sin characteristics of the old νόμος. His constant emphasis is that what we have in Christ is something different in kind from νόμος, and he is very far indeed from the conception of the author of the First Gospel that Christ is the new Law-giver, and farther still from the thought of Christ as the New Law. Again, if Paul, as Davies suggests, thought of Christ as the successor of the old Law, he must presumably have thought of the Old Torah as pre-existent in the same way as his contemporaries the Rabbis did. But, as we know, this is not so: the Law παρεισῆλθεν (Rom. 5.20); it had not only an ending in time, but also a beginning, and that beginning was subsequent to the creation and fall. Davies might perhaps reply that according to Paul Christ *was* the pre-existent Torah; but if so how does he explain Paul's slighting references to the Torah under the Old Testament dispensation? Above all, if Paul saw Christ as the New Torah, how is it that he never refers to him as the καινὸς νόμος? He was apparently so steeped in the idea that he forgot to use the term. Nor can we rightly compare John's treatment of the Logos with Paul's treatment of the Torah. John, we may say, claimed the Logos for Christ. But he never suggested that there was an old Logos that was superseded or ineffective, which is precisely what Paul says about the Torah. Davies attempts to explain Paul's apparent hesitation to apply the term Wisdom to Christ in Colossians by saying that he was thinking of him primarily as Torah, not Wisdom. The same argument is used to explain why Paul does not use Logos of Christ. But all these arguments encounter the same fatal objection: if so, why does Paul never call Christ the New Torah? After all, he does call Christ the Wisdom of God in 1 Cor. 1.30; he never calls him the Law. Davies brings other evidence earlier on in his book, but it is no more conclusive. On p. 69 he says that Paul kept the Law all his life, though he concedes that this was probably in order to secure an evangelistic entry among the Jews. In the same way one could cite instances of converted Brahmins in India who, though wholehearted members of the Christian Church, maintained their vegetarian diet, partly out of sentiment, partly out of habit, and partly for the same reason that Davies allows to Paul, that by all means they might gain some. The truth is no doubt that Paul realized that in his day the Jewish doctors were using the term Torah in two senses: by Torah they meant both a code by which to live, and also the complete revelation of God. Paul himself thought of the Law as a code and not as a complete revelation; the code, he believed, was outmoded and transcended by Christ. The revelation was given in Christ, but that did not mean that he thought of Christ as the New Law. Christ was not a Law at all; he was the New Man, a person, not an impersonal code.

APPENDIX 5

THE MEANING OF πυρὸς ζῆλος IN HEBREWS 10.27

WHAT exactly does πυρὸς ζῆλος mean here? The quotation seems to be from a Greek version of Isa. 26.11:

> But they shall see thy zeal for the people and be ashamed,
> yea fire shall devour thine adversaries.

The R.V. margin offers in the first clause "be ashamed in their envy of the people", and in the second "the fire of thine adversaries shall devour them". The M.T. version runs:

וְיֵבֹשׁוּ קִנְאַת־עָם אַף־אֵשׁ צָרֶיךָ תֹאכְלֵם׃

The LXX as we have it offers:

γνόντες δὲ αἰσχυνθήσονται· ζῆλος δὲ λήμψεται λαὸν ἀπαίδευτον, καὶ νῦν πῦρ τοὺς ἐναντίους ἔδεται.

It will be seen at once that πυρὸς ζῆλος is not an exact translation of either of these versions. In the M.T. קִנְאָה is not connected with אֵשׁ at all, but applies to the people, not to God. In the LXX ζῆλος and πῦρ belong to different clauses. Editors emend the M.T. in various ways. Kittel (*Biblia Hebraica* in loc.) would omit as a gloss the reference to being ashamed, and Cheyne would read "zeal for thy people". But no editor suggests any alteration of the text that would produce קִנְאַת־אֵשׁ, which is what πυρὸς ζῆλος would naturally seem to translate. An expedient is to suggest that this is not a quotation in Hebrews but an echo half remembered (e.g. Th. Robinson in the Moffatt ed. of Hebrews (London 1933, in loc.) says the phrase is coloured by the LXX translation of Isa. 26.11). But if it is only an echo, why does it take the unnatural form πυρὸς ζῆλος instead of the quite familiar ζήλους πῦρ? As a matter of fact all editors without exception assume that though the author has written πυρὸς ζῆλος he means ζήλους πῦρ "a fire of jealousy". For example Wickham (ed. Heb., West. Comm., London 1910, in loc.) actually quotes Zeph. 1.18, where the LXX quite accurately translates אֵשׁ־קִנְאָה as ζήλους πῦρ. Having turned πυρὸς ζῆλος into ζήλους πῦρ, editors then go on to explain ζῆλος in terms of more or less emotional wrath. Westcott for instance says: "The word ζῆλος suggests the thought of love which has been wronged, just as πῦρ describes one aspect of the divine nature", and he compares 12.29: ὁ Θεὸς ἡμῶν πῦρ ἀνάλισκον. But our author does not describe God as πῦρ here; it is not πῦρ that is in the nominative. We must therefore conclude either that out author knew a different Greek text of Isa. 26.11 to what we know, or that πυρὸς ζῆλος is a translation, not of קִנְאַת־עָם, but of אֵשׁ־קִן. Going only on the two versions of the text which we have, πυρὸς ζῆλος is actually nearer to אֵשׁ־קִן than to any other phrase either in the Hebrew or in the Greek. If this be so, our author is not translating קִנְאָה at all, but אֵשׁ, and this is more like an ὀργή passage than a ζῆλος one. Assuming that the author of Hebrews had a different text of the LXX to what we know (an assumption which Kahle in his work already referred to tends to confirm), we may ask: can we guess at the Hebrew behind the πυρὸς ζῆλος of our author's text of the LXX? Was it קִנְאַת־אֵשׁ? If so, the phrase is unparalleled in the Old Testament. It seems therefore much more likely that, whatever our author's Greek text, there lay behind it אֵשׁ־קִן. Perhaps some Greek translator rendered אֵשׁ־קִן as πυρὸς ζῆλος. But we cannot entirely eliminate the possibility that our author knew a Hebrew version from which he translated אֵשׁ־קִן for himself, but used ζῆλος in deference to his Greek version. At any rate we may conclude that this reference to the ζῆλος of God has not necessarily got the overtones of קִנְאָה, but is more like the ὀργή. This is confirmed by the anonymity of the reference (it is not called the ζῆλος τοῦ Θεοῦ), and the suggestion that the wrath is something which we bring upon ourselves. N.B. אֵשׁ־קִנְאָה occurs several times in the Old Testament. Driver and Briggs in their ed. of Gesenius' Lexicon (Oxford 1892) wrongly cite Isaiah 26.11 as such an example.

APPENDIX 6

THE WRATH OF GOD AND FAITH IN CHRISTIAN THOUGHT COMPARED WITH THE CONCEPTS OF *KARMA* AND *BHAKTI* IN HINDU THOUGHT

THERE is a remarkable parallel to the concept of the wrath of God as we have described it to be found in Hindu thought. It is the doctrine of *karma*, to which we have had occasion to refer once or twice already. An examination of this parallel leads us on to a comparison of the Christian conception of faith with the Hindu conception of *bhakti*; so we must treat the two pairs of corresponding ideas together.

We have already noticed (see p. 196) that the concept of the wrath in the New Testament has certain resemblances to the Hindu concept of *karma*, in so far as it is essentially an impersonal process. *Karma* was in Hinduism originally an answer to the problem of the inequality of men's fortunes in this world. Apparently unmerited disasters were explained by the theory that they were in fact punishment for the sins of the unfortunate in previous existences. This was elaborated into the belief that everything we do and suffer in this life is the exact consequences of our good or bad deeds in previous existences. Later Buddhism elaborated this still further (see L. de la V. Poussin, art. "Karma" in *E.R.E.*, Edinburgh 1909), and it seems to have represented man's personality as being nothing but his *karma*, the consequences of his good and bad deeds working themselves out in the world, a series of events and experiences which possess no real personal centre. *Karma* was also extended to cover all the operations of the universe. By *karma* the stars held their courses, the rains came or failed to come, and so on. *Karma* was also independent of God: even Brahma could not change *karma*. *Karma* also had its positive side; Hinduism had its doctrine of works (not Buddhism, which offered salvation through Nirvana, ceasing from action). There could be good *karma* as well as bad *karma*. After the Rigveda period *karma* came to be thought of as almost entirely the correct performance of sacrifices. It is important to notice also that good *karma*, doing good deeds, could not offer salvation, but only a more advantageous position on the wheel of life in the next incarnation (see R. L. Turner, art. "Karma Marga" in *E.R.E.*). Later still came the conception of *Gnana Marga* as opposed to *Karma Marga*. And *Gnana Marga*, the way of knowledge, did offer release from the cycle of births and deaths. Through self-knowledge, that is the realization of one's identity with Brahman, one could contract out of the sphere of *karma* altogether and be absorbed in the absolute. But the two ways subsisted side by side; the orthodox procedure was to spend most of one's life doing one's duty according to the law of *karma*, and then at the end of one's life to leave the world of men and live as a *sanyasi*, seeking to realize one's identity with the absolute by means of *Gnana Marga*.

So far we can claim only a very general resemblance between the wrath of God in the Scriptures and the concept of *karma* in Hindu thought. This resemblance has been noted by E. W. Thompson in his book *The Word of the Cross to Hindus* (London 1938). After outlining the doctrine of Karma he writes: "So stated, the doctrine of *karma* appears to be identical in some respects with the Christian doctrine of moral retribution" (p. 172), and he quotes Gal. 6.7,8 and 2 Cor. 5.10. He has not, however, connected the Christian doctrine of moral retribution with the wrath of God in the New Testament. Moreover the differences between the doctrine of *karma* and corresponding concepts in Christianity are very obvious. In the first place, *karma* is apparently essentially individualistic: "the terrible power of evil, as expressed in and through society, its sinister persistence in the form of heredity, the suffering it brings to the innocent and the unborn, its cohesiveness, its putrescent contagion, its malignant capacity to thwart the progress of human welfare", none of these qualities of evil is really included in the concept of *karma* (quotation from M. T. Kennedy, *The Chaitanya Movement*, Calcutta 1925). Indeed the fact that the wrath in its origins in the Old Testament is so much concerned with the destiny of nations rather than individuals is a strong proof of its fundamentally social character. This same criticism of the concept of *karma* is made by Thompson (op. cit., p. 180). Another difference between *karma* and wrath is that the former is bound up with the doctrine of metempsychosis. The doctrine of *karma* attempts the same task as do, for instance, Job's friends, the vindication of divine justice in terms of rewards and punishments in this life. *Karma*, since it calls in a doctrine of metempsychosis, is much less easy to disprove than is the ingenuous

APPENDIX 6

theodicy of Job's friends or that of the author of Ps. 37. But the transmigration of souls has its own problems. (They have been very well pointed out by the famous Telugu scholar of the last century, Rao Bahadur K. Viresalingam, in his lecture *Janmantaramu*, published by the Hithakarini Samaj, Rajahmundry). The New Testament concept of the wrath of God is not primarily a theodicy at all. It is not an explanation but a description. Moreover, impersonal though the wrath is in its operation, it is still called the wrath of God: the essence of the wrath is that it is a state of being alienated from God (Eph. 2.12). *Karma* has no necessary relation to God at all. Again, *karma* is a double process: it can mean merit as well as sin; there is good *karma* as well as bad. Because Christianity is a religion of faith, there can be no such counterpart to wrath in the New Testament. Indeed the pith of St Paul's argument in Romans is that the attempt, whether made by Jews or Gentiles, to gain salvation by doing good *karma* has failed.

On the other hand, the apparent resemblance between the wrath and *karma* is not entirely illusive. The state of those who are thought of as being under the wrath in the New Testament, and of those who are conceived as being caught in the cycle of births and deaths in Hindu thought, is similar. In both the sufferer seems to be the helpless victim of circumstances; of both we can say that the further a man is from salvation (however salvation be defined) the more impersonal is his condition. When we also remember the Aeschylean principle of δράσαντι παθεῖν, and the difficulty that Aeschylus experiences in the *Eumenides* in escaping from that principle, we must surely conclude that in this conviction, that "what a man sows that must he reap", we can discern a principle of natural theology. The way in which this principle is fitted into the various religious systems is, however, the touchstone of their specific differences, and it is in this that the greatest divergency appears between Christianity and Hinduism.

When we turn to the concept of *bhakti*, the resemblance to Christianity is much more remarkable. Indeed Sir G. A. Grierson states (art. "Bhakti Marga" in *E.R.E.*) quite definitely that the Bhakti cult in its developments, though not in its origin, was influenced by Christianity —an opinion which does not seem to have found much support among subsequent scholars. Though the concept of *bhakti* is found far earlier, the real history of the *bhakti* cult begins in the twelfth century A.D. It was in effect a protest against throughgoing Vedantism or orthodox Hindu pantheism. Its champions were Ramanuja and Madhva. The former retained as much of Vedantism as he could, the latter was much more independent. For the out and out *bhakti* worshipper the *Bhakti Marga* was a third way of life beside *Karma Marga* and *Gnana Marga*. Scholars have not found it easy to get an exact translation of *bhakti*: "Devotion" seems to be the nearest. Bishop Appasamy (in *Christianity as Bhakti Marga*, London 1927, p. 22) says that it is essentially man's self-giving love to God, rather than faith alone. The element of surrender and dependence is certainly most marked, and some of the great *bhakti* poets express their utter dependence on God in language which would certainly not be inappropriate for a Christian. As early as the Bhagavad Gita, which, in this section at least, is dated by most scholars at about the fourth century B.C., we find the concept of the *nishkama* or disinterested work. This was interpreted by later *bhakti* worshippers as meaning that the only works valuable in the eyes of God are those offered without any thought of reward or merit, but done only out of devotion to God. This certainly is not far from the "reasonable, holy, and living sacrifice" of Romans 12. This *bhakti* attitude could not fail to afford a contrast to the *Karma Marga*: "A favourite comparison is with a paid workman and a slave born in the house. If a paid workman (i.e. a doer of interested works) does any damage, he has to make it good to his employer; but if damage is done by a faithful slave (i.e. the doer of disinterested works), who works for love and not for reward, the master bears the loss, and none of it falls on the slave" (Grierson, op. cit., p. 544). Macnicol represents *Bhakti Marga* and *Gnana Marga* as entirely unreconciled opposites (*The Living Religions of the Indian People*, London 1934, p. 88): "Orthodox *bhakti* worshippers", he says, "are drawn in the one direction or the other by contrary desires— the desire for fellowship with God on the one hand, and the desire for release from rebirth on the other." And he quotes a scholar, Gnanesvar, as saying that there are some to whom is "so dear the faith of *bhakti*, they despise the great release". Appasamy on the other hand quotes authors who would reconcile *karma* with *bhakti*, saying that the determination to be devoted or opposed to God is decided by a man's previous *karma*. "It is his *karma* which enables him either to have or not have *bhakti*" (Appasamy, op. cit., p. 54). On this he comments: "If

APPENDIX 6

bhakti is determined by factors like *karma* for which we are not responsible, it cannot be the deep personal relationship it ought to be" (p. 57). This previous determination of *bhakti* was in fact a conclusion to which Paul very nearly comes in Rom. 9, and one which Calvin boldly accepted. But Paul was perhaps saved from adopting it by his deeply personal conception of God, which enabled him to see the gift of faith as dependent not on *karma*, but on the will of God. And in the last resort he could not believe that the will of God had predestined any to wrath.

It is very interesting to try to answer the question: From what is *bhakti* conceived as rescuing the devotee? In the case of the great exponents of the Bhakti cult, the answer seems to be unequivocally, *karma*. Thus the Tamil Saivite poet, Mannika Vasagar, quoted by Sydney Cave (*Redemption Hindu and Christian*, Oxford 1919, pp. 128–9), in describing his condition before conversion, says:

> I gave no thought on thronging births and deaths,
>   but dwelt on tricks and wiles and glancing eyes
> Of maids with wealth of braided tresses fair . . .
>   He [God] wisdom gave and made me all His own.

That is, the poet felt he should have been concerned with the great problem of escape from *karma*, but when salvation came it brought with it release from *karma* through *bhakti*. Similarly Appasamy (op. cit., p. 74) claims that the *bhakti* worshippers found in their cult "a release from the ever recurring cycle of births and deaths". Here is M. T. Kennedy's summary of the faith of the great *bhakti* revivalist Chaitanya: "But when the soul, becoming conscious of its rightful relation to Krishna as its lord and saviour, turns to him in faith, it is rid of illusion and finds salvation through the experience of *bhakti*."

There is certainly a remarkable parallel to be found between the New Testament conception of faith in God through Christ which delivers us from the sphere of the wrath, and the Hindu conception of *bhakti* towards the deity (be he Krishna or Siva) which delivers the devotee from the sphere of *karma*. Many Christian scholars have failed to see the full force of this parallel, as they have not fully realized the *impersonal* nature of the divine wrath in the New Testament, and *impersonality* is the hall-mark of *karma*. But when we have said this we have said all that can be claimed about the resemblance between *bhakti* and πίστις, *karma* and ἡ ὀργὴ τοῦ Θεοῦ. We must not fail to go on and note the outstanding differences between the two sets of ideas. The main difference undoubtedly lies in that from which *bhakti* and πίστις respectively deliver one. The Hindu claims deliverance from *karma*, the Christian from sin. When the Christian speaks of being delivered from the wrath, he means the wrath as primarily a state of alienation from God. The Hindu means by *karma* either suffering, or merely worldly existence, or illusion. Thus the Tamil Saivite *bhakti* poet Appar, quoted by Appasamy, p. 100, cries:

> I am caught in the tangle of supporting my wife and children, who have merely physical wants.

In the quotation given on p. 279 from Kennedy's account of Chaitanya the soul is described as "rid of illusion", and later on in his book (p. 228) Kennedy says: "In its conception of that from which the soul is saved Vaishnavism falls back upon the traditional ideas which are strange to Christian thought. It is illusion, Maya, ignorance—the realm subject to the working of *karma* and transmigration." (The Vaishnavites were pre-eminent as *bhakti*-worshippers; Krishna, Chaitanya's special devotion, was an incarnation of Vishnu; but the Saivites had their *bhakti*-worshippers too, e.g. Appar, quoted above). The *bhakti* cult tended, despite the religious background from which it sprang, to grope its way towards a really personal conception of God: "To him the very ideal of salvation involves personal consciousness, and a real relationship between lover and beloved", says Kennedy of Chaitanya (p. 98). But it never quite attained a truly personal conception of God, and always inclined to fall back on the monistic thought of God as that which is in its ground identical with the creation. Small wonder that, according to Grierson (op. cit.), there was in the Middle Ages in India a rumour of a fair-skinned race in the West that had a perfect doctrine of *bhakti*. The consequence is that sin is never treated seriously enough; as Cave says (op. cit., p. 136): "Sin is not treated as the act of a responsible personality. All Siva's grace can do is to illuminate the soul by revealing its identity with himself." Moreover, since *Bhakti Marga* is essentially irreconcilable with *Gnana Marga* or *Karma Marga*, the relation of *bhakti* to *karma* was never satisfactorily

APPENDIX 6

decided. The historian of Hindu thought must pronounce that fundamentally *karma* is one thing and salvation by *bhakti* another. They both (like much else that is irreconcilable) happen to come under the category "Hinduism", but they have no essential relation to one another. In Christian thought, on the other hand, salvation by faith is intimately related to the law–sin–wrath sphere from which the believer is saved. Wrath works according to Law; without Law sin could not be known to be sin; and salvation through faith is essentially salvation from sin.

Bhakti, then, as salvation from *karma*, cannot be exactly equated with faith in Christ as salvation from wrath. There is a great difference which springs from two different conceptions of God, one as impersonal and the other as personal. But this does not mean that Christian thinkers can afford to dismiss the *Bhakti Marga* as of no interest to them. On the contrary, there is sufficient truth in the conception of *bhakti*, especially as developed in the *bhakti* poets, for us to be able to say that in the *bhakti* cult of India we can trace the activity of the Logos. Just as the Alexandrian Fathers of the first three centuries A.D. claimed that they could trace the activities of the Logos in the writings of Plato, so Christian theologians in India should surely be ready to see in the *bhakti* concept of Hinduism a trace of the Logos as revealed outside the Christian dispensation. This does not mean that we should receive into Christianity the whole *bhakti* cult with all its implications and accompaniments, but that we should be ready to acknowledge that the *bhakti*-worshippers did understand something of God's way with men. Their understanding was imperfect, it is true; because of the deeply rooted principle of monism from which they set out, they could never fully apprehend the personal encounter of God in Christ. Because their account of the incarnation of God was legendary and mixed up with all sorts of mistaken and (by Christian standards) positively immoral circumstances, they could not see the Word made flesh; but they did apprehend something of what Paul is emphasizing in the Epistle to the Romans. They at least approached the conception of a righteousness which is not of the Law; they knew something of a God who saves from the wrath. Because their understanding of God was not sufficiently personal, that righteousness was thought of too much as absorption in deity, and not enough as personal communion with God; and the wrath was conceived of too much as a state of suffering and illusion and not enough as a state of alienation from the holy God. Indian Christian theologians in the past have tended too much to deny any resemblances between Christianity and Hinduism. To-day a few of them are tending not to emphasize the essential differences enough. The Alexandrian Fathers could have taught them otherwise; they were ready (perhaps too ready) to recognize the activity of the Logos in the Greek philosophy which formed the intellectual climate of their age. But they never doubted that that activity had been overlaid and obscured by much that was untrue and misleading; and their test of truth and purity was always the Word as he had been revealed in Jesus Christ.

We have said that the account which the *bhakti* worshippers gave of the incarnation of God was legendary and mixed up with misleading and even repulsive details. Even this is not true of the Saivite *bhakti*-worshippers, who did not worship their deity as incarnate. But the Vishnavite *bhakti*-worshippers have always been the majority and their *bhakti* cult centred on Krishna as an incarnation of Vishnu. Both the shortcomings and the insights of this Indian *bhakti* cult of the incarnate deity are clearly discernible in the career of Chaitanya, the famous Bengali leader of the Vishnavite *bhakti* cult, who flourished in the early sixteenth century of our era. Chaitanya led a great revival of *bhakti* worship, which took firm hold for a time in Northern India. It was a reaction against the formalism of Vedantic Brahmanism. Chaitanya was born in 1486; the parallel with Luther is remarkable, and has been noted by Kennedy (p. 227). The differences from Luther are equally remarkable, and the fact that Luther's work has stood, while Chaitanya's movement is apparently nothing but a memory, is also significant. Chaitanya eventually settled down at the famous shrine of Jagannadh in Puri in Orissa, and there devoted the rest of his life to meditation on, and devotion to, Krishna as the incarnation of Vishnu. The precise phase of that incarnation on which he concentrated was the legend of Krishna's amorous exploits with Radha, the girl who left her wedded husband in order to devote her whole life to the service of Krishna. Chaitanya deliberately took as his exemplar for love toward the deity the love which Radha had for Krishna. He encouraged his disciples in their meditations to imagine themselves in Radha's situation and to try to recapture her experiences (for these details see Kennedy, op. cit., pp. 108f.). This must seem astonishing and indeed offensive to

Christians. We are familiar in some medieval mysticism with the thought of the individual soul as the bride of Christ being elaborated with great imaginative detail—even though such a concept could hardly be called anything but peripheral in the Bible. But deliberately to think of the soul as the concubine of the deity seems outright blasphemy. Before condemning, however (as we must condemn as Christians), we should pause to ask how Chaitanya, a man undoubtedly of deep religious instincts, could have come to adopt so grotesque and (to us) repulsive an idea. What apparently appealed to him in this legend was the risk which Radha took for the sake of Krishna. Krishna in the legend had a lawful wife of his own, but for Krishna's wife to devote herself to her husband would not be an unusual display of self-sacrifice, but only what convention demanded. The fact that Radha was ready to risk everything, including reputation and morals, for the sake of Krishna was what appealed to Chaitanya. As Christians we ought at least to be able to understand this: that element of risking all for the sake of God is very prominent in the Bible. More than that, when Paul speaks of the "foolishness of God" (1 Cor. 1.25) what he means surely is that God himself was willing to take a risk for the sake of men. He was willing to take the risk of putting himself unreservedly in their hands and permitting them to do what they would with him. And it is this element of risk apparent in the Cross that is perhaps the source of its deepest appeal to men. When we compare the risk that God really took in Christ with the risk that Radha is supposed to have taken in the legend, we cannot for a moment hesitate in deciding which is true and noble and which is imperfect and ambiguous. But at least we can understand what it was that attracted Chaitanya, and we can recognize, even in this doubtful and distorted cult, a gleam of the Light that is the Life of men.

BIBLIOGRAPHY

PRE-OLD TESTAMENT

G. A. Cooke: *A Text Book of North Semitic Inscriptions* (Oxford 1903)

M. Jastrow: *Die Religions Babyloniens und Assyriens* (Giessen 1905)

A. Jeremias: *The Old Testament in the Light of the Ancient East* (tr. Beaumont, London 1911)

W. F. Albright: *Archaeology and the Religion of Israel* (Baltimore 1946)

—— *From Stone Age to Christianity* (Baltimore 1946)

C. H. Gordon: *The Loves and Wars of Baal and Anat* (Princeton 1943)

—— *Ugaritic Handbook* (Rome 1947)

—— *Ugaritic Literature* (Rome 1949)

OLD TESTAMENT GENERAL

Hermann Schultz: *Old Testament Theology* (tr. Paterson, Edinburgh 1892)

S. R. Driver, C. A. Briggs, & F. Brown: ed. Gesenius' *Hebrew Dictionary* (London 1892 ed.)

H. B. Swete: *An Introduction to the Old Testament in Greek* (2nd ed., Cambridge 1902)

P. Kuechler: "Der Gedanken des Eifers Jahwehs in A.T.", *Zeitschrift f.d. A. T. Wissenschaft*, pp. 42–53 (Giessen 1908)

W. O. E. Oesterley & T. H. Robinson: *A History of Israel*, 2 vols. (Oxford 1932)

W. O. E. Oesterly: *An Introduction to the Books of the Old Testament* (London 1934)

H. Wheeler Robinson: ed. *Record and Revelation* (Oxford 1938)

N. Snaith: *The Distinctive Ideas of the Old Testament* (London 1944)

P. Kahle: *The Cairo Geniza* (London 1947)

R. Kittel: ed. *Biblia Hebraica* (4th ed., Stuttgart 1949)

H. H. Rowley: *Studies in Old Testament Prophecy* (Edinburgh 1950)

L. Koehler & W. Baumgartner: *Lexicon in Vetus Testamenti Libros* (Leiden 1953)

OLD TESTAMENT COMMENTARIES

GENESIS:

S. R. Driver: *West. Comm.* (London 1907)

J. Skinner: *I.C.C.* (London 1910)

BIBLIOGRAPHY

Exodus:
B. Baentsch: *Handkommentar z. A.T.* (Goettingen 1900)
A. H. McNeile: *West. Comm.* (London 1908)
S. R. Driver: *Camb. Bible* (Cambridge 1911)

Leviticus:
A. T. Chapman & A. Streane: *Camb. Bible* (Cambridge 1914)

Numbers:
A. Dillmann: ed. *Numbers, Deut., Joshua* (Leipzig 1886)
G. B. Gray: *I.C.C.* (Edinburgh 1903)
L. E. Elliott-Binns: *West. Comm.* (London 1927)

Deuteronomy:
C. Steuernagel: ed. *Deut.* and *Joshua* (Goettingen 1900)
S. R. Driver: *I.C.C.* (3rd ed., Edinburgh 1902)

Joshua:
J. Garstang: ed. *Joshua-Judges* (London 1931)

Judges:
G. F. Moore: *I.C.C.* (Edinburgh 1903)
C. F. Burney: ed. *Judges* (London 1920)

1 & 2 Samuel:
F. H. F. Smith: *I.C.C.* (Edinburgh 1899)
D. K. Kirkpatrick: *Camb. Bible* (Cambridge 1930)

1 & 2 Kings:
J. Skinner: *Century Bible* (Edinburgh 1900)
W. E. Barnes: *Camb. Bible* (Cambridge 1908)
I. W. Slotki: *Soncino Series* (London 1950)

1 & 2 Chronicles:
O. Zoeckler: ed. 2 *Chron.* (tr. Murphy, Edinburgh 1876?)
W. A. L. Elmslie: *Camb. Bible* (Cambridge 1915)

Ezra-Nehemiah:
L. W. Batten: *I.C.C.* (Edinburgh 1913)

Amos & Hosea:
R. F. Horton: *Century Bible* (London 1900)
W. R. Harper: *I.C.C.* (Edinburgh 1910)
R. S. Cripps: ed. *Amos* (London 1929)

MICAH:
R. F. Horton: *Century Bible* (London 1910)
J. M. P. Smith: *I.C.C.* (Edinburgh 1912)
ISAIAH:
T. K. Cheyne: ed. *Isaiah* (London 1884)
C. J. Bredenkampf: ed. *Isaiah* (Erlangen 1887)
F. Delitzsch: ed. *Isaiah* (Eng. tr., Edinburgh 1890)
J. Skinner: ed. *Isaiah 1-39, Camb. Bible* (Cambridge 1900)
G. H. Box: ed. *Isaiah 40-66* (London 1908)
G. W. Wade: *West. Comm.* (London 1911)
G. B. Gray: ed. *Isaiah 1-27, I.C.C.* (Edinburgh 1912)
G. A. Smith: ed. *Isaiah 1-39* (London 1927)
J. Skinner: ed. *Isaiah 40-66, Camb. Bible* (Cambridge 1929)
E. J. Kissane: ed. *Isaiah 1-39* (Dublin 1943)
I. W. Slotki: *Soncino Series* (London 1949)
JEREMIAH:
C. H. Cornill: ed. *Jeremiah* (Leipzig 1905)
S. R. Driver: ed. *Jeremiah* (London 1908)
A. S. Peake: *Century Bible* (London 1900)
B. Duhm: ed. *Jeremiah* (Tuebingen and Leipzig 1910-11)
L. E. Elliott-Binns: *West. Comm.* (London 1919)
H. Freedman: *Soncino Series* (London 1949)
LAMENTATIONS:
A. S. Peake: *Century Bible* (London 1900)
EZEKIEL:
C. H. Cornill: ed. *Ezekiel* (Leipzig 1886)
C. H. Toy: *Polychrome Bible* (London-Stuttgart-New York 1899)
R. Kraetschmar: ed. *Ezekiel* (Goettingen 1900)
A. B. Davidson: *Camb. Bible* (Cambridge 1900)
W. F. Lofthouse: *Century Bible* (1907)
H. A. Redpath: *West. Comm.* (London 1907)
G. A. Cooke: *I.C.C.* (Edinburgh 1936)
NAHUM:
J. M. P. Smith: *I.C.C.* (Edinburgh 1912)
C. G. V. Stonehouse: *West. Comm.* (London 1929)

HABAKKUK:
F. Delitzsch: ed. *Habakkuk* (Leipzig 1843)
W. H. Ward: *I.C.C.* (Edinburgh 1910)
G. W. Wade: *West. Comm.* (London 1929)
MALACHI:
T. T. Perowne: *Camb. Bible* (Cambridge 1898)
J. M. P. Smith: *I.C.C.* (Edinburgh 1912)
OBADIAH:
T. T. Perowne: *Camb. Bible* (Cambridge 1898)
J. Bewer: *I.C.C.* (Edinburgh 1912)
JOEL:
J. Bewer: *I.C.C.* (Edinburgh 1912)
JONAH:
T. T. Perowne: *Camb. Bible* (Cambridge 1898)
J. Bewer: *I.C.C.* (Edinburgh 1912)
ZECHARIAH:
T. T. Perowne: *Camb. Bible* (Cambridge 1898)
H. G. Mitchell: *I.C.C.* (Edinburgh 1912)
PSALMS:
F. W. A. Baethgen: ed. *Psalms* (Goettingen 1897)
T. Witton Davies: ed. *Psalms* 63–90, *Century Bible* (London 1900)
T. K. Cheyne: ed. *Psalms* (London 1904)
C. A. Briggs: *I.C.C.*, 2 vols. (Edinburgh 1907)
A. F. Kirkpatrick: ed. *Psalms* 42–89, *Camb. Bible* (Cambridge 1914)
W. E. Barnes: *West. Comm.* (London 1931)
W. O. E. Oesterley: ed. *Psalms*, 2 vols. (London 1939)
A. Cohen: *Soncino ed.* (London 1948)
PROVERBS:
T. T. Perowne: *Camb. Bible* (Cambridge 1898)
C. H. Toy: *I.C.C.* (Edinburgh 1904)
JOB:
G. H. A. von Ewald: ed. *Job* (Eng. tr., London 1882)
E. C. S. Gibson: *West. Comm.* (2nd ed., London 1905)
S. R. Driver: ed. *Job* (Oxford 1906)
J. Strahan: ed. *Job* (Edinburgh 1913)

JOB—*continued*.
A. B. Davidson: *Camb. Bible* (Cambridge 1918)
S. R. Driver & G. B. Gray: *I.C.C.* (Edinburgh 1921)
E. J. Kissane: ed. *Job* (Dublin 1939)
V. E. Reichart: *Soncino Series* (London 1946)

DANIEL:
S. R. Driver: *Camb. Bible* (Cambridge 1912)
J. A. Montgomery: *I.C.C.* (Edinburgh 1927)
H. H. Rowley: *Darius the Mede* (Cardiff 1936)

INTER-TESTAMENTAL PERIOD

C. Tischendorf: *Apocalypses Apocryphae* (Leipzig 1866)
A. Wuensche: *Der Midrasch Bereschit Rabba* (Leipzig 1881)
S. A. Naber: ed. *Josephus Opera Omnia* (Leipzig 1888)
S. Bueber: *Midrasch Tehillim* (tr. Wuensche, Trier 1892)
R. L. Bensly: *Fourth Book of Esdras; Camb. Texts and Studies*, Vol. 3, No. 2 (Cambridge 1895)
T. C. Conybeare: "The Apocalypse of Moses", *Jewish Quarterly Review*, vii, 216–35 (London 1895)
G. N. Bonwetsch: *Die Apokalypse Abrahams* (Leipzig 1897)
R. H. Charles: *The Assumption of Moses* (London 1897)
M. R. James: Ἀποκάλυψις Βαρούχ, *Apocrypha Anecdota*, 2nd Series, *Camb. Texts and Studies*, Vol. 15 (Cambridge 1897)
C. Taylor: *Sayings of the Jewish Fathers* (2nd ed., Cambridge 1897)
Israel Lévi: ed. *Hebrew Text of Ecclesiasticus* (Paris 1898)
J. Geffcken: *Sibylline Oracles, Corp. Scr. Gr.* (Leipzig 1902)
A. Duff: *First and Second Books of Esdras* (London 1902)
W. Fairweather: *I and II Maccabees* (London 1903)
W. B. Stevenson: *Wisdom and the Jewish Apocryphal Writings* (London 1903)
L. Cohn & P. Wendland: ed. *Philonis Opera* (Berlin 1906)
R. H. Charles: *The Greek Version of the Testament of the Twelve Patriarchs* (Oxford 1908)
J. A. F. Gregg: ed. *Wisdom of Solomon, Camb. Bible* (Cambridge 1909)
J. H. A. Hart: ed. *Greek Text of Ecclesiasticus* (Cambridge 1909)
S. Schechter: *Documents of Jewish Sectaries*, Vol. 1 (Cambridge 1910)

BIBLIOGRAPHY

J. Viteau: *Les Psaumes de Salomon* (Paris 1911)

W. O. E. Oesterley: ed. *Ecclesiasticus, Camb. Bible* (Cambridge 1912)

R. H. Charles: ed. *Apocrypha and Pseudepigrapha of the Old Testament*, 2 vols. (Oxford 1913)

H. J. Wicks: *The Doctrine of God in Jewish Apocryphal and Apocalyptic Literature* (London 1915)

W. O. E. Oesterley: *The Books of the Apocrypha* (London 1916)

C. W. Emmet: *III and IV Maccabees* (London 1918)

F. H. Colson & G. H. Whittaker: tr. *Philo*, Loeb ed. (London 1929)

H. Danby: *The Mishnah* (tr. and ed. London 1933)

J. Bonsirven: *Le Judaisme palestinien au temps de Jésus Christ*, 2 vols. (Paris 1934)

W. O. E. Oesterley: *An Introduction to the Books of the Apocrypha* (London 1935)

C. G. Montefiore & H. Loewe: *A Rabbinic Anthology* (London 1938)

Bulletin of the American Schools of Oriental Research: No. 112, pp. 8–18 (Jerusalem–Baghdad, December 1948)

E. L. Sukenik: *Megilloth Genuzoth* (Jerusalem 1948–50)

M. Burrows: *The Dead Sea Scrolls of St Mark's Monastery*, Vol. I: *The Isaiah Manuscript and the Habakkuk Commentary* (New Haven 1950)

G. R. Driver: *The Hebrew Scrolls* (Oxford 1951)

H. H. Rowley: *The Zadokite Fragments and the Dead Sea Scrolls* (Oxford 1952)

A. Dupont-Sommer: *The Dead Sea Scrolls* (Eng. tr., Oxford 1952)

Chaim Rabin: *The Zadokite Documents* (Oxford 1954)

NEW TESTAMENT GENERAL

G. Kittel: ed. *Theologisches Woerterbuch z. N.T.*: arts.: γενέα, ζῆλος, θυμός, ὀργή (Stuttgart 1933–)

C. H. Dodd: "The Mind of Paul", etc., *Bulletin of Rylands Library*, Vol. XVIII, No. 1, p. 69 (Manchester 1934)

T. W. Manson: *The Teaching of Jesus* (Cambridge 1935, 2nd ed.)

A. T. Hanson: "Theophanies in the Old Testament", etc., *Hermathena*, Vol. LXV (Dublin and London 1945)

O. Cullmann: *Christ et le temps* (Neuchâtel and Paris 1947)

W. D. Davies: *Paul and Rabbinic Judaism* (London 1948)

E. H. Blakeney: Letter to *The Guardian*: "Wrath of God", 4 October 1950.

D. E. W. Harrison: "The Apostolic Testimony to Christ Crucified", *The Churchman*, Vol. LXV (London 1951)

J. H. Moulton & G. Milligan: *The Vocabulary of the Greek Testament* (London 1952 ed.)

R. Fuller: *The Mission and Achievement of Jesus* (London 1954)

NEW TESTAMENT COMMENTARIES

1 AND 2 THESSALONIANS:
W. Milligan: ed. 1 and 2 Thess. (London 1908)

GALATIANS:
J. B. Lightfoot: ed. *Galatians* (London 1881)
E. de W. Burton: *I.C.C.* (Edinburgh 1921)
A. W. F. Blunt: *Clarendon Bible* (Oxford 1925)
G. S. Duncan: *Moffatt Comm.* (London 1934)
E. Middleton: ed. *Luther's Comm. in Gal.* (London 1940)

1 CORINTHIANS:
F. Godet: ed. 1 *Corinthians* (tr. Cusin, Edinburgh 1887)
A. L. Goudge: *West. Comm.* (London 1903)
A. Robertson & A. Plummer: *I.C.C.* (Edinburgh 1911)
E. Evans: *Clarendon Bible* (Oxford 1930)
J. Moffatt: *Moffatt Comm.* (London 1938)

2 CORINTHIANS:
A. Plummer: *I.C.C.* (Edinburgh 1915)
A. L. Goudge: *West. Comm.* (London 1927)
R. H. Strachan: *Moffatt Comm.* (London 1935)

ROMANS:
W. Sanday & A. C. Headlam: *I.C.C.* (Edinburgh 1907)
C. H. Dodd: *Moffatt Comm.* (London 1932)
K. Barth: ed. *Romans* (tr. E. Hoskyns, Oxford 1933)

PHILIPPIANS:
J. B. Lightfoot: ed. *Philippians* (London 1890)

COLOSSIANS:
J. B. Lightfoot: ed. *Colossians* (London 1892)
T. K. Abbott: *I.C.C.* (Edinburgh, no date)

BIBLIOGRAPHY

EPHESIANS:
T. K. Abbott: *I.C.C.* (Edinburgh, no date)
J. Armitage Robinson: ed. *Ephesians* (London 1907)
C. Gore: ed. *Ephesians* (London 1909)
MATTHEW:
A. Plummer: ed. *Matthew* (London 1909)
W. C. Allen: *I.C.C.* (3rd ed., Edinburgh)
A. H. McNeile: ed. *Matthew* (London 1915)
MARK:
H. B. Swete: ed. *Mark* (London 1898)
LUKE:
A. Plummer: *I.C.C.* (Edinburgh 1901)
JOHN:
B. F. Westcott: ed. *John* (London 1889)
J. H. Bernard: *I.C.C.* (Edinburgh 1928)
E. C. Hoskyns & F. N. Davey: *The Fourth Gospel* (London 1940)
C. H. Dodd: *The Interpretation of the Fourth Gospel* (London 1953)
JOHANNINE EPISTLES:
B. F. Westcott: ed. *Johannine Epistles* (London 1886)
W. H. Bennett: *Century Bible* (London 1900)
H. Pakenham Walsh: *Indian Church Comms.* (Madras 1910)
C. H. Dodd: *Moffatt Comm.* (London 1946)
ACTS:
A. W. F. Blunt: *Clarendon Bible* (Oxford 1922)
E. R. Rackham: *West. Comm.* (10th ed., London 1925)
F. J. Foakes-Jackson: *Moffatt Comm.* (London 1931)
F. J. Foakes-Jackson & Kirsopp Lake: *The Beginnings of Christianity*, 5 vols. (London 1933)
HEBREWS:
F. Rendall: ed. *Hebrews* (London 1883)
B. F. Westcott: ed. *Hebrews* (London 1903)
E. C. Wickham: *West. Comm.* (London 1910)
H. Windisch: *Handbuch z. N.T.* 4th vol., 3rd book (Tuebingen 1913)
W. H. G. Holmes: *Indian Church Comms.* (Calcutta 1917)
T. H. Robinson: *Moffatt Comm.* (London 1933)

PASTORAL EPISTLES:
E. F. Browne: *West. Comm.* (London 1917)
E. F. Scott: *Moffatt Comm.* (London 1936)
R. Falconer: ed. *Pastoral Eps.* (Oxford 1937)

1 PETER:
J. R. Lumby: *Expositor's Bible* (London 1893)
W. H. Bennett: *Century Bible* (London 1900)
C. Bigg: *I.C.C.* (London 1901)
J. W. C. Wand: *West. Comm.* (London 1934)
E. G. Selwyn: ed. *1 Peter* (London 1946)
F. W. Beare: ed. *1 Peter* (Oxford 1947)

JAMES:
A. Plummer: *Expositor's Bible* (London 1897)
J. B. Mayor: ed. *James* (London 1897)
W. H. Bennett: *Century Bible* (London 1900)
E. H. Plumptre: *Camb. Bible* (Cambridge 1909)

2 PETER AND JUDE:
W. H. Bennett: *Century Bible* (London 1900)
C. Bigg: *I.C.C.* (Edinburgh 1901)
E. H. Plumptre: *Camb. Bible* (Cambridge 1909)
J. W. C. Wand: *West. Comm.* (London 1934)

REVELATION:
H. B. Swete: ed. *Revelation* (London 1909)
R. H. Charles: *I.C.C.* (Edinburgh 1920, 2 vols)
R. H. Preston & A. T. Hanson: *Torch Comm.* (2nd ed., London 1951)
A. T. Hanson: "Studies in Texts: Rev. 14.20", *Theology*, Vol. XLIX, No. 311, p. 141 (London 1946)
A. Farrer: *A Rebirth of Images* (London 1949)

DOCTRINE OF THE WRATH

A. Ritschl: *De Ira Dei* (Bonn 1859)
J. McLeod Campbell: *The Nature of the Atonement* (London 1873)
R. W. Dale: *The Atonement* (London 1884)
J. Hastings: ed. *Dictionary of the Bible* (London 1898)
A. Ritschl: *The Christian Doctrine of Justification and Reconciliation*, Vol. 3 (Eng. tr., Edinburgh 1900)

BIBLIOGRAPHY

R. C. Moberly: *Atonement and Personality* (London 1901)
F. R. Tennant: *The Source of the Doctrine of the Fall and Original Sin* (Cambridge 1903)
P. T. Forsyth: *The Work of Christ* (New York and London 1910)
H. Rashdall: *The Idea of the Atonement in Christian Theology* (London 1919)
E. G. Selwyn: ed. *Essays Catholic and Critical* (London 1926)
A. E. J. Rawlinson: *Essays on the Trinity and the Incarnation* (London 1928)
K. Barth: *Doctrine of the Word of God* (Eng. tr., G. G. Thompson, Edinburgh 1936)
Edwin Bevan: *Symbolism and Belief* (London 1938)
A. B. Macaulay: *The Death of Jesus* (London 1938)
L. Hodgson: *Towards a Christian Philosophy* (London 1943)
Sydney Cave: *Doctrine of the Work of Christ* (London 1947)
R. V. G. Tasker: *The Biblical Doctrine of the Wrath of God* (London 1951)
Gordon Rupp: *The Righteousness of God* (London 1952)

RELATION TO HINDUISM

J. Hastings: ed. *Encyclopaedia of Religion and Ethics* (Edinburgh 1909)
   arts. "Bhakti Marga", G. A. Grierson
      "Karma", L. de V. Poussin
      "Karma Marga", R. L. Turner
Sydney Cave: *Redemption Christian and Hindu* (Oxford 1919)
M. T. Kennedy: *The Chaitanya Movement* (Calcutta 1925)
A. J. Appasamy: *Christianity as Bhakti Marga* (London 1927)
E. W. Thompson: *The Word of the Cross to Hindus* (London 1933)
Nicol Macnicol: *The Living Religions of the Indian People* (London 1934)

INDEX OF REFERENCES AND CITATIONS

OLD TESTAMENT

Genesis	
6.6	207
6.7	56
18.30	207
31.35	207
44.2	29
44.5	29

Exodus	
4.14	206
15.7	11, 206
19.12	139
19.22–24	3
21.13	60
22.24	206
32.6	144

Leviticus	
10.6	206
18.5	211
23.29	128
26.28	206

Numbers	
11.1	4
11.4	76
11.10	3
11.33	206
12.9	4, 162, 206
12.10	4
14.34	22, 162, 207
15.30	59
16.26	206
16.31–35	4
16.46	22
21.6	4
22.20	3
22.22	3
25.11	4
32.10	4, 162, 206
32.14	162, 206

Deuteronomy	
1.34	6
1.37	207
3.26	6
4.24	140
6.16	78
7.4	162, 206
9.18	207
11.17	206
13.17	162
18.15	128, 129
21.23	74
29.18	131
30.12,13	210
31.17	162
31.29	207
32.16	207
32.21	77
32.27	11, 207
32.33	49
32.35	11, 93
32.36	207

Judges	
6.39	207
19.27	35

1 Samuel	
6.19	1, 183
15.11	148, 208
26.16	103
26.19	2, 39
28.18	11

2 Samuel	
6.6,7	23, 183
6.7,8	1, 2
6.8	3, 208
24.1	1, 2, 3, 23
24.25	2, 3

1 Kings	
22.21	72

2 Kings		18.49	99
3.27	5, 43, 208	35.19	144
		60.3	33
1 Chronicles		69.4	144
13.10	1	69.9	98, 99
15.13	23	69.25	131
21.1	23	75.8	34, 36, 57
27.24	22, 23	78.21	23
		78.31	23
2 Chronicles		78.49	58, 87
19.2	22, 53	78.37	131
19.10	22, 23	82.6	146
24.18	23	85.1–7	18
26.19	22	85.3	39
28.9	23	85.4–6	18
28.11	23	85.8	18
28.13	23	85.10, 11	19
32.25, 26	22	91.11, 12	99
36.16	22, 24	95.10	133
		99.1	171
Ezra		105.44	54
7.23	23	106.23	39
9.14	23, 25	106.30	39
		111.7–11	19
Nehemiah		119.9	148
9.5	26	119.17	148
13.18	23	119.67	148
		119.101	148
Job		119.158	148
4.9	20	Proverbs	
7.17	51	3.1	148
9.5	21	11.4	24
10.17	20	11.23	24
13.16	81	11.30, 31	151
14.13	20, 46	24.18	24
16.9	21		
19.11	21	Song of Songs	
21.20	36, 192	1.16	55
40.11	21	Isaiah	
Psalms		2.10	72
2.2	171	3.19	35
2.8, 9	168	5.25	7
6.1	39, 44	6.9	117, 130, 144
7.11	55	6.10	115, 117
11.6	36	8.14	120
16.5	36	9.8	7

INDEX OF REFERENCES AND CITATIONS

Isaiah (cont.)

9.12	7
9.17	7
9.21	7
10.3	119
10.4	7
10.5	7, 10, 33, 164
10.24–7	12
11.4	167
13.3	207
13.5	46. 90
13.9	26
13.13	26, 204
26.11	213
26.20–21	46
28.21	11
29.10	48, 52
30.27, 33	12, 26
33.14	27, 140
34.2	27
42.1–4	123
42.25	13
48.9	13
49.4	81
49.8	82
51.1–58	205
51.17	34, 126, 160, 204
51.17–23	32
51.20	10
53.1	211
53.4, 5	135
57.16, 17	14, 108
59.18	15, 207
60.10	14
63.1–6	15, 174
63.3	176
63.5	16
63.7–64.12	7, 16, 18
63.17	16
64.1	17
64.6, 7	16
64.9	16
64.11	16
66.1	27
66.14	207
66.14, 15	27
66.16	27

Jeremiah

3.12	207
4.4	8
6.11	8, 9
7.18, 19	9
7.20	35
8.18, 19	9
10.25	35
13.13	30
14.7–9	26
14.19–22	26
18.8	209
20.9	8, 10
23.9	10
23.19	208
23.20	13
23.29	8
25.15–31	204
25.15	32
30.23, 24	208
42.10	209
42.18	35
44.6	8, 35
48.26	36
49.12	36
49.37	12
50.25	90
51.7	32, 35, 36, 163
51.39	36
51.57	36

Lamentations

1.15	162
2.6	207
4.21	32

Ezekiel

5.12	167
11.13	199
16.38	10
16.42	10
21.9	45
21.31	207
23.25	10
23.31–4	31, 34
24.1–14	39
25.14	11
25.17	11

237

Lamentations (cont.)		Obadiah	
30.15	11	16	36, 192
36.5, 6	11		
38.18, 19	11	*Nahum*	
		1.6	35
Daniel		2.4	35
2.34, 35	120	3.11	30, 192
2.44	120		
8.19	24	*Habakkuk*	
9.16	25	1.5	129
9.26	24	2.3, 4	137
9.27	24	2.15	30, 50, 202
11.22	25	2.16	30, 161, 202, 203
11.36	25	3.8	207
12.2	143		
		Zephaniah	
Hosea		1.18	213
5.10	6, 35	3.8	35
5.14	168		
8.5	6	*Haggai*	
10.8	124, 170	2.6	139
11.8, 9	6		
13.11	6	*Zechariah*	
		6.8	14
Joel		12.2	34, 36, 192
3.2	175		
3.12	175	*Malachi*	
3.13	162, 173	4.5	42

INTERTESTAMENTAL

2 Esdras		Wisdom	
8.30	51	5.18	108
8.34	51	5.20	45, 46, 108
		11.9	44, 45, 46
		12.2	45
Judith		13.11	91
		16.5	45
3.8	173	18.15	46
6.2	173	18.20	45, 46
		18.21	46
		18.23	46
Greek Additions to Esther		18.25	45, 46
13.14	173	19.1	45, 46

INDEX OF REFERENCES AND CITATIONS

Ecclesiasticus
5.4	42, 155
5.6	41
7.16	41
16.6	41
16.11	41
18.24	41
23.16	41
39.28	42
39.28–31	46
48.10	42

Baruch
1.15–3.8	26
4.25	46, 155

1 Maccabees
1.64	43
2.49	43
3.8	42

2 Maccabees
5.17	43
6.12–14	44
7.33	43, 44
7.38	42

4 Maccabees
4.21	44
6.27, 28	43
9.24	43
9.32	44
12.18	43
17.22	43, 189

Jubilees
21.22	150

Martyrdom of Isaiah
5.13	52, 192

Enoch
50.2	166
55.3	47
62.12	47
64.4	47
67.4–7	157
67.10	156

Testaments of the XII Patriarchs
Levi 6.11	47, 71
Gad 4.7	155

Sibylline Oracles
III, 309	103
III, 632	59
III, 766	59

2 Baruch
12.4	53
13.8	52, 192
64.4	53

Psalms of Solomon
8.15	48, 52, 192

Apocalypse of Moses
3.2	103

Apocalypse of Abraham
chap. 25	53

Zadokite Fragment
(Refs. as in Charles, op. cit.)
1.5	49
2.6	49
2.10	49
3.7	48
9.19, 20	31, 49
9.40	49

Habakkuk Commentary
comm. in Hab. 2.15	50

Psalms of Thanksgiving
Ps. c	50

War of Sons of Light and Sons of Darkness
P. 82 (Dupont-Sommer)	50

Rabbis
Judah the Prince	54
Huna II	54
Samuel ben Nahmani	54

Rabbis (cont.)		De Vita Mosis		
Tanhuma	55	I, para. 119		59
Genesis Rabbah	54	II, para. 147		59
Canticles Rabbah	55	II, para. 166		59
Berakot 7a	55	III, para. 121, 122		61
		III, para. 129		61
Letter to Aristeas		III, para. 136		61
para. 254	56	De Specialibus Legibus II, para.		
		209		59
		De Virtutibus		
Philo		para. 171, 172		59
Legum Allegoria III		para. 174		59
para. 115	62	De Providentia		
para. 123, 124	62	Frg. 2, para. 39		61
De Sacrificiis Abelis		Frg. 3, para. 41		61
para. 96	58			
para. 133	60	*Josephus*		
Quod Deterius Potiori, para. 69, 60		Archaeologia		
De Gigantibus, para. 17	58, 87	I, (50)		63
Quod Deus Immutabilis		III, (315)		64, 84
para. 51	56	III, (321)		65
para. 52	57	IV, (130)		63
para. 60	57	V, (132)		65
para. 70	57, 61	VI, (167)		63
para. 79	57	VII, (81)		63
De Fuga et Inventione, para. 65	60	VII, (147)		63
Quod a Deo Mittantur Somnia		VII, (151)		63
I, 234	58, 59	VII, (321)		63
I, 236	58	VII, (328)		63
II, 179	58	XV, (299)		64
De Abrahamo		Bellum Judaicum		
para. 41	59	II, (135)		65
para. 143	60	VIII, (328)		64

NEW TESTAMENT

Matthew		10.34	167
2.16	86	10.42	126
3.7	128	12.9–14	113
4.6	99	12.11	137
4.7	78	12.20	123
5.25	122	12.39	128
5.26	122	13.13–15	115, 116
7.23	148	17.17	128
8.2–4	113	18.23–35	120, 121
10.18	118	18.26	154

INDEX OF REFERENCES AND CITATIONS

Matthew (cont.)
19.13–15	113
20.22	127
21.41	120
22.2–10	177
22.7	121
23.29	125
23.32	169
23.35, 36	122
23.36	122, 128
25.14–30	121
25.25	121
25.46	97, 149
26.39	127
26.42	127
27.43	98

Mark
1.40	113
1.41	113
3.5	113
4.12	114
4.29	174
6.11	118
8.12	128
9.19	128
9.49	140
10.14	113
10.38	126, 176
10.38, 39	127
12.9	119
13.9	118
13.22	72
13.30	128
14.36	127

Luke
2.35	167
3.7	112, 128
4.10	99
4.28	86
5.12–16	113
6.6–11	113
8.10	115, 130
9.41	128
10.30	137
11.22	166
11.28	148
11.29	128
11.49–51	122, 128
12.56	122
12.58	122
14.15	177
14.17	177
14.21	121
18.1–8	123, 153
18.6–8	185
18.7	42, 91
18.15–17	113
19.12–27	121
19.44	119
20.16	120
21.13	118, 193
21.23	112
21.32	128
22.42	127
23.30	124, 142, 170

John
2.17	78, 99
3.16–21	141
3.34	147
3.36	142, 148, 182, 193
5.22–4	143, 147
5.28, 29	143
5.38	146
5.45	143
5.47	147
6.31, 32	144
6.48	144
6.63	147
6.68	147
7.48	75
7.49	75
8.21–28	145
8.31	147
8.37	147
8.43	147
8.44	145
8.47	147
8.51	146, 147, 148
10.19	148
10.35	146
11.4	150
12.31	145
12.37–41	144

John (cont.)		1.26	108
12.40	118	1.27	85, 94
12.47, 48	145	1.28	83, 108, 152
13.18	145	1.29–32	94
14.23	146	2.1–16	85
14.24	147, 148	2.4	153
15.3	146	2.5	86, 112, 142
15.7	147	2.8, 9	86, 87
15.20	148	3.4	100, 166
15.25	144, 148	3.5	41, 88, 184
17.6	146	3.9	88
17.8	147	3.19	105
17.14	146	3.21	185
17.17	146	3.25	184
18.11	127	3.26	193
		3.27	211
Acts		4.15	88, 89
1.18–20	131	5.3	87
2.3	140	5.9	89
2.40	128	5.10	107
3.19	128	5.17	89
3.23	128	5.20	212
3.26	128	6.21	101
4.21	149	7.8	81
4.22, 23	170	8.2	211
4.25	170, 171	8.7	107
4.29, 30	170	8.35	87, 88
5.1–11	131	8.36	100
5.9	78	9.7	81
8.20	131	9.14–33	90, 91
9.15	91	9.17	81, 90
12.22	131	9.21	91
12.23	131	9.22	10, 90, 150, 153, 154, 179, 185
13.8	131	9.23	91
13.10, 11	131	10.5	211
13.41	129	10.6	208
13.46	130	10.8	81
17.31	130	10.16	211
18.6	130	10.19	78
26.16	98	11.11	78
28.27	130	11.14	78
		11.22	92, 179
Romans		11.23	179
1.17	84, 184	11.28	107
1.18–32	83	11.31	179
1.18	4, 70, 81, 84, 85, 112, 183	12.1	218
1.21	94	12.12	87
1.24	85, 108	12.19	92, 97, 191

INDEX OF REFERENCES AND CITATIONS

Romans (cont.)
12.21	166
13.1–7	60, 93, 97
13.4	90, 98, 167, 191
13.5	95
13.6	96
13.9, 10	95
15.3	80, 98, 99, 100
15.9	99, 100
15.16	98
16.10	83

1 Corinthians
1.18	116
1.25	223
1.30	185, 212
2.7, 8	100
3.13–15	140
4.1	98
4.11–13	100
5.5	77, 79
5.12, 13	76, 79, 95
9.27	83
10.1–13	76
10.4	144
10.6	76
10.7	144
10.11–13	78, 180, 183
10.22	77, 179
11.19	79, 83
11.27	95, 105
11.30	77, 168, 179, 198
11.31, 32	79
15.26	106
15.55	166

2 Corinthians
2.4	87
2.15, 16	79, 85, 101, 119
4.7	91
4.8	88
5.10	216
5.17	82
5.19	82
5.20–6.10	80, 82
5.21	75, 80, 81, 98, 185, 187
6.2	80
6.6	153
7.10	88, 149
10.18	83
11.2	78
11.15	101
12.20	86
13.1–10	82, 83

Galatians
3.7–22	73, 74
3.10, 11	74
3.13	73, 75, 80, 81, 82, 98, 187, 188
3.19, 20	75
3.22	75, 172
4.27	81
5.22	153
6.7, 8	75, 216

Ephesians
2.1	104
2.2	104
2.3	102, 182, 183
2.5	105
2.12	217
2.14–16	105
4.2	153
4.18, 19	108
5.5	142
5.6	102, 103
6.2	81
6.10–20	108
6.12	96
6.13–17	15
6.13	167

Philippians
1.19	81
1.28	101, 116
2.16	81
3.9	185
3.18	107
3.19	101

Colossians
1.11	153
1.21	101, 107
2.13, 14	101
3.6	102, 103
3.12	153

243

1 Thessalonians

1.10	69, 71
2.15	107
2.16	47, 69, 71, 72, 84, 94, 112, 116, 123, 130, 142, 181
4.4	91
5.9	71

2 Thessalonians

1.3–10	71
1.5	71
1.6	86, 87
2.1–12	72
2.3–11	72, 73
2.4	73
2.7	65, 72
2.11	72, 73

1 Timothy

1.16	153, 154
3.6	137
3.7	137
6.9	137

2 Timothy

2.15	83, 152
2.20, 21	91
3.8	152

Titus

1.16	152
3.1	96
3.11	152

Hebrews

2.2, 3	132
2.10	102
3.7–4.13	76, 132
3.16–19	133
4.1	133
4.12, 13	46, 134, 136, 148, 167
6.2	136
6.4–8	134
6.8	101
6.12	155
6.15	155
7.19	140
9.27, 28	134
10.26–31	136
10.27	78, 140, 191, 213
10.38	137
10.39	137
11.7	138
11.26	100
12.15	138
12.17	138
12.18–28	138
12.29	214
13.10–16	175
13.13	140

James

1.15	152
1.20	186
2.12, 13	152
3.6	140
4.4	183
5.20	152

1 Peter

1.23	148
2.12	119
2.13, 14	96
2.14	98
3.7	91
3.20	154
4.12	140
4.13	151
4.14	100
4.17, 18	151

2 Peter

2.1	156
2.4	156, 157
2.9	97, 150, 156
2.15, 16	156
2.17	157
3.9–15	155, 157

1 John

2.19	148
3.4	89
3.14	148
3.20, 21	149
4.17, 18	149
5.16	150

INDEX OF REFERENCES AND CITATIONS

Jude	
4	155
6	156, 157
13	156

Revelation	
1.15	140
1.16	166, 167
2.3	172
2.10	87, 172
2.12	167
2.13	172
2.16	167
2.19	172
2.22	87, 167, 179, 198
2.23	87, 179, 198
2.26, 27	168
3.10	172
3.21	165, 168
4.11	102
5.5	165
5.5, 6	168, 173
6.2	165, 173
6.4	167
6.8	167
6.11	169
6.15	169
6.16	71, 124, 142
6.17	72, 169
9.6	142
9.12	125
9.20	177
10.7	173
11.7	165, 166
11.14	125
11.16–19	170
11.18	160
12.9	145
12.11	165, 168
12.12	160, 173
12.17	160, 173
13.1	125, 177
13.3	173
13.4	72, 173
13.7	165, 166
13.10	167, 172
13.14	167
13.16	173
14.8	96, 161, 163
14.10	161
14.12	172
14.14–20	173
14.19	162
14.20	140
15.1	160
15.2	165
15.7	159
16.9	177
16.14	167
16.19	96, 159, 162
17.2	163
17.3	164, 177
17.4	33, 163
17.5, 6	163, 173
17.14	165, 167, 175
17.16, 17	199
18.3	31, 50, 96, 161
18.6	164
18.10	164
18.24	71
19.9	177
19.11	167
19.11–16	175
19.13	138
19.15	159, 162, 163, 167
19.17	177
19.19	167
19.21	167
20.8	167
20.10	145
21.7	165
21.9	178
22.18, 19	178

GENERAL INDEX

Abbott, T. K., 102, 103, 106, 183
Aeschylus, 196, 217
'*ālāh*, 24
Albright, W. F., 11, 29, 30
Alexander the Great, 30
Allen, W. C., 115, 122
Ambrose, 32
'Anat, 28
Andrews, H. T., 56
Antiochus Epiphanes, 24, 25, 51, 172
'*aph*, 141
Appar, 220
Appasamy, A. J., 218, 219, 220
Aramaic Targum, 117
Aristotle, 58, 65
Artaxerxes Ochus, 16
Augustine, 80, 150, 187

Baal, 28
Baethgen, F. A., 34
Barnes, W. E., 5
Barth, K., 89, 190
Batten, L. W., 23
Baumgartner, W., 202 (*and see* Koehler, L.)
Beare, F. W., 151
Bennett, W. H., 149, 150
Bernard, J. H., 141, 143, 144
Bevan, E., 191
Bhagavad Gita, 218
bhakti, 215f.
bhakti marga, 217f.
Blakeney, E. M., 92
Bonwetsch, G. N., 53
Book of Common Prayer, 196
Box, G. H., 16, 32, 51
Brahma, 197, 215, 216
Brahmins, 212
Bredenkampf, C. J., 17, 35
Briggs, C., 18, 24, 34, 214
Brownlee, 202
Buddhism, 215
Bueber, S., 55
Buechsel, 87, 128, 163
Buhl, F., 34

Burrows, M., 16, 202
Burton, E. de W., 74

Calvin, John, 196, 219
Campbell, J. McLeod, 182, 187
Cave, S., 75, 219, 220
Chaitanya, 219f.
Charles, R. H., 47, 48, 49, 51, 52, 56, 159, 160, 161, 162, 164, 169, 171, 173, 175, 178
Chemosh, 5
chesed, 19
Cheyne, T. K., 16, 26, 34, 213
Chrysostom, 106
Claudius, Emperor, 98
Codex Ambrosianus, 208
Codex Bezae, 113
Codex Marchalianus, 207
Cohen, A., 19
Colson, F. H., 60 (*and see* Whitaker, G. H.)
communicatio idiomatum, 197
Cooke, G. A., 5, 11, 31, 35, 40
Cornill, C. H., 30, 33, 204
Cranmer, Thomas, 196
Cullmann, O., 95, 166

Dale, R. W., 183, 184, 187, 196
Davey, F. N., 142, 146 (*and see* Hoskyns, E. C.)
Davidson, A. B., 40
Davies, W. D., 210, 211, 212
de Jonge, M., 47
Delitzsch, F., 17
Diatessaron, 113
Dodd, C. H., 69, 85, 86, 88, 89, 90, 93, 98, 100, 148, 149, 150, 169, 179
Driver, G. R., 50
Driver, S. R., 24, 74, 214
Duff, A., 51
Duhm, B., 9, 16, 26, 30, 33, 204
Duncan, G. H., 74, 75
Dupont-Sommer, A., 50, 51

GENERAL INDEX

Elliott-Binns, L. E., 4, 204, 205, 208
'*emeth*, 19
Emmet, C. W., 43
Ephraem, 113
'*erek 'appayim*, 153
Essenes, 65
Eucharist, 77
Eumenides, 196, 217
Eusebius, 61
Evans, E., 76

Falconer, R., 152, 154
Farrer, A. 162, 174
Foakes-Jackson, F. J., 78, 130 (*and see* Lake, K.)
Forsyth, P. T., 187
Freedman, H., 205
Fuller, R. H., 70

Gesenius, W., 214
gnana marga, 216f.
Gnanesvar, 218
Godet, F., 77
Gordon, C. H., 28, 29
Gore, C., 104, 107
Goudge, A. L., 77, 79, 80, 82
Gray, G. B., 4, 8, 26
Gregg, J. A. F., 45
Grierson, G. A., 217, 218, 220

Hadad, 35
Hanson, A. T., 99, 162, 173, 177 (*and see* Preston, R. H.)
Harrison, D. E. W., 192
Hastings, J., 186
Headlam, A. C., 4, 80, 83, 85, 86, 88, 89, 90, 93, 98, 99, 100, 210 (*and see* Sanday, W.)
Hegel, 196
Hicks, F. C. N., ix
Hippolytus, 176
Hodgson, L., 188
Holmes, W. H. G., 132, 135
Hooke, S. H., 30
Hort, F. A., 113, 165 (*and see* Westcott, B. F.)
Hoskyns, E. C., 142, 146 (*and see* Davey, F. N.)

'*Il*, 28

Jagannadh, 222
Judas Maccabaeus, 47
Justin Martyr, 139

Kahle, P., 123, 214
Kant, 196
Karaite Movement, 50
karma, 105, 196, 197, 215f.
karma marga, 215f.
$k^e ley$ $za'am$, 90
Kennedy, M. T., 216, 219f.
Kilpatrick, T. B., 186
Kirk, K., 189
Kirkpatrick, A. F., 18
Kissane, E. J., 15, 16, 21, 32
Kittel, G., 26, 128, 163
Kittel, R., 32, 34, 213
Knox, R., 104
Koehler, L., 202 (*and see* Baumgartner, W.)
kōs, 126, 159–160
Kraetzschmar, R., 31
Krishna, 16, 219f.

Lactantius, 84
Lake, K., 78 (*and see* Foakes-Jackson, F. J.)
Leo, Pope, 197
Lévi, I., 41, 42
Liddell, H. G., 65, 208 (*and see* Scott, R.)
Lightfoot, J. B., 74, 86, 101
Loewe, H., 54 (*and see* Montefiore, C.)
Lofthouse, W. F., 40
Logos, 211, 221f.
Luther, Martin, 17, 73, 222

Macaulay, A. B., x, 191, 192
Macnicoll, N., 218
Madhva, 218
Mannika Vasagar, 219
Manson, T. W., 117
māya, 220
Mayor, J. B., 152
McNeile, A. H., 115, 116, 118, 123
Menelaus, High Priest, 51

247

Middleton, E., 74
Milligan, G., 65, 92, 102 (*and see* Moulton, J. H.)
Milligan, W., 70, 73
mishpāt, 19
Moabite Stone, 5
Moberly, R. C., 186, 191
Moffatt, J., 77
Montefiore, C. J., 54 (*and see* Loewe, H.)
Montgomery, J. A., 25
Moulton, J. H., 65, 92, 102 (*and see* Milligan, G.)

Naber, S. A., 63
ne'ᵉmānim, 19
necheratsah, 25
Nero, 199
Nero Redivivus, 173
Nirvana, 215
nishkama, 218

Oecumenius, 106
Oesterley, W. O. E., 15, 18, 24, 34, 35, 41, 42, 44
Onias, III, 25, 51
Oresteia, 196
Origen, 176
Orissa, 222
Orr, J., 186

Pakenham-Walsh, H., 149, 150
Peake, A. S., 9, 30, 32, 33, 204
Plato, 57, 58, 221
Plummer, A., 77, 80, 112, 115, 116, 120, 122, 123, 125 (*and see* Robertson, A.)
Plumptre, E. H., 152, 156
Polybius, 208
Poussin, L. de la V., 215
Preston, R. H., 99, 162, 173, 177 (*and see* Hanson, A. T.)
Puri, 222
pyly, 160

qīnāh, 141
qubba'āh, 32
qūt, 133

Rackham, E. R., 129, 130
Radha, 222f.
Rama, 16
Ramanuja, 218
Rashdall, H., 188, 189
rᵉ'u baggōyim, 129
Rigveda, 215
Ritschl, A., ix, 181, 186
Robertson, A., 77 (*and see* Plummer, A.)
Robinson, A., 103, 106
Robinson, T. H., 15, 213
Robinson, W., 5, 12
Roman Empire, 160, 161, 162, 163, 170, 199, 200
Rome, 161, 162, 163, 164, 169, 177, 199
Rowley, H. H., 24, 30, 50, 51

Salathiel Apocalypse, 51
Samaritan Lament, 16, 18
Samaritan Temple, 27
Sanday, W., 4, 80, 83, 85, 86, 88, 89, 90, 93, 98, 99, 100, 210 (*and see* Headlam, A. C.)
Schechter, S., 48, 49
Schultz, H., 38
Scott, E. F., 152
Scott, R., 65, 208 (*and see* Liddell, H. G.)
Selwyn, E. G., 151, 189
shālōm, 19
sheteph, 25
shūbh, 39
Simon Maccabaeus, 35
Šiva, 219f.
Skinner, J., 5, 8, 26, 27
Slotke, I. W., 5
Smith, G. A., 15
Smith, J. M. P., 1, 2
Snaith, N., 19
Stevenson, E. B., 46
Strachan, R. H., 21, 81
Stumpff, 78
Swete, H. B., 56, 115, 171, 175, 176, 206

Tasker, R. V. G., x, 70, 84, 90, 93, 96, 104, 113, 121, 126, 159, 184, 187

GENERAL INDEX

Tatian, 113
$t^e n\bar{u}'\bar{a}h$, 22
Tennant, F. R., 104
Tertullian, 139
testimonia, 123
Thackeray, H. St J., 208
Theodotion, 143
Thompson, E. W., 216
Thompson, G. G., 190
Torah, 210, 211, 212
Toy, C. H., 40
tsedeq, 19
Tübingen School, 70
Turner, R. L., 215

Ugaritic, Language, 28
Ugaritic Literature, 28

Vaishnavism, 220
Vedantism, 218
Vespasian, 199

Viresalingam, K., 217
Vishnu, 16, 222
Viteau, J., 48

Wade, G. W., 8, 26, 129
Wand, J. W. C., 156, 157
Ward, W. H., 129
Weinel, 189
Westcott, B. F., 113, 134, 136, 139, 140, 141, 142, 145, 146, 147, 149, 150, 165, 214 (*and see* Hort, F. A.)
Whitaker, G. H., 60 (*and see* Colson, F. H.)
Wickham, E. C., 213
Wicks, H. J., 53

yāda', 13
yāshār, 19

Zenzirh, 35

www.ingramcontent.com/pod-product-compliance
Lightning Source LLC
Chambersburg PA
CBHW050848230426
43667CB00012B/2194